MEDITERRANEAN PERSPECTIVES

Philosophy, Theology, Aesthetics

MEDITERRANEAN PERSPECTIVES
Philosophy, Theology, Aesthetics

Edited by
Robert M. Berchman

Dowling College Press
2000

Library of Congress Cataloging-in-Publication Data

Robert M. Berchman, *Mediterranean Perspectives: Philosophy, Theology, Aesthetics*

1. Mediterranean Studies 2. Philosophy 3. Theology
4. Aesthetics

ISBN 1-586840-56-8

Published by Dowling College Press
Distributed by Global Publications
IGCS, Binghamton University
Binghamton, NY USA 13902-6000
Phone: (607) 777-4495 or 6104; Fax: (607) 777-6132
email: pmorewed@binghamton.edu
http://ssips.binghamton.edu

MEDITERRANEAN PERSPECTIVES

ANNOUNCEMENT

Selected papers from *The Dowling College Mediterranean Conference* are published in the series entitled '*Mediterranean Perspectives.*' The aim of this series is to trace out the main lines of intellectual, cultural, and scientific development from which emerge the fundamental features of our contemporary perspectives on the Mediterranean.

On behalf of the Editorial Board, I am pleased to express our appreciation for the support from the Dowling College administration; we especially thank President Albert E. Donor.

Robert M. Berchman
Editor-in-Chief

Norman Holub
Editor (*ex-officio*)

Table of Contents

Foreword

This volume, like the others in the series, is intended to serve as a "perspective" into the scholarship celebrated at the Dowling Mediterranean Conference XX held in Valencia, Spain in 1998, and Dowling Mediterranean Conference XXI held in Castellemare di Stabia, Italy, in 1999.

With the appearance of this volume, we have completed the first of the two tasks that this series set for itself in publishing selected papers from the Rome, Istanbul, Paris, and Bordeaux Mediterranean Conferences held in 1996 and 1997. This was to trace out in general terms the processes of 'give and take' by which Mediterranean philosophers, writers, and historians have continually interacted with their wider cultural and social environments when engaged in such conversation. In this volume we have attempted to characterize several lines of intellectual development by which some of the fundamental features of ancient, medieval, and modern pictures of God, Nature, Beauty, the State, and the Self came to be accepted as common knowledge in the Mediterranean world today.

Throughout the centuries of intellectual endeavor touched upon in these essays, the growth of metaphysical and historical consciousness across subjects, ranging from theology and physics at one extreme to music and social history at the other, took closely parallel forms. Just how closely parallel they are emerges from the papers offered here. The other concern these articles address has to do with the recurrent patterns of theory manifested in all the disciplines examined here. Whenever thinkers with quite different subject matters, such a philosophy, theology, music, or history, have faced common forms of problems, they seem to resort to similar strategies. To this extent thinkers today have more to learn than they yet recognize from the theoretical quandaries facing their predecessors in philosophy, political theory, and even in theology.

The principle of unity appropriate to this collection is not suggested by the Platonic paradigm of one-in-many, but by Wittgenstein's image of a rope with many strands and family resemblances. That is to say, although the topics that surface in these studies are limited, they are, nonetheless, related, for they highlight a series of conceptual and social moments in which a Mediterranean past still remains visible in a Mediterranean present.

The debts we owe to colleagues range more widely than ever before. One service that the editor and contributors to this volume are glad to perform is to thank Professor Norman Holub of Dowling College for creating and sustaining these conferences over some twenty-five years. It is to his genius that we owe a remarkable and memorable academic achievement—the Dowling Mediterranean Conferences.

Much of the academic ground for these conferences, in particular, was mapped out by Dr. Riccardo Campa, Vice Rector of Siena University, and Dr. Gaetano Massa of the Garibaldi Institute in Rome. The history of ideas still remains a 'subject' in the Italian academic world. We can only hope that this publication may help to awaken a greater interest in this field of thought in other more sleepy worlds.

As things stand, it appears that institutions, such as the Dowling Mediterranean Conference, are the only real means by which novel, exciting, and even eccentric ideas get off the ground. Of all institutions this one has earned an outstanding reputation for its liberality, flexibility, and generosity. It has promoted research into some of the fundamental features of earlier Mediterranean cultures that are accepted as foundational in the Mediterranean world of today.

We welcome this opportunity to offer our gratitude to all for their support in publishing the papers of these conferences. We are, once again, deeply grateful to Maureen Volpe of Dowling College who "typed" and completed this volume. We owe her more than we can say. Without Maureen's spirited patience and sustained resolve this collection of essays would not have been possible.

Robert M. Berchman
Jamesport, NY
June, 2000

I.

PHILOSOPHY

The Ethics of Politics and the Politics of Ethics

John P. Anton
University of South Florida

I.

The thoughts I am about to share with you may not provide the answers to the problem under consideration, i.e. what is the proper education for the individual in order to meet his/her community responsibilities. However, I plan to try it. In fact, I will try to employ a model of theorizing that is quite old and goes back to classical antiquity, when ethics and politics were inseparable twin enterprises. The model, that is, goes back to a time before ethics and politics went their separate ways in the course of Western civilization. However, more about this divorce between ethics and politics later. Today we see strange things happening, among them a new specialist taking over the tasks of ethics and subsuming them under the rubric of moral rules: the "ethicist" of this and the "ethicist" of that. Also, we see everywhere the old type of the wise statesman being replaced with professional politicians, while we, the ordinary people, are trying to keep our lives in order by obeying rules and laws that pile up at an amazing rate.

To make my point clear I will go back to the tragic poet Euripides and cite Fragment 910 from one of his lost tragedies to illustrate the type of conduct I will discuss as the model that fits my theme. The Fragment in translation runs as follows:

Happy is he who has knowledge
That comes from inquiry.
He stirs no evil for his townsmen,
Nor gives himself to unjust doings.
But surveys the deathless nature
Of the never-aging worlds, of what it is made,
And whence and how.
In men of this kind, the thought
Of doing base acts never finds a home.[1]

The person Euripides had in mind and for whom he wrote these lines was Anaxagoras of Clazomenae, who is credited with bringing philosophy to Athens and then becoming a member of the illustrious Periclean circle. Though not a citizen of Athens, Anaxagoras gave to the city more than he ever took from it. I should also mention at this point that he was sentenced to death on the charge of impiety for having taught that the sun was a fiery stone larger than the Peloponnesus, not a divinity. His friend Pericles got him out of Athens just on time to prevent the Athenians from carrying out the death penalty. Years later, the Athenian poet Euripides made the proper amends, as the Fragment tells us.

In case you wonder why I have cited this Fragment and what is its significance in relation to the theme of my lecture, allow me to draw attention to two central ideas: (a) relying on of human reason for the study of nature, and (b) cultivating the mind to prevent evil acts against one's fellow citizens. It makes little difference whether Anaxagoras was not in fact a citizen of Athens to recognize his integrity and excellence. His contribution to the culture of Athens as part of the Golden Age of Greece became a landmark in the history of philosophy and science.

Euripides took this contribution a step further. He emphasized the idea that science and philosophy as rational activities are profoundly political. As such, they illustrate how the human mind, cultivated and dedicated to the study of nature, including human nature, conditions our conduct as the guide to constructive citizenship. To put it somewhat differently, science in the broad sense of the term goes hand in hand with the development of the character needed for political *ethos,* the right habits required for public life.

Euripides' Fragment, connecting as it does science and philosophy to the public good as parts of one's political character, was hardly an isolated statement on the development of culture in the classical age of Greece. Let us not forget that Euripides as a tragic poet was convinced that his own art, dramatic poetry, belonged to the community and the public good. In fact, the theater belonged to the collective good of the *polis.* The same demand holds for all the institutions and activities that belong to the society as a *polis,* what we call today the city-state. Nothing that human beings do can be evaluated properly apart from the good of the community. None of the arts, none of the sciences, no religious practice, can rise in importance beyond the general human good. Aristotle said summarizing the cultural experience of Greece in the next century:

> The attainment of the good for one person alone is, to be sure, a source of satisfaction; yet to secure it for a nation and for the city, is nobler and more divine (*Politics* 1094b 9-11).

He also remarked in the same work that for a person "to live alone one must be either beast or god." Of course, he could have just as easily added at this point that for a human being to live alone is by nature impossible. The argument supports the rejection of the idea of absolute individualism. That the idea became something close to a cult in modern times is another story, one that has haunted many a social thinker ever since.

I need to stress at this point the idea about the converging goals of all public institutions and human activities, as the Greek philosophers understood them, to sustain the pursuit of the common good. One may be tempted to raise an objection concerning the existence of such a common good that is over and above the individual good. We are all familiar with many of the failed experiments in the history of humankind to build communities based on some version of a common good. That many such experiments turned out to be neither good nor common is hardly surprising. There are explanations for those ideological and political failures, not least among them is the explanation that the principles upon which such experiments rested were either half-understood or misconceptions of human nature. Once in operation as political programs they forced the citizenry into submission to the tyrannical rule dressed as the protector of the alleged common good. When the idea of this good is cast in so misleading an ideal, the evils of dissent and injustice threaten whatever cohesion the community may have achieved in the past. That is why the rule of force and the idea of freedom have always been opposing vectors in the lives of communities.

Nevertheless, even under adverse circumstances, the coherence of community life is neither a lost cause nor an impossible objective. Human beings have always had to work hard and with real dedication, often at the risk of receiving severe punishment for defying the tyrant, to clarify and defend the meaning of the common good as a feasible goal. A great portion of what is recognized as political philosophy has been precisely the formulation of ideas that state the means to effect the common good in action. It will surprise no one if I say–actually repeating what has so often been said–that the first time in the history of mankind this task was undertaken and brought to fruition was in classical

Greece. It was a task to which artists, poets, statesmen, sculptors, architects, dramatists, lawgivers, jurists, not only philosophers, contributed in their own way to clarifying the meaning of the common good. Therefore, the individual good became a basic ingredient of the common good itself, blending harmoniously with the concept of the individual as citizen. Aeschylus decided to write his own Epitaph, stating in it not that he served the Muses but that he was the citizen who fought at Marathon:

Aeschylus of Athens, Euphorion's son, this tomb
Covers, who died at wheat-bearing Gela;
His valor of high repute the grove of Marathon would attest,
And the long haired Mede who came to know it well.[2]

This shared sense of responsibility tied the individual citizens as creative agents working for the general welfare to the same power of the human soul, the logical nature of the mind, or to use another phrase, *the power of intelligence.* As Euripides has suggested in the Fragment I read, once the mind is trusted, he who does it "stirs no evil for his townsmen, nor gives himself to unjust doings." However, when the mind is turned into a tool and is forced to serve the passions and the appetites, zillions of failures, personal and communal, inevitably follow. One has but to read Thucydides to learn from his account of the events at Corcyra how an otherwise peaceful and throbbing *polis* is driven to civil war under the strong influence of the inflamed eruption of the passions.

Was the discovery of the mind a Greek achievement? Yes and No. Their achievement was not a literal invention, something that was not there before and was put together for the first time. After all, the mind has been and is a universal feature of all humankind. Never did the Greeks claim that they were the only people endowed with reason. What they actually claimed, and to their great credit, was how the mind is to be understood as the source of reasoning. They conceived of the mind as both a tool and as an end in itself, as an activity, endowed with a purpose of its own. It was in this context that they saw the mind as a good and as the foundation of the common good. The greatest gift of the Gods to humanity was not fire, although it was this element that Prometheus stole from heaven and that proved most useful for mankind's survival. The greatest gift was the power of reason, the ability to choose and to discriminate, to plan, to build and to avoid errors. Thus Homer sings in the opening book of the *Odyssey,* where at the council of the Gods, he tells the gathering why human beings alone are responsible for whatever disasters and sufferings come from their own actions:

> Oh for shame, how the mortals put the blame on us gods, for they say evils come from us, but it is they, rather, who by their recklessness win sorrow beyond what is given.

Homer's dictum never lost its force of relevance. It was true then, it was true in the golden age of Greece, it is still true today. Simply put, it is not possible to escape the bitter and painful consequences of the way of life that, for whatever reasons, turns the mind into a tool for the gratification of the desires and the caprices of the passions. Those who adopt the mode of irrationality, especially if they happen to be philosophers, aggravate the existing illness by adding a terrifying cultural problem. The defenders of irrationality create a vicious circle. By using intelligence to degrade itself they force upon the mind tasks that humiliate its natural operations. The ensuing problem is worse than religious fanaticism, for it goes to the heart of education. Since what will be taught in this manner about the mind can affect the minds of the youth by conveying a false sense of cultural freedom, it becomes a serious aberration. We have already seen the results, for more often than not, youth slides almost effortlessly into the abyss of a life of greed. The outcome is always the same: either cultural anarchy or the tyranny of barbarism.

The way I see it, the meaning of individual education and the limits of cultural responsibility are questions no society can escape or give false answers. Nor did the Greeks sweep them under the carpet or try to treat them lightly. On the contrary, they felt the full force of their import and tried to give answers to the best of their ability. Socrates comes to mind immediately. The whole issue of the life of reason was placed at the center of the public affairs of Athens throughout the fifth century. When the great Sophists arrived on the scene, teaching how to use effectively the skills they declared themselves qualified to teach, the aspiring pupils paid to acquire them for a fee. Assurances were given that through these skills they would gain fame, wealth, power and success. The newly developed powers of the mind, for example, the art of rhetoric, and even beyond that, the art of arguing, logic and dialectic, became precious commodities. Having them in one's possession meant the most secure means to rise to the top of success. One of these sophists, Callicles, who figures impressively in Plato's dialogue, the *Gorgias*, argued with unusual force against the position that Socrates has taken, that "might makes right." And another sophist, Protagoras, made a name for himself with his doctrine that "man is the measure of all things." He visited Athens and took the city by storm.

To be sure, many great ideas were proposed at the height of the fifth century, when Anaxagoras and Protagoras, Euripides and Socrates, Pericles and Thucydides were all contemporaries. The idea of the common good had become an issue of general interest. On the ritual side of civic life, it was actually celebrated all along at the public festivals, as in the case of the Panathenaia, in honor of the goddess Athens, whose temple was the most holy shrine of the city. Being also of practical value to the citizenry, it was cherished as a brave action to defend the *patria*. The new challenge to the traditional meaning had to be faced. It became the work of the new freedom in the name of the mind, except for one thing: the bond between the life of reason and the traditional meaning of the common good was being weakened. The two ideals were suddenly moving in opposite directions. The leading sophists had inadvertently added to the rift. The cohesion of the community's institutions was in mortal danger of collapsing. Cultural anarchy and disintegration were on the march, all in the name of the new freedoms, painfully won with the aid of successful democratic reforms.

The wave of the rising individualism carried the day. To make a long story short, the trouble came not with the dawn of democracy as a novel political system but with the limited arsenal of means that intelligence had in storage at that time. What had to be fully understood to prevent the continuous confrontation between community cohesion and cultural anarchy, caused by what historians call the rising tide of subjectivism and relativism against universal values, was the nature of human reason. The cultural leaders had to take reason a step beyond the point that the Ionian scientists and the great sophists had done.

It was this cultural crisis, i. e. the other face of the golden age of Periclean Athens, that brought about the greatest intellectual revolution of all times with Socrates at the helm. He was the one who forced into the open the issue of the ideals of public life. Socrates in his personal life as well as his public conduct explored the full range of human intelligence and made it the basis for evaluating every institution from government and law to art and religion. The thrust of his dialectic was how to conceive of reason not merely as a tool but as an end in itself as well. For Socrates, the cohesive power of the life reason was to serve as the replacement of tradition and unreflective loyalty to the city. Without the bond of reason, the grand virtues, civic and personal, ran the risk of falling apart. Such was the importance of the Socratic teaching about the unity of the virtues: courage, prudence, piety, justice and wisdom. Without this doctrine, the educated individual could somehow become sophisticated, efficient and skillful but hardly a citizen responsible and accountable for the promotion of the common good. Without the rational defense of the unity of the virtues, the popular version of the common good was too weak a motive to share intelligently in community existence. This explains why classical individualism did not become a doctrine of personal and inalienable rights.

Two thousand years later the West will come up with an individualism of its own, the modern version, in all its varieties and shapes, its own theories of human nature to support them and its own brand of personality models. It also came up with its sense of community and its own demands for educating the individual to meet the responsibilities of political life. Small wonder then that modern individualism had to invent new models of bonds to link individuals to their communities. The most conspicuous model of such constructed bonds has been the theory of social contract. With it came the new wave of education and the modern doctrine of rights.

II.

I hope that the few remarks I am about to make regarding the post-classical changes of the political use of reason will not force the conclusion that I am being either hyper-critical or favoring only the philosophy of Socrates. Something did in fact happen during the Hellenistic period following the conquests of Alexander of Macedonia and the rise of the Roman Empire that led gradually to the divorce of ethics and politics. As a movement, it first appeared as an intellectual phenomenon and started with certain disillusioned philosophers who felt deeply the loss of the *polis*. We easily recognize the movement now as a case of estrangement or alienation, if one prefers. The "Garden" of Epicurus was the first sign of withdrawal into a private space, a club as it were, within the city. Almost parallel to that withdrawal, another intellectual development took place, Stoicism, distrusting the outer perimeter of the *polis* while extending it indefinitely. Stoicism declared the inhabited world a *cosmopolis*. Neither philosophical school being able to respect or cultivate the bonds of the citizens of the *polis*, each urged its members to find solace in the cultivation of personal ethics. Having made their withdrawal complete from the affairs of the *polis*, the political community, these disillusioned thinkers, these *sophoi*, had moved in a different direction from what Aristotle had written about the art and science of politics. The great discovery of the political mind in the age of reason was over. Its gradual eclipse became obvious when two new movements that were brewing for quite some time took charge of the human affairs in the Mediterranean world: the Roman Empire and Christianity. The Greek *polis* was taken over by the *Pax Romana* while the ethics of self-realization and human excellence was being steadily replaced with the salvational drama of the Christian soul.

Ever since the coming of the Hellenistic age the problem that urgently needed solution but did not find one was the re-integration of ethics and politics. To put the issue differently, the problem, then and now, was and continues to be, like one coin with two sides, the re-integrating of the ethics of politics and the politics of ethics. The issue is not whether in the history of post-classical Western civilization people had codes of ethics and systems of government. Rather, the issue was and remains whether these two fundamental components of practical life can converge to form a unified pattern of conduct. I could put the issue more simply by asking the question: Why is it that the individuals in organized societies follow one code of conduct in their ethics and another in the politics?

Let me press the matter a step further. A closer look into our current college curricula shows that a peculiar development has taken place. We have witnessed recently the proliferation of ethics courses and their replacement with many mini-courses, all specialized as medical ethics, business ethics, administrative ethics, athletic ethics and so on, with no end in view. What is lacking in this situation is a clear thesis concerning the common principles that could serve as the connectives for their continuity. Something comparable has happened in the field of political theory. The departments entrusted with the teaching in this area have undergone a change of name after the adoption of quantitative methods from Political Science to Departments of Government, etc. etc. Respectable as these academic disciplines are, one still feels lost in the maze of their information systems. We have moved away from what ethics and politics meant to the classical thinkers who started these inquiries as the arts and sciences of human conduct. We are nowadays asking different questions and arriving at different answers but none that gets us closer to the old fundamental question of the relationship between ethics and politics. An old-fashioned issue? Yes, it is, but no less essential and no less vital at that. If this old-fashioned question had no bearing on our goals of education and the development of character, I would be the first to say "Dump the issue once and for all." However, to do that would be to encourage another negative move, i.e. to dump the question of looking into the purpose of human life. Being negative about this last question is too easy. Seeking a positive answer is the greatest challenge.

If many answers to the question can be given, as they have, so much the better. Selecting the best answer and giving reasons for doing so is what philosophy in fact is all about. Here Aristotle is still our great teacher. Let me explain briefly why Aristotle, who wrote the *Nicomachean Ethics,* is still ahead of us, despite the fact that he composed that work close to twenty-four centuries ago. I will illustrate my point by quoting from a recent article that was published about three months ago in *The New York Times*. Not once did it occur to its author or to the scientists to which the article refers that the problems reported and investigated had been thoroughly studied and effectively disposed of in the first chapter of Aristotle's book. It was in that chapter that the ancient sage systematically explored the issue of the purpose of human life and what qualifies as the pursuit of the highest good. But first the excerpts from *The New York Times* article (in the "Science" section, Tuesday, February 2, 1999) written by Alfie Kohn:

> Over the last few years,...psychological researchers have been amassing an impressive body of data suggesting that satisfaction is not for sale. Not only does having more things prove to be unfulfilling, but people for whom affluence is a priority of life tend to experience an unusual degree of anxiety and depression as well as a lower overall level of well-being. Likewise, those who would like nothing more than to be famous or attractive do not fare as well, psychologically speaking, as those who primarily want to develop close relationships, become more self-aware, or contribute to the community.
>
> Dr. Ryan and Dr. Kasser said their studies provided a look at the "dark side of the American dream," noting that the culture in some ways seemed to be built on precisely what turned out to be detrimental to mental health.

> A preoccupation with money bodes ill regardless of how much money one already has. The effects also appear not to be limited to any one culture. Dr. Kasser and his associates have now collected data from subjects in 13 countries, including Germany, Russia and India.

More data and more data, but to what end, one may ask. That there has always been a dark side to the American dream hardly requires further documentation. Ever since the classical critiques of the pursuit of pleasure, wealth, fame and other comparable values as the ultimate goals of life, other ideals were introduced and defended. Numerous theorists have proposed Liberty and Equality, for instance, as satisfying the criteria to serve as the highest good in human life, but despite their high degree of desirability they have enjoyed objections that have not been wanting. It has been a commonplace to argue that these values belong to the good as means to other ends. Equally well known is the fact that once one becomes prisoner of these attractive means and suffers loss of soul, the usual result is a weakening of community bonds. The analysis of the cited article is old hat and hardly helpful or leading to novel assessments. Not even once do the researchers in question raise the substantive issue behind the "dark side of the American dream," that is, the view that intelligence is only a means for securing the goods that shine in the bright side of the American dream. Dark or bright, whichever side one pursues, the mind is treated only as a means, hardly getting any credit as an end in itself, as a self-contained value. Now we are surprised that the culture that promotes the mind as means "turned out to be detrimental to mental health." Worse, it is detrimental to the very idea of human happiness.

I am about to say the final words and end this lecture. At the risk of repeating myself, I would like to reiterate two concepts:

(1) The bond between ethics and politics is rooted in the life of reason. To the classical Greek thinkers who discovered it, explored and defended it as an ultimate purpose of life, the mind became the cornerstone in the education of the individual and the conduct of the political community.

(2) The separation of ethics and politics was a post-classical development. Despite all the ideological systems in modern times to minimize the distance between them, the cleavage persists and causes a variety of types of alienation.

I can only say in conclusion that since this basic problem has been solved once in the course of history, it can be solved again. What I cannot say is "how" it can be unhinged from the condition of the modern. The way out I could confidently recommend is through the re-introduction of the principle of reason as mind in the fullest sense and as the Greeks understood it in our education and our other institutions. The tasks required for its success are not confined to what the philosophers write. They belong even more fittingly as practical goals to the political leaders. Anyway, Plato was right when he said that there would be no end to human suffering until such time as when "either the philosophers become kings or the kings be philosophers."

Endnotes

[1] Ὄλβιος ὅστις τῆς ἰσστορίας
ἔσχε μάθησιν,
μήτε πολιτῶν ἐπι πημοσύνὴν
μήτ᾽ εὶς ἀδίκους πράξεις ὁρμῶν,
ἀλλ᾽ ἀθανάτου καθορῶν φύσεως
κόμον ἀγήρων, πῇ τε συνέστη
καὶ ὅπῃ καὶ ὅπως
τοῖς δὲ τοιούτοις οὐδέποτ᾽ αὶσχρῶν
ἔργώ μελέδημα προσίζει.

[2] In *Aeschylus: A Collection of Essays*, ed. March H. McCall, Jr. (Englewood, N.J.: Prentice-Hall, 1972), 2; Aeschylus died in 456 BC. at Gela in Sicily.

On the Relation Between Dialectic and Metaphysics in Aristotle: Re-examination of Some Texts in Confrontation With E. Berti's Interpretation

Horst Seidl
Pont. Lateran University, Rome

Aristotle's texts on dialectic offer a partly positive, partly negative, perspective on the art of debate. Dialectic is said to be distinctly inferior to the sciences. At the beginning of *Topica* I.1, Aristotle describes dialectic as "a method able to argue by conclusion about any given problem starting from probable premises" (100a 18-20: μέθοδον ἀφ' ἧς δυνησόμεθα συλλογίζεσθαι περὶ παντὸς τοῦ προιεθέτος προβλήματος ἐξ ἐνδόξων). At the end of *Sophistici elenchi,* ch. 43, he calls it "an ability to draw conclusions about the given problem from existing, most probable premises" (*183a 37-39*: δύναμίν τινα συλλογιστικὴν περὶ προβληθέντος ἐκ τῶν ὑπαρχότων ὡς ἐνδοξωτάτων). Since probability is based on opinion rather than on knowledge, dialectic is inferior to science. However, dialectic is sometimes presented in a positive light. For example, in *Topica* I.2 Aristotle points out a threefold utility of dialectic: first, it promotes exercise of conclusive argumentation (πρὸς γυμνασίαν); second, in conversation we are able to relate the opinions most widely accepted (πρὸς τὰς ἐντεὐξεις); thirdly it is useful for "the philosophical sciences"; for when we are able to argue both sides of a problem (πρὸς αμφῶτερα δοἄπρῆσαι), "we shall more easily understand the true and the false at every point". Since dialectic is helpful in acquiring "the ultimate first principles applied in every science", it leads, as the ability to prove, "to the principles (premises) of all methods (disciplines, sciences)" (ἐξεταστικὴ γάρ οὖσα πρὸς τὰς ἀπασῶν τῶν μεθόδων ἀρχὰς ὁδὸν ἔχει).

Some contemporary scholars judge Aristotle's metaphysics as a miscarried "First Philosophy" of being—P. Aubenque speaks of a "failure"—of which only dialectical argumentation remains. Such scholars are committed to taking dialectic as the proper method of philosophy. This essay focuses on Enrico Berti, who has interpreted dialectic in this way. We will re-examine the Aristotelian texts to which he refers. A discussion of the relationship between dialectic and metaphysics in Aristotle is complicated by current controversies about interpreting his metaphysics; those controversies turn on the understanding of Aristotle's epistemology as applied to his metaphysics. We begin with some remarks on this topic.

1) Preliminary Remarks on Aristotle's Metaphysics as Based on his Epistemology

In *Metaph.* IV.1 and VI.1, Aristotle relies on his theory of science, as presented in the *Analytica posteriora.*[1] According to *Apo*, every special science has its specific object and its specific properties; each science attempts to demonstrate that these properties belong necessarily to this object. To this end a science looks for the internal essential causes of the object, for those will enter into the middle terms of demonstrations. Thus the essence of the object is no longer demonstrable, but must be defined. Every science presupposes for its definitions and demonstrations: 1. That the object exists (ὅτι ἔστιν), and 2. That it is something (τί ἐστιν, with an essence). In *Metaph.* IV.1 and VI.1, Aristotle introduces his "First Philosophy", comparing it with the special sciences. It has in common with them a scientific structure, like them starting from an object and going back to certain causes. However, in contrast to the particular sciences, First Philosophy has no specific material object other than those of the particular sciences; rather it has a formal object, common to them all, namely their being as such (IV 1, 1003a 21-24: ἔστιν ἐπιστήμη τις ἥ θεωρεῖ τὸ ὄν ᾗ ὄν καὶ τὰ τούτῳ ὑπάρχοντα καθ' αὐτό). First Philosophy deals with that which the particular sciences presuppose for their objects, i.e. their being, their existence (ὅτι ἔστιν), and being something (τί ἐστιν, with an essence). Metaphysics proceeds, then, to "the causes of being as such", (a 31: διὸ καὶ ἡμῖν τοῦ ὄντος ᾗ ὄν τὰς πρώτας αἰτίας ληπτέον).

Thus on the one hand Aristotle's metaphysics is grounded on an epistemological consideration of the presupposition of all acquirable knowledge, especially knowledge of the particular sciences, leading to "being as such", thematized as the object of metaphysics. On the other hand, when metaphysics proceeds to the essential features or causes of things, it lays the groundwork for epistemology itself, referring to the essential causes of the objects of the sciences, defined in their premises.

A more empiristic approach to Aristotle's epistemology has difficulty accepting its metaphysical implications. Terry Irwin[2] settles some problems in a very instructive way; we can review his findings only very briefly here:

a) The problems begin with Aristotle's distinction between "principles better known to us" and "principles better known in themselves" (or by nature). In either case the principles can be either prepositional principles or non-prepositional—"the things and their relations" to which the prepositional principles refer. Prepositional principles "better known to us" are provisory first intuitive opinions; "better known in themselves" are reflective, argued opinions. Irwin rightly underlines the Aristotelian realism according to which such propositions refer to things. However, this claim requires justification; Aristotle tries to provide that by way of dialectic argumentation, taking it as a constructive method, as Irwin correctly points out (o.c., 3-7).

> There are, however, "puzzles about dialectic" (Irwin 8): On the one hand, dialectic should be "the road to objective first principles". But on the other hand, "serious difficulty arises. Aristotle's description of dialectical method seems to offer no grounds for believing that it systematically reaches objective first principles. It examines commonly held beliefs (*endoxa*), and if it is successful, it reaches a more coherent version of the beliefs we began with. . . But coherence within common beliefs does not seem to be a ground for claiming to have found objective principles".

b) Aristotle's realism is confronted with two objections (Irwin 9): 1. The sceptical claim that our opinions about things existing independently of us is false cannot be excluded. 2. Dialectic arguments rely on "intuitive beliefs", whose coherence must be demonstrated. However, they are never cogent, for they may be destroyed by "scientific inquiry".

c) Certainly Aristotle distinguishes between dialectic and science. The latter pretends to rely on "objective first principles". However, it fails to demonstrate such objectively necessary principles (Irwin 10), "for it is not clear how Aristotle can show that any discipline meets the conditions he imposes on scientific knowledge. Each Aristotelian science must assume, but cannot prove, the objective truth of its own first principles, and apparently no scientific argument can show that the principles themselves are objectively true". We may remark concerning the problems raised by Irwin as follows:

Concerning a) Although Aristotle uses the term "principle" (ἀρχή) in *Apo* to refer to first premises in the sciences, its primary reference is to the causes or essences in things, the objects of the sciences. Thus also the distinction between "the better known by us" and "the better known in itself (by nature)" is aimed primarily at two aspects of the things themselves: the sensible, particular aspects (that which is caused), on the one hand, and the intelligible essential features (the causes), on the other. An interpretation of the Aristotelian distinction that primarily points out two sorts of opinions—provisional intuitive opinions and argued opinions—does not seem to be correct. Nor do we find in Aristotle a problem about whether to any given opinion there corresponds an objective principle. On the contrary, in his procedure the sciences try to gain insight of certain principles (in the things), and if these have been reached, then they are expressed in scientific propositions.

It is true that the dialectical method does not offer grounds for objective (scientific) principles. But this does not damage to Aristotle's doctrine. Indeed, in *Apo* he develops the scientific method to find the principles of a science, not the dialectical way of opinions, but through the scientific inductive way of definition. There are beautiful examples of definitions taken from astronomy—e.g., the definition of eclipse as the interruption of the sun's light cast on the moon, by interposition of the earth—or from geometry—e.g., the definition of circle as equidistant circumference about a central point. These definitions are not derived from opinions, but by definitory method; this is not the place to explain that method.

Concerning b): Aristotle does teach that opinions can be destroyed by scientific inquiry. But his First Philosophy is an exercise of science, not of opinions. The existence of the things independent of us is not a belief, but a first evident presupposition, according to the *Apo*, underlying to all acquisition of knowledge, including all doubts and refutations. Necessary knowledge is always related to the being of things in themselves, excluding the opposite.

Concerning c): The distinction between dialectic and First Philosophy is that between the way of opinions and the way of scientific research, as we have said above. The former refers to the sensible changing component of things, the latter to the intelligible essential component. Scientific procedure toward the essential features, causes, principles, of things is the method of definition, referring to this essential side of things. According to Aristotle's doctrine in *Apo,* there is no proof of principles, but there is definition, which is not proof because proofs depend on definitions, which enter into the premises of the proofs.

How can one be sure to have obtained an objective principle? By the inner evidence of the knowledge itself which perceives the essential causes in things. But this traditional interpretation runs up against modern empiricism, which looks only for those features of things based ultimately on sense-perception, and does not attend to intelligible features and causes; these are not "things and their relations". Empiricism is one-dimensional, following empirical phenomena and losing the intelligible causal dimension.

The simple being of things already has an intelligible aspect—it is no longer a sense-datum, not visible, audible, sniffable. It is thematized by the *Metaphysica* IV and VI as "being as such". In VII.1, Aristotle points out that being as such is "primary being" or "substance" (οὐσία), different from all accidental being, according to his categories, and then he proceeds, in chapter 3 and following, towards essential being (τὸ τί ἦν εἶναι). Indeed, empirical things have not only accidental features, but also essential ones that belong to them *per se*, καθ' αὑτό, i.e. not accidentally, but essentially and necessarily—with the exclusion of the opposite—which the sciences have to work out as specific differences in the definition, for example: human being as animal, human being as rational.

Let us return to the question of the relationship between dialectic and metaphysics as proposed by E. Berti.[3] In the following we discuss three items, re-examining the texts: whether dialectic "has only a methodological character" (Berti p. 119), as instrument of refutation; whether First Philosophy is a science or not and whether it is essentially dialectical.[4]

2) Is Dialectic Only a Method of Refutation?

As Berti and others interpret *Top* I.1-2, *Soph. El.* 9-11, and *Metaph.* IV.2, these texts represent dialectic essentially as a method or art of criticism and refutation. As δύναμις and τέχνη it is an "ability to produce something" (Berti 110), a "technique" of "producing arguments" (Berti 120), συλλογίζεσθαι, coinciding with the syllogistic of the *Analytics* or with logic (Berti 111).[5] The object of dialectic is universal in the sense that it is occupied with every argument. It applies the universal principles of non-contradiction and excluded middle as necessary for refutation (Berti 111f).

Top I.2, which speaks about the usefulness of dialectic for the "philosophical sciences", more precisely, "for the first principles among those which are applied in all sciences", πρὸς τὰ πρῶτα τῶν περὶ ἑκάστην ἐπιστήμην ἀρχῶν, and signifies the dialectic as an art of examination, ἐξεταστική, is interpreted by Berti thus: The philosophical sciences are the single sciences, and τὰ πρῶτα are their "proper principles", "not the common principles or axioms (τὰ κοινά, τὰ ἀξιώματα)" (Berti 117).[6] The refutation, ἔλεγχος, as συλλογισμὸς ἀντιφάσεως, seems to be a detection of contradictions or errors and to turn out as a *reductio ad absurdum*. The fact that the premises of dialectical arguments have only probable contents, τὰ ἔνδοξα, is due "to the essential relation with the interlocutor as well as to the critical character of dialectic as πειραστική". The fact that it starts from opinions does not form a motive inferior to that of proof and science ("non costituisce dunque un motivo di inferiorità"), but is indispensable for it, because it does not propose to attain the truth or to being a science; rather it aims at prevailing in discussions ("inquanto essa non si propone di raggiungere la verità, cioè di essere scienza, ma di prevalere nella discussione"), by refuting the opponent and criticising his presumed knowledge (115).

In the important passage of *Metaphys.* IV.2, 1004b 17-26, dialectic and sophistic are opposed to First Philosophy or metaphysics: dialectic is opposed because of the mode of its faculty, τῷ τρόπῳ τῆς δυνάμεως; sophistic because of its choice of life, τοῦ βίου τῇ προαιρέσει. According to Berti the expression "mode of faculty" does not indicate another mode of the philosophical faculty, weaker than that of the First Philosophy or metaphysics, but two different faculties, of which the philosophical is "theoretical", whereas the dialectic is "poetic", a critical activity which produces refutations (Berti 120). "One cannot compare them, because they belong to totally different domains, namely a theoretical and a poetic" (Berti 121).

This interpretation is convincing in some respects and not others. When Aristotle speaks of dialectic as a δύναμις and τέχνη, he does not use these terms in the narrow sense as "productive faculty" or "productive art", but in a broader sense that embraces all psychic faculties, including the cognitive and its method or discipline, e.g. rhetoric and medicine.[7] Every science is a δύναμις συλλογιστική, an ability of "making arguments"; dialectic is one example of this ability.[8]

Dialectic surely can discuss the principles proper to the various sciences; τὰ πρῶτα, mentioned in *Top.* I.2, perhaps refers to these principles, in addition to the universal "first" principles. *Soph El* 11, 172a 19, cites both sorts of principles together: τά γε πρῶτα καὶ τὰς οἰκείας ἀρχάς, and explains that dialectic, when discussing principles of the particular sciences, refers also to the common principles, τὰ κολνά (a 30, 32, 37foll.). But the latter are the very object of dialectic: a 14-15 says about "all", "the being" that there are certain properties and relations common to all things: unity and plurality, identity and difference, movement and rest and the like. The fact that dialectic has no specific proper object but discusses everything, so to speak, does not mean that it has no object, being only a technique or art of argumentation. Its object covers, in a certain sense, that of the First Philosophy, i.e. "being" (cf. *Metaph.* IV.2, 1004b 17ff). However, whereas philosophy acquires "science" (in the classical meaning) about being, dialectic remains in the field of probable assumptions and of the discussible opinions.[9]

The reason why dialectic does not perform demonstrations like those of the sciences, is not to be found in the generality of its discussions about all things (Berti, 112), but in its essential limitation to the domain of opinions, i.e., of probability. *Soph El* 11 tells us explicitly that dialectic does not demonstrate, because it introduces every premise in a "question-begging way", admitting always the possibility of the opposite premise. Thus it argues "from both" (premises): "If it were concerned to prove things, it would have refrained from putting questions, even if not about everything, at least about first things and about the specific principles", 172a 15-20. In other words, even when its object is not general or universal, dialectic proceeds nevertheless by question and examination (ἐρωτητική, πειραστική), because it is concerned with opinions.

Yet there is a connection between the generality of its object and its limitation to opinions, as the text indicates: indeed, the dialectician, busy on the pre-scientific level, presupposes in his interlocutors no specific knowledge, but only general or common knowledge which everyone has, including non-experts ("idiots", in the original sense, a 30), in the form of trustworthy opinions about general matters. Therefore everyone uses dialectic as an art of examination (πειραστική) and tries to put critical questions to "the professionals" about those common themes (τὰ κοινά); "for they have no less knowledge about that" than these, 172a 23-24. It turns out that everyone, when discussing in their common opinions, shares unmethodically (ἀτέχνως) in the same activity that dialecticians develop methodically (ἐντέχνως); for the dialectician proceeds in his examination with syllogistic technique (ὁ τέχνῃ συλλογιστικῇ πειραστικὸς διαλεκτικός, a 34-37). Hence dialectic is inferior to science, but functions as a preliminary to science.

From *Soph El* 11, as well as other passages in the *Soph El* and *Top*, it becomes manifest that dialectic is more than a mere technique of refutation. The term πειραστική does not mean "critical refutation". The root word πεῖρα, "proof", "trial", indicates the proper sense of the verb and adjective built on it: "to take a proof of something, to test something". Compare too the beautiful expression: περὶ ἁπάντων πειρᾶν λαμβάνειν (172a 39, cf. a 23); it does not mean "to refute everything critically", but "to test everything" (of which we do not yet have knowledge, μὴ εἰδώς) and to discuss on the basis of general opinions. In the *Topica,* we often find the expressions πειρατέον γνωρίζειν 105b 28, πειρατέον τοὺς λόγους ἀποδιδόναι, 106a 4, et passim, which show a positive endeavor of arriving at knowledge.[10] Furthermore, the art of examination, πειραστική, is only one part of the dialectic.[11]

From the relevant texts we cannot conclude that the syllogistic refutation as put in operation by dialectic always finds a contradiction in the argumentation of an opponent. Nor does it always have the form of a *reductio ad absurdum*, leading the interlocutor to conclusions opposed to his prior assumptions or premises,[12] in order to prove the opposite assumption. The texts, especially in *Apr* II.14 and 20, teach us something different: The *reductio ad absurdum* does not prove a given thesis directly, but only indirectly, proving that the assumption of the opposite thesis leads to an absurd conclusion.

True premise 1 opposite thesis 2
/ | } *reducio*
/ | } *ad*
/ | } *absurdum*
true thesis 1 absurd conclusion 2
(conclusion 1)

Further, identifying with the *reductio ad absurdum* with the elenctic proof (ἔλεγχος), Berti interprets the latter one as instrument of refutation, revealing contradictions in the interlocutor's argumentation. However, according to *APr* II.20, the elenctic proof has a different structure from reduction, namely that of a direct proof. Parallel to an already available proof with a correct conclusion (1), it tries to accomplish another proof, starting from another premise—contrary to the former conclusion (1)—and leading to an opposite conclusion (2).

```
Premise 1                  Premise 2
                       (contrary to concl.1)
   |    \ /               |      ] reductio
   |     V                |      } ad
   |     Λ                |      ] absurdum
   |    / \               |
Conclusion 1 —— — conclusion 2
      (contrary to premise 1,
       or contradictory to concl.1)
```

As can be seen from many examples in *Topica,* the elenctic proof does not try to detect contradictions in the opponent's argumentation, but (given a thesis, derived from certain premises) it tries to proof the opposite thesis from other premises, from another viewpoint. Thus, the elenctic enriches dialectical discussion on any given problem.

> The ἐξέτασις, too, has not only the negative intention of "revealing contradictions" ("smascheratrice delle contraddizioni"), but moreover the positive one of promoting discussion, by enrichment of its material. For this purpose, Aristotle has worked out some means, ὄργανα, which he describes in *Topica* I.13: 1. To establish premises, 2. To distinguish the meanings of every word, 3. To discover the differences between things, 4. to consider their affinities. Means 2 through 4 serves the first, i.e. to establish premises. In general, the dialectician is characterized (*Top* VIII. 14, end) as a person capable of establishing premises and making objections. The *reductio ad absurdum* does not offer that positive, constructive moment.

Aristotelian dialectic manifests itself not only as a technique of obtaining or maintaining superiority in discussions. In the passage just cited (164b 8ff), we read that this behaviour also has something ignoble. This remark is coupled with the advice not to discuss dialectically with just anyone, because discussion can deteriorate: "for with those who try to escape (refutation) it is certainly justified to argue syllogistically by all means, but it is not fine". The true objective of dialectic, like that of science and First Philosophy, is true knowledge; even if it does not achieve scientific insight, it can, like these, pave the way in this direction.[13]

After all, we can say that in Aristotle dialectic is a cognitive faculty alongside science and First Philosophy, differing from them by another mode of activity, exercising a proper method on an inferior level of knowledge. This is the meaning of the expression in *Metaph.* IV.2, 1004b 24: διαφέρει τῷ τρόπῳ τῆς δυνάμεως, confirmed in other places in *Topica* that employ the term τρόπος in a similar sense, aiming at the mode of activity of a faculty. Thus in I.3, dialectic is compared with other faculties (δυνάμεις), like rhetoric and medicine. Aristotle observes there that these try, "not in just any way" (οὔτε. . .ἐκ παντὸς τρόπου), but with every faculty in a determined way, to achieve their intended task "with the possible means" (i.e. with the means at their disposition). In the case of the dialectic these "means at their disposition" are the more or less probable opinions, which are appropriate for discussions of a general (not specifically scientific) nature. In the case of First Philosophy, however, the premises at one's disposition are certain universal true presuppositions concerning the being of all things.

Top I.18 mentions that the distinction of meanings of words does not only help us to detect paralogisms of the opponent, but also to form paralogisms. But the text continues that "this mode is not the proper one of dialectic" (108a 33-34: οὐκ οἰκεῖος ὁ τρόπος οὗτος). Indeed, the mode proper to it is arguing from probable premises, not from the appearance of paralogisms.

In *Metaph* IV.2, cited above, dialectic is distinguished from sophistic, which is considered to be only apparent wisdom. Dialectic differs from metaphysics as πειραστική from γνωριστκή. In other words: that which metaphysics treats "knowingly" from true presuppositions, dialectic treats only in a "testing" way. Thus dialectic exercises "another mode of faculty", not differing from metaphysics, as if they were two different faculties.

Berti refers to a place in *De Part An* I.1, 639a 1-10, which distinguishes, about every consideration and method, "two modes of comportment" (δύο τρόποι τῆς ἕξεως), a "scientific" mode and a "generally educated" mode; the latter could be the dialectical. But here again Aristotle does not speak about science and education as about two different dispositions. Both belong to one and the same disposition (note the singular τῆς ἕξεως). They differ only in terms of the mode of actuating this disposition. Therefore also the passage in *Metaph* IV.2 does not speak about a distinction of faculties ("distinzione di facoltà", Berti 122), but about two different modes of activity of one and the same cognitive faculty, active on different levels of knowledge. In the lower mode, it deals only with probability, whereas in the higher it achieves necessary true knowledge.

3) How is First Philosophy Related to the Other Sciences and to Dialectic?

In two further steps, Berti tries to show that (first) philosophy contrasts with science, as dialectic does, and that the latter is the proper method of philosophy.

Whereas the particular sciences deal always with a partial sector of reality, First Philosophy or metaphysics is concerned with all "being as such", with total reality. Correspondingly, the particular sciences assume their specific principles, i.e. existence and definition of their objects, by hypothesis or intuition, whereas metaphysics, just because its object is total reality, "cannot assume anything as true, but has to question everything" (Berti 121-122). "Not only that it does deal with particular principles, but must question also the universal principles of all being, or axioms, like the principles of non-contradiction and excluded middle" (*ibid.*). Intellect (νοῦς) is the intuitive faculty only for the proper principles of the sciences, but "has nothing to do with philosophy" which is concerned with the universal principles of all things in problematizing way (Berti 118, note 40). Furthermore, metaphysics does not construct deductive proofs as do the particular sciences, but only indirectly refuting proofs in an elenctic way (e.g., against those who deny the principle of non-contradiction). If, as a matter of fact, the sciences assume their principles, and metaphysics does not, but problematizes the principles, then it is obvious, according to this interpretation, that dialectic cannot serve as method in the sciences, but will do well in metaphysics.

We may remark about this interpretation as follows: It is true that the particular sciences deal always with a partial sector of reality, in contrast with metaphysics which concerns all being as such. However, it does not follow from this fact that only the particular sciences presuppose being/existence and the essence of their subjects, and metaphysics does not. Rather, also metaphysics presupposes and considers the being and the essence of the things, thematizing "being as such" as its very object. Reflecting on being, metaphysics does not question or problematize it. Moreover, starting from being, as a first evidence of all things, it searches the causes of being, finally finding a first transcendent cause.

I cannot share in the interpretation that identifies "being as such" with the totality of all beings, including the first cause. Thus, the expression of "being as such" is not a formula of a question of being. The famous question in *Metaph* VII, "What is being, what is substance?", aims at substantial being in the sense of first causes; Aristotle refers to the various endeavours of the Presocratics and Plato, who tried to determine the principle(s)—ἀρχή, αἰτία of all things, either as material elements (Presocratics) or as immaterial ideas (Plato).

The way in which the sciences assume their specific principles is not mere intuition. Rather it is an inductive way (ἐπαγωγή)[14] which, in addition to intuitive functions (of νοῦς), includes also discursive functions, operating for example in divisions (διαιρέσεις) of essential concepts of each object. Aristotle states expressly in *EN* VI.7 that wisdom/metaphysics is "intuitive intellect (νοῦς) and science" (1141a 19), "science and intuitive intellect about the most esteemed things" (b 2–3). Even if metaphysics does not accomplish deductive proofs, as the other sciences do, it nevertheless draws inductive conclusions about the first causes of all being, i.e. the immanent formal-efficient-final causes, *Metaph* VII.17, and the first transcendent, divine cause *Metaph* XII.6-7. Aristotle's metaphysics is not limited to apolitical discussions, but arrives at positive insights. Nor is its proper mode of argumentation elenctic refutation, although many scholars consider paradigmatic the "refutation" of those who deny the principle of non-contradiction, in *Metaph* IV.3 and following.

4) Is Aristotle's First Philosophy Itself Dialectic?

In the interpretation of P. Aubenque and E. Berti Aristotle's First Philosophy or metaphysics is not science, but is a problematisation of being as such, using as its proper method, dialectic. We examine here Berti's argument (pp. 124 foll.), oriented mainly toward Aristotle's defence in *Metaph* IV 3, and following, of the principle of non-contradiction (PNC) by means of "dialectical argumentation". This principle "has not been assumed by Aristotle as presupposition, but has been questioned, i.e. problematized" (Berti 128).

According to this interpretation, the procedure of refutation corresponds to the one elaborated in the *Topica*: The thesis to be refuted is the negation of the PNC. "The starting point for the refuting proof of the PNC is its negation. The proof does not consist in showing that such negation is unsuccessful in itself, if not by the position of that which it intends to deny, i.e. by negation of its negation" (Berti 130). "The procedure begins when he who answers makes a concession which concerning the present problem is this to say something. . ." (Berti 129). We following schema shows what he means:

Premise, conceded by the
opponent, that something
has a determined meaning

	re-futa-tion
Thesis: the negation of the principle of non-contradiction	Antithesis: the negation of the negation of the pr. of non-contradiction

However, the Aristotelian text, upon re-examination, presents something different. It is not Aristotle who problematizes the PNC, but the sophisticated opponent. In other words, it is not Aristotle who attempts a dialectical refutation, starting from the possible negation of the PNC as thesis in order to reach the antithesis, the negation of the negation of the PNC, as if Aristotle were the question begging interlocutor, and his opponent the answering. In fact, the procedure is the other way around: the initial thesis of the discussion is the PNC, and the opponent tests it by the antithesis, negating the PNC, asking from the philosopher the proof of his thesis. Aristotle is not dialectically questioning his interlocutor, but is the answerer who defends his thesis against the opponent, the non-philosopher:

Thesis: the principle of non-contradiction	>--------<	Antithesis: the negation of the principle of non-contradiction

The opponent tries "by ignorance" to contest the PNC, because he does not know that one cannot ask a proof of everything, and that the first principles of all proofs, like the axioms, above all the PNC, are no longer provable, *Metaph* IV.3, 1006a 5-11.[15]

> Aristotle does not ask for a premise, as the dialectician asks it from the opponent, but only that the opponent says something with a determined meaning (or, at least, not with any meaning). He remarks that it is not even necessary that his opponent "predicates something of something", but simply names something. Thus, Aristotle does not ask for a premise from his opponent—that would be a proposition with a subject and a predicate—

> but insists only on the indispensable condition of every conversation or discussion, that words with determinate meanings be used, that it be recognised that every thing has some determined reality and unity, and is not indeterminately many or opposite things.

Thus, *Metaph* IV.3 et seq. does not offer a "typically dialectical" situation (Berti 129). We do not find here, to start with, a thesis with a proof which must be refuted by another proof, as happens in dialectical discussions. Rather we find an unproven "thesis" and the opponent's demand of proving it—in order to refute the proof and initiate a dialectical dispute—is refused by the philosopher *a limine*, right from the beginning. For the philosopher points to the fact that the PNC is a primary axiom, not provable because a constitutive condition of every conversation. The opponent appears to be ignorant of this fact, for the PNC would be applied in every form of counter-argument, as soon as speech begins—"naming something with words". Thus, Aristotle's answer does not prove a thesis, but advises us that the negation of the PNC is impossible *a priori*. He does not prove the negation of the negation of the PNC (as Berti would have it), but points to the impossibility of the negation itself. Neither operation is allowed. Aristotle states expressly that the PNC is the most evident of all cognitive principles, "about which it is impossible to deceive ourselves", 1005b 12. His "refutation" of the opponent consists simply in pointing to this impossibility: ἔστιν δ' ἀποδεῖξαι ἐλεγκτικῶς καὶ περὶ τούτου ὅτι ἀδύνατον, 1006a 11-12. The PNC becomes evident as the most certain principle, not only by the negation of its negation, but immediately of itself, so that its negation is impossible from the start. Therefore in *Metaph* IV.3 et seq. the starting point is not the negation of the PNC, but the principle itself, and since its negation turns out to be impossible, it remains in its original position. We do not find here the procedure of a double negation, in a quasi Hegelian manner.

From *Metaph* IV.3 et seq. I cannot see that dialectic is "the refutation of any claim of an absolute knowledge" (133). Rather we apprehend here the limit of dialectic or of its critical function. The text does not articulate "a knowledge of non-knowing, i.e. a knowledge of the insufficiency of experience", nor does the text express a problematic nature of metaphysics regarding the principle of non–contradiction ("il principio di non contraddizione. . . non è altro che la stessa problematicità", ibid.), so that its defence is "the dialectical regaining of such a problematic nature" (*ibid.*).

Furthermore, there is a direct connection between the fact that, according to Aristotle, the PNC has to be recognised by everybody as evident principle (*APo* I.2 and 10), and the thematization of "being as such", referring to existence and essence of the things, which is presupposed as something evident by the particular sciences for their objects. Aristotle characterises the PCN as the "most evident" of all principles (*Metaph* IV 3, 1005a 17, 22) and defends it against any sophisticated problematization. In doing so, he confirms that also "being per se" is not a name of a problem, but the initial object of the metaphysics, as mentioned above.

Since Aristotle's metaphysics is a science, not a problematization of being as such, and since dialectic as cognitive faculty is inferior than science, dialectic can hardly be the proper method of metaphysics. Rather dialectic is, as we have seen in the passage in *Soph El* 11, a method of the "common sense", the natural opinions of humanity. The general themes about which people put questions and speak "unmethodically" (ἀτέχνος), are discussed by the dialectician "methodically" (ἐντέχνως). Thus, dialectic is a method for "lay people" or also for practical politicians and rhetors, not for "professional" scientists or philosophers. It can prepare the way to a scientific or philosophical argument at a stage where one has not yet achieved it.

Further, it would be a misunderstanding to consider every refutation as dialectical. Indeed there is also a scientific elenctic. The dialectical elenctic is only one kind among others (*Soph El* 9, 170a 37-38). Nor can it be maintained that dialectic is the only suitable method of questioning everything, even the PNC. Aristotle states clearly the limitations of dialectic in comparison with science, to which it is inferior. In *Rhet* I.2, 1358a 8ff, he says that dialectic and rhetoric argue from probable premises of general content. The more someone in the discussion succeeds in finding specific premises, proper to the discussed object, "the nearer one comes, unconsciously, to setting up a science that is distinct from dialectic and rhetoric. Indeed, when one arrives at (specific) principles, it will be no longer dialectic, nor rhetoric, but that (science), at which one has arrived". In this and similar passages it is made clear that dialectic operates in a preliminary domain of science, ending where science begins. If we ask when reason has obtained scientific knowledge, surpassing dialectic, the evidence must come from this knowledge itself, applicable universally and necessarily to all instances of the species with which the science is occupied.

Limits of another sort are mentioned in *Top* I.10-11: according to chap. 11, 105a 7-9, the object of dialectic "should not border upon that of which proof is too nearby, nor upon that of which proof is too far, for the former does not cause a problem, whereas the latter causes too great problems for the dialectical exercise". From this point of view, discussing the negation of the PCN is no job for dialectic, because that would concern the presupposition for all acquirable knowledge and for all dialogue. About this one does not dispute "for the sake of exercise". One the one hand, the PNC is too evident to provide problems which should be discussed; one the other hand, to explain this fact against deniers is too difficult for dialectic, because that requires a philosophical epistemology, as worked out in the *Analytica posteriora.*

Accordingly, Aristotle in *Metaph* IV.3 attributes the task of defending the PCN to First Philosophy, and takes it away from the claims of dialectic and sophistic.

In *Top* I.10 he indicates this limit of dialectic: "It is not every proposition nor yet every problem that is to be set down as dialectical; for no one in his senses would make a proposition of what no one holds, nor yet make a problem of what is obvious to everybody; for the latter admit of no doubt, while to the former no one would assent" (104a 4-7, ORT). Hence the most evident of all principles, the PNC, cannot be object of a dialectical discussion, but it can be the object of philosophical reflection about the condition of all humanly acquirable knowledge, as well as about the being as such of all things.

There remains a problem: Even if Aristotle's conceptions of metaphysics and dialectic both are different so that the metaphysical method is not dialectical method, is it not still a fact that nevertheless in his metaphysics he proceeds dialectically, as modern scholars often like to say? In order to answer this question, we must first understand why dialectic and metaphysics are different for Aristotle. The relevant texts indicate that the dialectician deals with opinions in a non-scientific way, whereas First Philosophy is a science that concentrates on "being per se", or substance, and is justified by epistemology. Furthermore, the dialectician does not have available the division of the categories, introduced by Aristotle as a critique of dialectic. Indeed, dialectic deals more with accidental than with substantial being. Using these and similar criteria we will be able to determine whether we are dealing with a dialectical argument or with an argument in Aristotelian First Philosophy.

Certainly, we do find dialectical arguments in Aristotle's *Metaphysica*, but those always appear in his examination of earlier philosophers, either in reference to their dialectical arguments, or in his confrontation of their opposed positions, for example in Book III between materialists and Platonists. Another example would be in VII.3: his opponent's dialectical argument is that "substance" is identical with "matter". But wherever Aristotle arrives at conclusions in his own metaphysical position with his own arguments—for example, in Book XII, where he arrives at the existence of the first divine substance, its immaterial nature, and to its self-knowledge as νόησις νοήσεως—these arguments are by no means dialectical.

If we can distinguish dialectical arguments from Aristotle's own arguments in his metaphysics, then the question arises how the one sort proceeds from the other. But this question goes beyond the scope of the present paper. We may mention here just two examples of such a procedure:

a) Zeno's dialectical reductions *ad absurdum* to hold indirectly the thesis that there is no motion, based on the mathematical implications of infinite divisibility, stimulates Aristotle to argue that there is no actual infinity in nature, distinguishing divisions in natural things from mathematical (ideal) divisions.

b) The opposite theses of the Presocratics that the causes of natural things are only matter and of Plato that there are immaterial ideas represent, at first glance, a dialectical situation that remains in opposition, as sketched out in *Metaph* III. But Aristotle surpasses this opposition in Book VII et seq. with his own arguments that detect the formal cause or essence (τὸ τί ἦν εἶναι) in the natural things themselves.

(I have to thank warmly Professor Dr. Anthony Preus for having revised the English and given useful amendments of the content.)

Endnotes

[1] This is explained in more detail in two of my publications in which I recover some aspects of traditional interpretations: *Beiträge zu Aristoteles' Erkenntnislehre und Metaphysik,* (Elementa vol. 35, Edit. Rodopi Amsterdam-Atlanta, Georgia), Würzburg-Amsterdam 1984, and: *Aristoteles' Zweite Analytiken,* (Elementa-Texte, vol.11, Edit. Rodopi) Würzburg-Amsterdam 1987.
[2] T. Irwin, *Aristotle's First Principles*, Oxford 1990.
[3] E. Berti, *Dalla dialettica alla filosofia prima,* Padua 1977.
[4] The theme has been treated in detail in my 1984 book, pp. 153ff.
[5] Berti refers to *Rhetorica* I.1, 1355a 9, in this connection.
[6] ἐξεταστική is translated as detecting the contradictions ("smascheratrice delle contraddizioni"). Note 39 refers to *Rhet* 6, 1427b 12-14.
[7] Cf. *Top* I.3.
[8] δύναμίν τινα συλλογιστικήν, *Soph.El.* 34, 183a 37. The expression, quoted by Berti from *Rhet* I.1, 1335a 3ss, does not mean that dialectic is identical with syllogistic or logic. We read there that the rhetorical "conclusio", the enthymema, is a syllogism: "Since it belongs to dialectic—on the whole or partially—to have knowledge equally of every syllogism, he who is best able to deal with it, namely from which and how a syllogism proceeds, is expert also in the enthymema". Hence, the dialectician must know how a syllogism works, as was set forth in *Top* I.1, but he must not know the whole syllogistic, which is an instrument for science (cf. the beginning of *APr).*

The text continues that the consideration of the true and of the probable—scientific and dialectical considerations—rests on the same faculty: τό τε γὰρ ἀληθὲς καὶ τὸ ὅμαιον ἀληθεῖ τῆς αὐτῆς ἐστιν δυνάμεως ἰδεῖν. . ., a 14-15. [9] In *APo* I.11, 77a 26ss, we read about dialectic that it discusses τὰ κοινά, i.e. certain universal principles, common to all sciences which refer to them in various specific ways. Thus, dialectic has "community with all sciences". Its object is no specific genus of being so in this way it is similar to First Philosophy or metaphysics. But unlike metaphysics, dialectic proceeds by questions and always admits opposite assumptions in order to promote argumentation on the same matter in these and antitheses. Science, however, argues from ascertained principles, previously established by definition.
[10] See also 163b 14, 17. At *APo* I.11, 77a 30, dialectic. . .πειρῷτο τὰ κοινά. Here the positive meaning is evident: to try something; in the present instance, in discussion with an interlocutor to try out his opinions.
[11] See *Soph El* 8, 169b 25.
[12] Berti, p. 127: ". . .che la tesi dell'avversario contraddice alle premesse da lui stesso concesse".

[13] Cf. 163b 9-14; I 2, 101b 3-4; I 11, 104b 1-3; 105b 30-31. Furthermore we observe in many places the repeated use of knowledge terms: γνῶσις, γνωριζειν, εἰδὲναι and the like, e.g. I.11, 104b 2, 6, 8, 11, 12. Cf. 11, 105b 28; 18, 108a 19, 27, 28, 31, b 1, 4, 13 et passim.

[14] The inductive way is explained by Aristotle in several places, like *Ethica Nicom.* I.2, *APo* II.19.

[15] Cf. 1005b 2-5, with reference to *APo* I.1-2.

Deus Ex Ontologia Aristotelea

Martin J. Henn
University of Kansas

Abstract

Scholars are divided over Aristotle's true position on the feasibility of universal ontology. Some (esp. T. H. Irwin, Charlotte Witt, Walter Leszl) emphasize Aristotle's own denial of such a science (cf. *SE* 170a20-3, *EE* 1217b25-35, *DeInt.* 16b22f.).

Others (esp. G.E.L. Owen) show that Aristotle eventually amended his claims in *Metaphysics Γ* due to a new found application of focal meaning analysis to 'Being'. But Owen never adequately states why the analysis works because he overlooks God—the much-needed ontological linchpin between universal and particular. Aristotle's God represents both (1) the primary *instance* of Being, and (2) a *universal ideal* applicable in formula to all beings.

Owen claims that "it is Γ, not Λ, that moves decisively beyond the old polemic, the denunciation of any general inquiry into the 'elements of things', that is still audible in *Metaphysics Λ*" (Düring 1960, p. 181). I demonstrate, rather, that it is Λ, not Γ that allows Aristotle's new found application of focal meaning analysis to work. (147 words)

I. Aristotle's Changing Attitude about the Feasibility of Universal Ontology

Scholars are divided over Aristotle's true position on the feasibility of universal ontology. Some, especially T. H. Irwin emphasize his denial of such universal science in the *Organon* (*cf. SE* 170a20-3, *DeInt.* 16b22ff.; *EE* 1217b25-3). Irwin thinks that Aristotle's rejection of one comprehensive science of the good (*NE* I 6 1096a29-34) unavoidably infects the feasibility of one comprehensive science of Being:

> At Top. 107a3-12 (cf. EN 1096a23-9, EE 1217b26-38, Ackrill [1972], 21f) Aristotle argues that goods are homonymous because goodness differs according to the different categories of being; it is hard to believe that he does not intend, here as elsewhere, to mark a similar homony in

> beings. . . Just as the question 'What is it?' Requires a different type of answer according to the category of the item considered, so also the statement 'x is F' must be understood differently according to the category of x, and being will be defined differently according to the categories.[1]

Other scholars, especially G. E. L. Owen, show that Aristotle eventually amended his claims in the *Metaphysics*. Owen argues that Aristotle's new found application of 'focal meaning analysis' in the *Metaphysics* is responsible for this change:

> In *Metaphysics I* 992b18-24) he says that because of this variety in the use of '*onta*' it is a mistake to engage in a general search for the *stoicheia ton onton* ('elements of *existing things*', Oxford translation). In *Metaphysics XIV* (1088b35-1089b33) he argues this thesis at length (concerning 'existing things' or 'things that are',/O.T.). In the *Eudemian Ethics* I (1217b25-35) he maintains that the same multiplicity shows that there can be no single comprehensive science of *to on* ('being', O.T.). In *Metaphysics IV* (1003a21-b16), resuming the same subject, he amends his claim: despite this multiplicity of use there can be a single comprehensive science of *to on* and *ta onta*, and those who looked for the elements of *ta onta* were very likely on the track of this science.[2]

Owen, however, never adequately accounts for the cause of the workability of this new found application of focal meaning analysis because he overlooks God as the much-needed linchpin between universal and particular. Aristotle's God represents both (1) the *primary instance* of Being, and (2) a *universal ideal* applicable in formula to all beings.

In his youth Aristotle did not apply focal meaning analysis to 'Being', even though he had fully worked out its dialectical mechanics, because he had no theological basis for regarding the concept of Being as anything more than an indeterminate cipher. For instance, he asserts in his refutation of the sophists that "we ought not attempt to grasp the number of things against which those who refute do their refuting without scientific knowledge (ἐπιστήυη) of all beings; *but this is not the task of one art* (τοῦτο δ' οὐ μιᾶς ἔστι τέχνῆς); for perhaps the are an infinity of sciences, so that obviously there would be an infinity of demonstrations as well (*SE* 170a20-23)."[3] This denial is reaffirmed at *SE* 172a13-15 where he denies that all beings fall under one genus, and again at *DeInt*. 16b22ff. where he claims that unqualified Being is a meaningless abstraction significant of nothing in particular.

But in *Metaphysics Γ* his attitude changes. Owen portrays Aristotle composing *Metaphysics Γ* as having "returned to, or newly arrived at, a belief in the possibility of a general metaphysics after a period in which he had denounced any such project as logically indefensible and castigated Plato and the Academy for pursuing it."[4] Aristotle claims in the *Metaphysics* that there is a universal science of Being which is different from the so-called special sciences "for none of the others examines *universally* about Being insofar as Being (1003a23)" and also that ".. .it belongs to one science to theorize not only on things spoken καθ' ἐν (as under a genus), but on things spoken in reference to one nature (πρὸς μίαν φύσιν); for these too are, in a way, spoken of καθ' ἐν" (1003b12-15). In the *Metaphysics* πρὸς ἓν analogical universals become scientifically admissible subjects of study. In the Organon works it is not clear whether they are admissible.

Why did Aristotle change his mind? The answer is not just because he discovered a new application of focal meaning analysis. Such analysis must be workable if there is to be any science of Being. *Why* does such analysis work when applied to 'Being'? The answer is that Aristotle discovered in God an entity who is at once universal and particular, ideal and real, absolute and cognizable, a One ever in the process of pluralizing its nature in a manyness of finite actualities; in short a synthesis of seemingly irreconcilable opposites.

II. Aristotle's Three Layers of Focal Analysis in the *Metaphysics* Converge in God as Focal Entity

Aristotle proves in *Metaphysics Λ* (1) that there exists an eternal primary *substance* (1071b3-12); (2) that this substance is pure *actuality* (1071b12-22); and (3) that this actual primary substance is *one* both in formula and in number (1074a31-38). Substance, actuality, and unity each represent a different layer in Aristotle's focal analysis of the term 'Being'. I.e. everything that exists is, insofar as it exists, substantial, actual, and unitary. Each of these demonstrations in Λ represents a layer of ontological reduction to God as primary entity. In this essay I plan to summarize each demonstration and then bring all three together thematically through an analysis of *Met. Λ 7*, 1072a26-b1 where God is identified as supreme object of desire, and is said to be contemplated through the notions of substance, actuality, and simplicity (i.e. intrinsic unity) each of which represents a positive notion in Aristotle's double column of contraries.[5] This double column (Λ *7*, 1072a26-b1) recalls the series of contraries mentioned in *Γ 2*. The interconnection of these texts is crucial to Aristotle's entire dialectical project because *Γ 2* sets up the general dialectical requirement for any speculation on the nature of the focal entity. In *Γ 2* this nature is still up for grabs; God is not demonstrated to be the focal entity until *Λ*. In *Γ 2* Aristotle merely claims that whatever this focal entity or primary instance of unity (τὸ πρῶτον, 1005a7) turns out to be, it will have its attributes subsumed under 'Unity' as positive head in a division of contraries. Once the focal entity is demonstrated to be God, the dialectical requirement set up in *Γ* 2 is fulfilled. The fulfillment of this requirement marks the end of dialectical ontology and the beginning of theology.

In *Met. Λ 4 & 5* Aristotle shows that the notions of substance, actuality, and unity are, when considered analogically, insufficient to count as true principles because they differ in application to things located in different contexts. Aristotle craves permanent existence. He does not cease until he finds a Prime Mover who remains the same for all things (Λ *5*, 1071a29-b2) in all contexts.

III. Aristotle's Focal Meaning analysis of Friendship in *EE VII 2*, 1236a8f. is Similar to His Analysis of 'Being' in the *Metaphysics*

The reason why these currents of analysis flow together in God is clear from the dialectical procedure of focal analysis itself. Before he wrote *Metaphysics Γ* Aristotle had long established the mechanics of focal analysis. When he applies such analysis, for the first time, to 'Being' in *Metaphysics Γ* we are asked to distinguish the universal notion of 'Being *qua* Being' from ordinary genera (e.g. 'Animal' and 'Tree'. Throughout *Metaphysics Γ 2* Aristotle emphasizes the difference between things spoken *according to one* thing (i.e. καθ' ἑν) versus things spoken *in relation to one* thing (i.e. πρὸς ἕν). The former are members of a genus, the latter each bear reference to one central primary instance. While the union of καθ' ἑν entities (like animals and trees) rests in an intrinsic generic nature; the union of πρὸς ἕν entities rests in an extrinsic nature, a focal entity which is not fully present in each of its secondary instances.

For example, Aristotle's focal account of φιλία in *Eudemian Ethics VII 2* (esp.1236a8ff.) is parallel, in dialectical method, to his focal account of 'Being' (τὸ ὄν) in *Metaphysics Γ 2*.[6] The following passage from *EE* describes in detail how the three forms of friendship (one based on utility, another based on pleasure, the third based on personal excellence, 1236a36-1236b1) are related to one central meaning or primary form, not through καθ' ἐν reference, nor through chance homonymy, but through πρὸς ἕν / focal reference:

> Therefore, there must be three kinds (εἰὅη) of friendship, but not all so termed under one thing (καῦ' ἕν) as species of one genus (ὡς ειςη ἑνὸς γένους), nor as sharing a name homonymously. For these kinds are spoken relative to a unitary and primary thing (πρὸς μίαν τινα καὶ πρώτην) (*EE* 1236a16-19, my translation)

Aristotle consciously employs the same dialectical procedure in his analysis of the kinds of friendship in the *Eudemian Ethics* as in his analysis of 'Being' in the *Metaphysics*. Consider this passage from *Metaphysics Γ*:

> 'Being' is spoken in many senses, but in reference to some unitary nature, and not homonymously—just as every healthy thing refers to Health, one thing by guarding it, another by producing it, another by being a sign of Health, and another by admitting of it (*Met.* 1003a33-b1, my translation)

The two cases of analysis are so similar, in fact, that they are connected by analogy to an analysis of 'the medical practitioner' (ὁ ἰατεικὅς: *EE* 1236a19 & *Met.* 1003b1ff.). I wish to prove in this essay *that the various forms of Being explored in the text of the Metaphysics (i.e. substance, actuality, unity) are tied together in focal reference to God. God is the primary instance of Being, because primary essence; and universal because primary.* Since God represents pure substantial form—i.e. supreme *ousia*—and is supremely actual and unitary, and since his formula must be present somehow in the formulae of all beings the way the formula of the medical doctor is present in the formulae of the medical mind, instrument, and operation (*EE* 1236a15ff.), it must therefore be the case that theology, in studying God, gains fundamental insight into the unity, substance, and actuality of all things, and that each of these areas of contemplation is a clue to unlocking the philosophical richness of the notion of Being *qua* Being.

The difference between καθ' ἑν and πρὸς ἕν unity is crucial. A genus is present uniformly in each of its members. The members are spoken "καθ' ἑν" with respect to their genus. All difference between members is accounted for by differences *outside the concept of the genus*. For instance, that which differentiates the animals man and ox is an idea outside the concept of animal. Perhaps the difference here is *rationality*. But, whatever the case may be, the nature of the primary instance functions differently in each secondary instance in virtue of the fact that the relation each has to the primary instance is different from individual to individual. All difference between πρὸς ἕν relata (like healthy things, medical paraphernalia, and beings) is accounted for in the different relationships that each secondary instance has to the primary one. Only the presence of the formula of the primary instance in the formulae of all secondary instances, along with the fact of πρὸς ἕν reference itself, is common to πρὸς ἕν relata. Nevertheless, this formula sameness is sufficient for scientific treatment of πρὸς ἕν relata.

The point here is that whatever is to serve as a primary instance of something (like the medical doctor in the case of medicine, or God in the case of beings) must be *independent* of the essence of each πρὸς ἕν relatum. For instance, a scalpel, an operation, a medical mind each depend upon the essence of the medical doctor. But not vice versa. The formula of the doctor must be understood before the scalpel can be recognized as a *medical* instrument, or the operation as a task of *medicine*. Likewise, Aristotle is searching for an entity whose being remains independent of beings. This inevitably requires proving the existence of an eternal indestructible substance. Aristotle does just this in *Metaphysics Λ 6*, 1071b3f.

The existence of God removes Aristotle from any suspicion of harboring Platonic Forms in the notions of being and unity. Both notions are made concrete in the primary instance universal called "God." Aristotle's God represents the much needed ontological linchpin between universal and particular. God is at once (1) *universal* because primary (God's primacy is responsible, in other words, for his formula being present in the formulae of all πρὸς ἕν relata), and (2) *individual* because an instance of Being.[7] A primary instance is an idealization of something that can't be specified. Being cannot be specified, nor can Health nor

Medicine—that is, none is a genus. The way to investigate these is to find a primary instance and study it. I.e. the medical doctor who has knowledge of the art of doctoring in his soul is, claims Aristotle *EE* 1236a19, the primary instance of medicine, and, in the case of Being, it is God who, through self-reflexive thinking, represents the Absolute, i.e. pure relation to self. The way to understand what makes instruments, bodies, and operations medical is to study the art of medicine which the medical doctor has in his soul. Similarly to study what makes existing things entities or beings is to study theology.

Just as the doctor represents that which is supremely medical, God represents that which is supremely Being and Unity. For Aristotle the universal is primary (*EE* 1236a23). In positing primary instances for concepts like Being and Medicine, Aristotle follows the classical Greek tendency to idealize forces in nature through individual models of excellence, archetypes which are easier to grasp than abstract notions that cannot be specified. The model is primary; things whose nature is parasitic on it are secondary. Think of a model friend, a model physician, a model of health, and you will begin to see the point. Each model possesses all the perfections that pertain to its form. A model physician possesses all degrees of medical knowledge and skill; his hands are steady and his vision is clear. A model friend is loyal to you out of love; not in order to gain riches and reputation. A model of health glistens with perfect muscle tone. And a model entity possess all degrees of perfection in existence. A model entity is supremely actual, is not moved by another—for this would imply imperfection in reliance on another being, is a primary essence, and is alone because supremely unitary.

Thus, where a genus cannot be found to characterize a community of objects, a perfect instance is described. That instance becomes something to which each member in the community refers. E.g. a medical mind, hand, and instrument each refer to the *medical doctor* by containing a reference to him in their respective formulae (*EE* 1236a20ff.). Since God is likewise involved somehow in the formula of every being, one can easily see why Aristotle conceived theology to be First Philosophy—as opposed to a mere branch. God in the form of his supreme attributes (unity, substance, and actuality) is universally present in all things. But now this must be illustrated from the text.

IV. Aristotle's Radical Reassessment of the Pre-Lambda Currents of Focal Analysis

In *Metaphysics Λ 4 & 5* we see a fundamental reassessment of the leading contenders for first principle and cause of all beings. These contenders are primary substance (and its elements form, matter, privation), the intelligibles Being *qua* Being and Unity, along with actuality and potentiality. Aristotle intends to show in *Λ* that each these elementary concepts are insufficient as first principles for various reasons. Dialectical tension emerges from Λ *4 & 5*. For, in one sense, the elementary concepts, when considered analogically, provide an intelligible basis for conceiving the Being of all there is, but, in another sense, none serves as a *separately existing* real basis for all there is. Aristotle's focal analysis has led him, it seems, into a dead end. His only way out is to search for an entity that would provide an objective basis of sameness and permanence for all there is in the universe.

Here is a summary of Aristotle's Λ *4 & 5* reassessment of the previous currents of focal analysis:

(1) *The argument against being and unity as principles*

The intelligible universals being and unity cannot serve as principles and elements of things common to the several categories and prior to them, because (a) no element can be the same as the complex which includes it, and (b) being and unity are predicable of concrete things—and so presumably not separable from, but included in them (*Met.* 1070a35-b10).

Aristotle has just undertaken (1070a36-1070b4) a search for a cause common to both relations and substances. This common cause would be applicable universally across these categories. But even the most universal of intelligibles, being and unity, do not possess the kind of independent existence that such a cause requires:

> Furthermore, in what manner is it permissible for the elements of all things to be the same? For no one element can be the same as that which is composed of elements; for instance, 'B' or 'A' cannot be the same as their composite 'BA'. Nor, therefore, can any of the intelligibles, e.g. being and unity <serve as elements of things>; for these are predicable of

> each composite entity (*Metaphysics Λ 4*, 1070b4-8, my translation, Ross ed.).

Aristotle's point here is that the intelligibles being and unity can have existence only in the composites of which they are predicable; since there are no separate freely-floating Platonic Forms. If there were, Aristotle would no longer need to search for a real basis of permanence in the cosmos. The Forms would be that basis.

(2) *The argument against form, matter, and privation as principles*

Because all sensible things have a form (e.g. heat), a privation (e.g. cold), and a matter, we can know *by analogy* that the elements of substance—form, matter, and privation—are the elements of all things; but, unfortunately, even these are different across genera (*Met.* 1070b9-21).

Again, just like being and unity, the elements of substance are only common when considered analogically. In reality they differ across genera; that is, the form, privation, and matter of triangles, animal bodies, and celestial spheres is different for each, but the same by analogy:

> Or as we say, there is a sense <in which the elements of all things are the same>, and a sense <in which they are> not <the same>. For instance, perhaps heat is the *form* of sensible bodies while cold is their *privation*, and *matter* is that which directly, in virtue of itself, is potentially these, while these <elements> along with the things composed of them, whose principles are these <elements>, are *substances*; i.e. any unity which comes to be from heat and cold, e.g. flesh and bone; for it is necessary for that which comes to be to be distinct from these. Now then the elements and principles of these things are the same (though different for different things), and it is not possible to speak of all things in this way, but <it is possible> by analogy—just as if someone were to say that the principles are three in number, the form, the privation, and the matter. But each of these is different for each genus. For instance, in color these are white, black, and surface—or again, light, darkness, and air, for from these come day and night (*Metaphysics Λ 4*, 1070b10-21, my translation, Ross ed.).

The elements of substance are common to things in different genera only by analogy. In reality they lack independent and permanent existence; and so, are not really the same for all things. For instance, color is a genus comprising the contrariety of white and black. These colors differ from each other the most of any two colors. And their difference is one of varying degree. I.e. there are intermediate shades of grey. The medium in which these contraries pass into and out of existence is surface. The form-privation-matter dynamic is played out differently in different genera. The genus *body* comprises the contrariety of hot and cold. And one medium in which these contraries are found constantly replacing each other is, as Aristotle says, flesh and bone. It is tempting to think that Aristotle wishes to get rid of form, privation, and matter (along with being and unity) because of their variability in application to things. But this would be a mistake. Aristotle seeks a permanent entity on which each of these elementary concepts converge.

(3) *The argument against actuality and potentiality as principles*

By analogy, says Aristotle, the principles of things are the same, for instance, actuality and potentiality. But these too, like form, privation, and matter, are different for different things in different circumstances (*Met.* 1071a3-11). By analogy actuality and potentiality are principles. But, once they are applied to a host of real objects existing in different genera, they fail as common factors because they lack the separate existence required to allow them to function as ontological points of reference for all things potential and actual. Notice, in the following passage, the sharp division between *separately existing* principles (Aristotle suggests possible examples: soul and body, or intellect, desire, and body, 1071a3) and *non-separate, analogical* principles (e.g. actuality and potentiality):

> Since, on the one hand, there exist *separate entities*, and, on the other, *non-separate entities*, the former will be substances. And for this reason the causes of all things will be the same, because, without substances, affections and movements would not exist. Perhaps then these will be soul and body, or intellect, desire, and body. And yet in another way, by analogy, principles are the same; for instance, actuality and potentiality. But these are different for different things in different contexts. For in some cases the same entity will at one time exist in actuality and at another time in potentiality; e.g. wine or flesh or man. (And of these fall under the aforementioned causes; for, on the one hand, both the form—if it is not separate—and the composite, and the privation (e.g. darkness or sickness) exist actually, but the matter only potentially; for it represents the potentiality for becoming both. But the distinction between actuality and potentiality assumes a different shape for things whose matter is not

> the same and whose[8] form is not the same but different; just as the elements serve as the cause of a man—fire and earth as matter along with an individual form—and, in addition to these, something else outside, e.g. the father, and besides these the sun and its slanting orbit, these being neither the matter, nor the form, nor the privation, nor the same species as man, but rather moving causes (*Metaphysics Λ 5*, 1070b36-1071a17, my translation, Ross ed.).

Aristotle is searching for substantial permanence to physical change in the cosmos. He even briefly speculates that this substantial permanence consists in soul and body, or perhaps in intellect, desire, and body. In *Λ 6* he concludes that there must be an eternal prime mover. But for the moment he finds that the notions of actuality and potentiality may serve well as common universal principles when considered analogically, though, just like being and unity, they differ in application to different things in different contexts. In some cases the same thing is both actual and potential. E.g. Socrates is *potentially* an escaped prisoner, but actually a man who accepts the sanction of law. On a deeper level different aspects of substance are at the same time actual (i.e. form) and potential (i.e. matter). Furthermore, when cause and effect have not the same matter the distinction between actuality and potentiality differs dramatically. The father of Socrates is a moving cause which has a different parcel of matter than the sun, which is another moving cause of Socrates. The sun and the ecliptic are neither the matter of Socrates, nor the form, nor the privation of that form, but are remote moving causes which allow Socrates to flourish in life. So, perhaps, it is not even accurate to limit the elements and causes of Socrates to just the matter, form, and privation present in his person. But if so, where does the regress of outside causes and principles cease? Aristotle's point here is that the elements of substance along with actuality and potentiality differ when applied to individuals in different contexts. Aristotle questions the *objectivity* of these notions. If they differ in different circumstances, how can they serve as objective standards for knowledge? Aristotle craves permanence. His dialectics demand a focal entity as standard of reference for all beings. The passages we have looked at from *Metaphysics Λ 4 & 5* make the radical suggestion that all the previous efforts expended in the dialectical search for principles and causes of existence have been in vain; for none has brought the philosopher to a separately existing, self-sustaining and substantial basis of permanence in the cosmos.

Aristotle wants to prove in these arguments that principles universally applicable to all things by analogy, are really not the same for all because they lack permanent independent existence. They are common *only* by analogy. They are just as suspect to criticism as Platonic Forms because they lack a principle productive of motion and change. A separate and permanent entity that is common to all there is across categories and prior to them *could* provide such a principle. Analogical universals satisfy neither the requirement for *separate existence* beyond the categories nor the requirement *kinetic impetus.*

V. Aristotle Demonstrates the Substantiality, Actuality, and Unity of an Imperishable Prime Mover

Only an eternal substance, whose existence is proven at 1071b3-12, fully satisfies both the requirement for separate existence and the requirement for kinetic impetus. To this end Aristotle constructs three proofs:

> **First Proof** An Eternal Substance exists:
>
> Because there were three substances, two of them natural and one unmovable, we must say concerning this latter that there must necessarily exist an eternal immovable substance. For substances are first of existing things, and if all <substances> are destructible, then all things whatsoever are destructible. But neither is it possible for motion to have come into existence or to have been destroyed (for it always existed), nor for time to do so; since it is not possible for there to exist a before and an after where there is no time. Motion, therefore, is in this way continuous, just as time is—because time is either the same thing as motion or an affection of it. And there is no continuous motion except for locomotion; and of locomotion, circular motion (*Metaphysics Λ 6*, 1071b2-11, my translation, Ross ed.).

The proof for the existence of an eternal immovable substance takes the form of a hypothetical syllogism in the *modus tollens*:

Major Pr.:	If all substances are perishable, then everything else is perishable (1071b6).
Minor Pr.:	*But, motion and time are not perishable* (1071b6-7).
	Therefore, not all substances are perishable.

> Therefore, there must exist an imperishable kind of substance.

There seem to be supporting arguments for both premises as well. Firstly, everything other than substance is posterior to and dependent upon substance. Whatever is posterior to and dependent upon something perishes with the perishing of it. Therefore, if substances perish, then all else perishes as well. Secondly, Ross tells us that the proof for the eternity of motion is to be found in *Phys. Viii. 1-3*.[9] Aristotle clearly borrows from *Phys. Viii. 1*, 251b10-15 when he proves that since time is either a number of motion or a kind of motion, it follows that if there is always time, then motion itself must be eternal. Further, in that same *Physics* passage, he claims that there cannot be a before and an after without the existence of time. The question is: How can we know that time always existed? Granted, if motion is eternal, then so is time; because time is a measure of motion. Aristotle's reasoning must be this: to assert a beginning to time is absurd because this would apply a measure of before and after to the whole span of time, which cannot be measured, since time is itself a measure of the motion of things.

Whatever the case may be Aristotle has just proven that there exists a separate eternal mover of all things. The existence of this first mover gives Aristotle's metaphysics a sound objective scientific basis in reality. However "Kant suggests," as Irwin claims, "that metaphysics is second-order in so far as it examines, not the questions about the world that directly concern inquirers into nature, but the questions raised by the assumptions made by these inquirers. Aristotle's universal science is second-order in this sense."[10] Surely the existence of a Prime Mover refutes Irwin's claims. What could be more first-order than a science of eternal substance? Perhaps Irwin wants to separate "ontology" as study of the principles of logic from "theology" as study of God.[11] "Ontology" would, in this case, be second-order because it studies logical axioms that first-order departmental sciences assume by hypothesis.[12] But the question concerns the meaning of "metaphysics" which, understood in the Aristotelian sense, signifies the combination of theology with ontology. Aristotle's ontology turns out to be a preliminary *dialectical* groundwork for theology, not a self-sustaining science. Theology, however, is a science because it *demonstrates* truths about the nature of existence in its demonstration of the divine attributes.

Second Proof There is a Principle whose Substance is Actuality:

> But if, in fact, there exists something capable of moving things or acting upon them, but not actually doing so, there will be no motion; for it is permissible for that which has a potentiality not to actualize it. There is, therefore, no advantage if we were to posit eternal substances, like those who posit Forms, unless there existed in them some principle capable of producing change. Now not even this <principle> is sufficient, nor some other substance besides the Forms. For if it does not act, there will be no motion. Nor, in addition, <will this principle be sufficient> if it fails to act, and its substance is potentiality; for there will not be eternal motion. For it is permissible for a potential being not to exist. Therefore, it is necessary for there to exist such a principle whose substance is actuality. In addition, these substances must exist without matter; since they must be eternal, if, in fact, something else is eternal. Therefore, they must be actuality (*Metaphysics Λ 6*, 1071b12-22, my translation, Ross ed.).

Ross remarks at 1071b21 that "so far Aristotle has spoken of the necessity of one unmoved mover of the universe. He now refers by anticipation to the unmoved movers of the several celestial spheres, for which cf. 1074a15."[13] These movers are the closest entities to the one divine nature. They exhibit eternal, circular locomotions. They exist as pure form without need of matter; and are pure actualities. Aristotle shows latter that the prime mover must be unitary (cf. 1074a31-38), otherwise, being many, it would need matter in order to exist, which contradicts what he is trying to prove at 1071b12-22. But 1074a31-38 contradicts 1071b20-21! The paradox appears irreconcilable from the text—perhaps an inevitable casualty of speculation.

In the above passage Aristotle proves that the eternal substance (whose existence he just been proven at 1071b3-12) must be pure actuality because, if it were capable of producing motion and change, but did not do so, there would never have been motion. Clearly there is motion, therefore the eternal substance must be an activating principle.[14]

Thus, nothing is gained by positing Forms, because these do not supply a principle of change and movement (1071b15). Even if there were a moving principle besides the Forms, this principle would be insufficient if it did not act and remained a mere stationary capacity for bringing about movement in things (1071b17). But even if this principle acts, it will still not be sufficient if its substance is mere potentiality (1071b18). Because, in that case, there would be no *eternal* movement; since it is possible for that which exists potentially not to exist at all (1071b19). Therefore, the substance of this principle must be actuality (1071b20). And, since these activating substances are eternal, they must exist without matter; if, indeed, there exists some other eternal thing (i.e. a prime mover).

Here is Aristotle's main argument (with its suppressed minor premise):

Major Pr.: If there exists some <principle[15]> capable of producing motion and acting on things, but does not actually do so, then there would be no motion in the cosmos (1071b12-14).

Minor Pr.: [*But, clearly there is motion in the cosmos.*]

Therefore, there does not exist some <principle> capable of causing motion, but not actually doing so.

Therefore, if there does exist such a principle, it must be an *activating* principle.

Aristotle then inserts this supporting argument (with minor premise again suppressed):

Major Pr.: Platonic Forms are not sources of motion and change.

Minor Pr.: [Only a source of motion and change can serve as a principle which would account *for the apparent movements of physical objects in the cosmos.*]

Therefore, Platonic Forms are not principles which would account for apparent movements.

Aristotle then rejects two kinds of principle as insufficient:

(A) Any principle which fails to act, and remains a mere potentiality for causing motion and change.

(B) Any principle which does act, but whose substance is potentiality.

Aristotle's cosmic principle must be active always in order to account for the apparent motions of things. There must, therefore, exist a principle which does act, and whose substance is actuality. Now the question remains: How many of these first principles are there?

Third Proof The prime mover, and the heaven that it moves, are one both in number and in definition (1074a31-38):

> Evidently the heaven is one. For if there were many heavens as there are men, the principle for each would be one in form, but many in number. But things many in number possess matter (for the formula of many things is one and the same; for instance <the formula> of man, though Socrates is one). But the Prime Essence does not have matter; for it is actuality. Therefore, the primary unmoved moving Being is one both in formula and in number (*Metaphysics Λ 8*, 1074a31-38, my translation, Ross ed.).

Aristotle's argumentative move here caps of a series of proofs for the substance, actuality, and unity of the prime mover. Each of these descriptors has a privative contrary. Substance has accident as contrary; actuality has potency; unity has plurality. Aristotle seems to opt for the positive over the privative in his description of the prime mover. This mover is pure form 1074a35-36 (positive), not matter (privation of form); actual 1071a12-22 (positive), not potential (privation of actuality); unitary 1074a36 (positive) not plural (privation of unity); substantial, i.e. existing on its own 1071b3-12 (positive), not accidental, i.e. dependent on another for existence (privation of substance).

VI. All Substances desire the Divine Perfection

Aristotle even makes explicit mention of the two columns of contraries when describing the πρὸς ἕν relationship that all beings have with the supreme Being (*Met. Λ 7*, 1072a26ff.) as one of *desiring* a final state of perfection:

> Since that which is moved and moves is intermediate, there exists a thing which moves without itself being moved; being eternal, substance, and actuality.[16] The objects of desire and thought move in this way. They move without being moved. Their primary attributes are the same. For that which *appears* beautiful is loved, while that which *is* beautiful, being primary, is an object of the will. We desire a thing because it seems good; a thing does not seem good because we desire it. For thinking is a principle. And thought is moved by the object of thought, and one column <of contraries> is an object of thought in virtue of itself, and in this

> column substance is first, and of this that which is simple and actual. (Unity and simplicity are not the same; for the unit signifies a measure, while simplicity signifies the manner in which the thing itself exists.[17]) But surely the beautiful and that chosen for its own sake belong in the same column <of contraries>; and the best is either always or by analogy the primary instance. The following distinction makes clear that that for the sake of which is found among the immovables: that for the sake of which may exist either (1) *for someone* <on the way to a goal>, or (2) *of something* <as goal>; of these, one belongs among the immovables, the other does not.[18] It <i.e. the primary instance> moves by being loved, and it moves the other things which are moved (*Metaphysics Λ* 7, 1072a24-b4, my translation, Ross ed.)

How can the prime mover be simple if there are 55 other immaterial movers of the celestial spheres? Ross suggests a solution at 1074a22-23: "the movers of the planetary spheres are here said to act as final causes on the planetary spheres, as God does on the sphere of the fixed stars; i.e. a sort of desire is ascribed to the planetary spheres; cf. *De Caelo* 292a20-b25. The relation of their movers to God is nowhere stated, but is presumably also one of desire." Accordingly *De Caelo* 292a18-21 "We think of the stars as mere bodies, and as units with a serial order indeed but entirely inanimate; but we should rather conceive them as enjoying life and meaningful activity"; again *De Caelo* 292ab1-7 "for this reason <292a18-21?> we must consider the meaningful activity of the stars to be similar to that of animals and plants. For on this earth the greatest number of meaningful activities belongs to man, since there are many goods that man can obtain, hence many meaningful activities and many ends beyond these activities. But that which holds the best condition possible has no need for activity, since it is the same as the end for the sake of which, and meaningful action consists of both an end and means to this end" (my translation, D. J. Allan ed.). Throughout this section Aristotle speaks of ἡ τῶν ἄστρων πρᾶξις which implies *action guided by intelligence*, as opposed to simple kinetic motion.

The main argument of 1072a24-b4 is that all substances *desire* the divine perfection as the end of their meaningful activities, and that, subsequently everything in nature occurs for a purpose relative to the divine. Nature does everything for the best and nothing in vain:

Major Pr.:	That which moves without being moved is an object of thought and desire (1072a26-7).
Minor Pr.:	*An eternal substance moves without being moved (1072a25).*
	Therefore, an *eternal substance* is the object of thought and desire (1072b3-4).

The external evidence for God as object of desire is copious. At *Phys. I. 9* 191b35-192a25 Aristotle corrects the Platonists by asserting that the underlying matter serves as a cause, as does the form, of the composite which comes-to-be now this quality now its opposite. I.e. it is not the case, as the Platonists suppose, that one contrary desires another, since contraries are mutually destructive. Rather matter desires form, as woman desires man, *Phys.* 192a20-25. Without underlying matter any given side of a Platonic contrariety would appear not to exist at all to one who focuses attention on it as an evil agent. Presumably, when Platonic contraries do battle one side must triumph over the other, so that, without underlying matter for support, the existence of the vanquished is blotted out entirely: "for there being something divine and good and longed for, we assert that there exists, on the one hand, a contrary to it, and, on the other, that which of its own nature longs for and desires it" (*Phys.* 192a16-19 my translation).

In *De Generatione et Corruptione II. 10* Aristotle says God guarantees that things come-to-be perpetually in the closest approximation to his own perfect nature, and goes on to assert that, since being is better than its opposite non-being, things strive to maintain their own existence while always seeking a better and more perfect state: "Coming to be and passing away will always be continuous, and will never fail owing to the cause we stated. And this continuity has a sufficient reason. For in all things, as we affirm, nature always strives after the better. Now being (we have explained elsewhere the variety of meanings we recognize in this term) is better than not-being; but not all things can possess being, since they are too far removed from the principle. God therefore adopted the remaining alternative, and fulfilled the perfection of the universe by making coming-to-be uninterrupted; for the greatest possible coherence would thus be secured to existence, because that coming-to-be should itself come-to-be perpetually in the closest approximation to the eternal being" (*De Gen. et Corr.* 336b27f., H.H. Joachim translation).

In Aristotle's biological works we again find divine governance *De Vita* 469a28 "what we have said makes it clear that the source of the sensitive soul, together with that connected with growth and nutrition, is situated in this organ [i.e. the heart] and in the central one of the three divisions of the body. But it follows by reason also; for we see that in every case, when several paths are open, Nature always chooses the best" (G.R.T. Ross translator); *De Partibus Animalium* 687a15f. "For nature adds that which is less to that which is greater or more important, and not that which is more valuable and greater to that which is less. Seeing then that such is the better course, and seeing also that of what is possible nature invariably brings about the best, we must conclude that man does not owe his superior intelligence to his hands, but his hands to his superior intelligence" (W. Ogle translator); *De Ingressu Animalium* 704b15f. "At the beginning of the inquiry we must postulate the principles we are accustomed constantly to use for our scientific investigation of nature, that is we must take for granted principles of this universal character which appear in all nature's work. Of these one is that nature creates nothing without a purpose, but always the best possible in each kind of living creature by reference to its essential constitution" (A.S.L. Farquharson translator).[19]

These external passages suggest that God is somehow an archetype expressing the most important positive states of things. All natural change occurs in matter shifting between positive state and privation. State and privation are contraries. Because natural objects always seek the God by seeking the better state, and because in all movement between contraries there is a better and a worse, the God must consist of attributes on the better (i.e. positive) side of the table of contraries. At 1072a31 Aristotle brings this theme to its logical climax. The faculty of thought is moved by an object of thought. One column in Aristotle's array of contraries lists those objects of thought which can be contemplated by themselves without need of other objects; while objects in the other column can be thought only in conjunction with their opposites.

Aristotle contemplates the following table of contraries at 1072a30f.:

Objects of Thought Per Se	*Objects of Thought Per Accidens*
(1) Substance (οὐσία, 1072a31)	(1) Accident
(2) Simple Substance (ἁπλῆ οὐσία, a32)	(2) Manifold Substance
(3) Actual Substance (καιʼ ἐνέργειαν οὐσία, a32)	(3) Potential Substance
(4) The Beautiful (τὸ καλόν, a34))	(4) The Ugly
(5) The Primary Instance (τὸ πρῶτον cf. 1072b1)	(5) Secondary Instances
(6) That chosen for its own sake (τὸ διʼ αὐτὸ αἱρετὸν, 1072a35)	(6) That chosen for another's sake

Contrary opposition plays a central role in almost all of Aristotle's discussions of first principles.[20] Commenting on Aristotle's use of contraries at 1072a31 Ross has "ἡ ἑτέρα συοτοιχία, cf. Λ. 986a23n., . 1066a15, Phys. 201b25. Not only is συστοιχία used of the Pythagorean list of opposites, but Aristotle himself recognizes a positive συστοιχία including such terms as being, unity, substance, and a negative συστοιχία including not-being, plurality, not-substance (Γ. 1004b27, *De Gen. et Corr.* 319a15, *De Sensu* 447b30, 448a16, *P.A.* 670b21). In each case the negative is known not *per se* but as the negation of the positive term."[21]

Certain Pythagoreans recognized ten sets of first principles which they arranged into opposing pairs of contraries (*Met. Λ.* 986a23f.):

Pythagorean Contraries

(1) Finite (πέρας)	Infinite (ἄπειρον)
(2) Odd (περιττόν)	Even (ἄρτιον)
(3) Unity (ἕν)	Plurality (πλῆθος)
(4) Right (δεξιόν)	Left (ἀριοτερόν)
(5) Male (ἄρρεν)	Female (θῆλυ)
(6) Resting (ἠρεμοῦν)	Being Moved (κινούμενον)
(7) Straight (εὐθύ)	Curved (καμπύλον)
(8) Light (φῶς)	Darkness (σκότος)
(9) Good (ἀγαθόν)	Evil (κακόν)
(10) Square (τετράγωνον)	Oblong (ἑτερόμηκες)

These Pythagoreans, says Aristotle, believed (a) that contraries were the principles of all things (986b3), and (b) that these first principles served as the *matter* out of which things were composed (986b6). Aristotle seems willing, in the *Metaphysics*, to accept (a) so long as we reject (b). Aristotle often criticizes (b) by positing a *tertium quid* in the matter upon which the contraries supervene. He thus distinguishes between matter in process of change between contraries, and the contraries themselves. Nevertheless, contrariety serves a central purpose in scientific explanation.

For instance, God is contemplated through a series of *per se* concepts; e.g. substance, simple substance, actual substance, the beautiful, etc. Parasitic on these are a series of privative concepts. Privation can be contemplated only *per accidens*, in reference to a corresponding positive. The dependence of the privative on the positive is evident in the following: *Met.K* 1066a13-16 "The reason why movement is posited as falling into these classes <i.e. difference, inequality, and non-being 1066a11> is that it is believed to be something indeterminate, and the principles in one of the columns of contraries are indeterminate because they are privations" (my translation). Compare *De Gen. et Corr.* 319a14f. "Those things, therefore, which do not signify substance are not said to come-to-be without qualification, but to come-to-be something. However, coming-to-be is said to take place in all things alike when a thing comes-to-be something in one of the two columns; for instance, in substance if it comes-to-be Fire, but not if it comes-to-be Earth, and in quality, if it comes-to-be knowledgeable, but not if it comes-to-be ignorant" (my translation). Fire and Earth are contrary *substances*; knowledgeableness and ignorance are contrary *qualities*. Note further *De Partibus Animalium* 670b17-23: "One the other hand, in such animals as have a bladder, and whose lung contains blood, the spleen is watery, both for the reason already mentioned, and also because the left side of the body is more watery and colder than the right. For each of two contraries has been so placed as to go together with that which is akin to it in another pair of contraries. Thus right and left, hot and cold, are pairs of contraries; and they are in the same column as one another, after the manner described" (W. Ogle translation).

VII. The Gamma-Lambda Connection

Aristotle did not import the division of contraries mentioned at *Met. Λ 7* 1072a30f. from someone else's philosophy, they were an inevitable outcome of his own philosophical development. For instance, in *Met. Γ 2* Aristotle undertakes the ambitious task of reappraising the principles of previous philosophers in terms of Unity-Plurality, what he calls "the principles of all contraries" 1005a4. He sets out to prove in *Γ 2* not only that one science investigates Being *qua* Being, but that this science is different from all of the so-called departmental sciences. The continuity between books *Γ* and *Λ* is remarkable. Both emphasize the dialectical role of a primary instance (τὸπρῶτον compare 1005a7 with 1072b1); but mark two distinct phases of philosophical maturity. In book Γ the identity of the primary instance is still up for grabs. In book *Λ* it turns out to be God unequivocally. In Γ Aristotle purposefully holds back commitment to any one entity or notion that would characterize the Being of beings, though he posits substance (οὐσία) and unity (ἕν) to be the guiding objects of study. But this is to say no more than that the notions of Medicine and Health represent *in abstracto* the guiding objects of medicine and dietetics. It does us little good if we cannot specify our object of study by means of a primary instance, a πρῶτον. Remember that Being, Medicine, and Health do not maintain separate existence as Platonic Forms; they cannot, therefore, be contemplated by themselves *in abstracto* without reference to a concrete instance. Their natures must be made concrete, but by means of just any instance, rather by means of studying an individual primary type or instance; e.g. the medical doctor (*EE VII. 2*, 1236a20f.) and, of course, God. Socrates and this scalpel are equally instances of Being and Medicine, but not *primary* instances. Our knowledge of either abstract notion is not enhanced in the least by knowing who Socrates is or what this scalpel does. We must come to grips with the nature of the *primary* instance.

Compare the passage quoted from *Met. Λ 7*, 1072a24-b4 above with the following from *Met. Γ 2* where Aristotle argues for a trans-departmental science of Being:

> In addition, one column of contraries is privation, and all things are reduced to being and not-being, and to unity and plurality; e.g. rest belongs to unity, motion to plurality. Nearly all thinkers agree that beings and substance are composed out of contraries; in fact, all assert that the principles are contraries. Some posit odd and even, some warm and cold, some limit and unlimited, and some friendship and strife. All other <contraries> apparently reduce to one and many (let us assume this reduction), and the principles of other thinkers fall entirely under these as genera. Therefore, it is clear from these considerations that it belongs to one science to theorize on Being *qua* Being. For all things are contraries or composed of contraries, and the principles of contraries are unity and plurality. These belong to one science, whether they are spoken *under a unitary notion* (i.e. καθ ' ἑν), or not—as is probably the case. Nevertheless, even if 'unity' has many meanings the other <positive

> notions> and, in like manner, their contraries will be spoken in reference to the primary instance <of unity>. Even if being and unity are not universal, and the same in all cases, nor separately existing—as they probably are not, some referring to unity, others unities one by one. For this reason the geometry does not theorize on what 'contrary', 'perfect', 'being', 'unity', 'same' or 'other' mean, but rather accepts their meaning by hypothesis. Therefore, it is clear both that one science theorizes on Being *qua* Being including its attributes *qua* Being, and that the same theoretical studies not only substances, but their attributes as well, both those mentioned and prior & posterior, genus & species, whole & part, and others like these" (*Metaphysics Γ 2*, 1004a27-1005a18, my translation, Ross ed.).

In this passage Aristotle tries to prove three things: (1) that only *one* science studies all there is, 1005a2-3; (2) that it is not the geometer's to investigate notions common to all there is (e.g. 'contrary', 'being', 'unity', 'same', 'other', etc.), 1005a11-12; and (3)—a combination of (1) and (2)—that it belongs to one science, in studying all there is, to study both substances and their attributes (both the ones mentioned in (2) plus 'prior' & 'posterior', 'genus' & 'species', 'whole' & 'part', and other binaries), 1005a15-17. Many of the reasons Aristotle provides here in *Γ 2* to uphold his conclusions anticipate directly some of his teachings in Λ *4 & 5* concerning the insufficiency of analogical universals like 'being' and 'unity' as well as the need for demonstrating the nature and the mode of operation of the first mover in *Λ 7*.

The First Argument from the *Γ 2* passage above is, like so many dialectical arguments, enthymematic. The major premise is suppressed. I summarized the reasoning as follows:

Major Pr.:	There is *one* science of x, when every set of attributes pertaining to x can be brought under one set of principles.
Minor Pr.:	Science of all there is has one such set of principles in the notions of Unity v. Plurality (1005a4-5).
	Therefore, there is one science of all there is (1005a2-3).

Aristotle gives two supporting arguments for the minor premise:

Supporting Argument I

Major Pr. All things are either contraries or composed of contraries—as nearly all thinkers agree (1005a3-4).

Minor Pr. All contraries (both those explicitly mentioned as originating from previous thinkers and those that were not) are subsumable under Unity v. Plurality as if under genera (1004b33-1005a2).

Therefore, Unity v. Plurality are principles governing all things.

Supporting Argument II

Major Pr: A science of all there is would require a set of principles governing all things. (This is evident from the fact that previous thinkers have searched for principles governing all things, 1004b29-33).

Minor Pr: The set of principles governing all things is Unity v. Plurality, (cf. 1004b33-1005a2, Supporting Argument I).

Therefore, a science of all there is would require Unity v. Plurality as principles.

The second argument in the passage stems from these: because (as proven at 1005a3) there is *one* science of all there is, Aristotle can now assert that this science, and not geometry, a departmental science, will study notions common to everything. Since such notions as ‘contrary’, ‘unity’, ‘prior’ & ‘posterior’, etc. are commonly assumed among the departmental sciences, there needs to be a science that studies these. Only philosophy has a broad enough subject-matter to do this. Philosophy is not a second-order science as Irwin (and Kant) imagine, precisely because there is a real unitary Being underlying all that is whose nature is the subject-matter of the philosopher.

This unitary Being, God, is not specifically mentioned in *Γ 2*, but is foreshadowed. Firstly, 1005a6: “whether these <i.e. the principles of Unity v. Plurality> are spoken *under a unity* (i.e. καθ’ ἐν), or not—as is probably the case”, there will still be one science of all there is. Even if the notions of Unity and Plurality turn out not to be genera, there will still be *one* science of Being.

Secondly, 1005a6-8: unity and plurality are the subject-matter of one science “but nevertheless even if the term ‘unity’ has many meanings, <there will still be one science of all there is, because> the others <i.e. the

other *positive notions* besides 'unity'>, and their contraries in like manner, will be spoken in reference to the *primary instance* <of unity>."[22] Aristotle deliberately leaves unclear in the context just *what* this *primary instance* (1005a7) of unity is. Determining the identity of this primary thing is the task of Aristotle's dialectic, i.e. the pre-lambda books *Met. Γ-Θ* which I call "ontology" in order to distinguish it from "theology" (*Met. Λ*) whose task is to demonstrate *the attributes* properly predicable of the primary entity. Theology undertakes to demonstrate that the primary unity of things is God. It then proceeds to demonstrate as much as can be predicated of this God. Ontology, on the other hand, is purely dialectical. There is no commitment to the existence of God, just as there is no final commitment on most of the dialectical questions originally raised in *Met. β*; Aristotle's purpose in ontology is almost always to give arguments for both sides of a question. He was concerned with leaving behind for his students certain templates of argument defending both sides of some of the foundational questions in philosophy.

There are subtle connections between books Γ and Λ. *Met.* 1005a6-8 anticipates *Met. Λ*, 1072a30-35 (translated above) in which the divine attributes are linked to universal notions that can be contemplated *per se* without reference to any other notion (e.g. *actual* substance as opposed to *potential* substance, *simple* substance as opposed to *manifold* substance, etc.). The *per se* notions mentioned in *Λ 7*, 1072a30ff. occupy the positive side of the list in Aristotle's double column of contraries. Compare this to Γ *2*, 1005a6ff.: even if 'unity' has many meanings, there will still be one science of all there is, because all notions subsumable under 'unity' (understood as positive head) will "be spoken in reference to the primary instance" of unity; just as all notions subsumable under 'plurality' (understood as privative head) will be parasitic on their corresponding positives. *Met.* 1005a6-8 does not make sense without knowing *what* the primary instance is, i.e. without 1075a30-35.

Further, (1005a8-11) "even if 'being' and 'unity' are not universal and the same in every instance nor separately existing—as is probably the case, but there are just things referring to unity and others which are unities taken one-by-one" there will still be one science of all there is.[23] Compare this to 1070b4-10 (quoted above) where Aristotle criticizes 'unity' and 'being' as principles just because they are applicable to all things only by analogy. There is no Platonic Form of Being or Unity. There are only individually existing instances of being and unity. Taken one-by-one these instances are unitary, but they manifest their unity differently in different contexts. Socrates, for instance, manifests his unity by being a *rational animal*, the Mausoleum of Augustus by exhibiting, perhaps, a *proportionality of structure agreeable to the senses*. There is, of course, a deeper transcategorial unity to these objects; i.e. they can be contemplated analogically insofar as they are just beings. But since unity is, in the context of *Γ 2*, purely analogical, it is merely an *intelligible* unity that is studied, not a palpable separately existing substantial unity. Aristotle discovers in Λ, but not in *Γ*, that he needs a basis of permanence in the cosmos for their to be a substantial Unity to which all of the instances of unity can be reduced. The reader of *Γ*, as yet unaware of what is to come in Λ, must inevitably ask: *How can there be one science of all there is given that, in all probability, the terms 'being' and 'unity' do not refer to universals in the sense of permanent separately existing Platonic Forms, nor apply to all things in exactly the same way?* The answer reveals itself only in book *Λ*: *Because all things bear πρὸς ἕν reference to God as primary Entity*.

On the way to *Metaphysics Λ* Aristotle experiments with three currents of focal analysis. First, in *Γ 2-8* he posits unity and plurality as contrary ontological principles; and proves *ad absurdum* that the laws of non-contradiction and excluded middle necessarily ensure entity's unity over time. If an entity did not maintain its unity over time, but just sporadically changed its identity from one moment to the next, then intelligent discourse would be impossible. Any term could change its signification at any time. Secondly, in the central books Aristotle experiments with the idea that 'being' denotes primary substance; i.e. a *this something* as opposed to a species or genus. But he does not state there what he takes to be *the* primary substance. The identity of this substance is still up for grabs. Thirdly, in book Θ he discuss actuality and potentiality in application to substantial and qualitative change over time. It is only when Aristotle reduces all of these currents to one primary instance in book *Λ* that he completes the dialectic and begins the theology. Aristotle's three proofs for the substantiality, actuality, and unity of the Primary Entity converge three currents of focal analysis into one study called "Theology."

Aristotle's Primary Entity is a God who represents the unifying substantializing cosmic *energy* behind all that is. God supplies a constant impetus for kinetic change, and, at the same time, marks that final state of perfection towards which all things strive in their own kinetic endeavors to

Exist. Cosmic *kinesis* is recursive: God impels the celestial spheres to remain in eternal circular motion, but these, like the terrestrial objects they encompass, seek return to God through an inborn desire for the divine perfection.

Works Cited

Anton, John P. *Aristotle's Theory of Contrariety*. London, 1957.

Apostle, Hippocrates G. *Aristotle's Metaphysics: Translated with Commentary and Glossary*. Indiana, 1966.

Barnes, Jonathan. *The Complete Works of Aristotle*. 2 vols. Princeton, 1984.

Bonitz, Hermann. *Index Aristotelicus*. (Fifth Edition). Berlin, 1870. Reissued 1955.

Cherniss, Harold F. *Aristotle's Criticism of Plato and the Academy*. Oxford, 1944.

Irwin, T. H. *Aristotle's First Principles*. Oxford, 1988.

Irwin, T. H. 'Homonymy in Aristotle', *The Review of Metaphysics*, vol. XXXIV, no. 3, March 1981, pp. 523-544.

Jaeger, Werner. *Aristotle: Fundamentals of the History of His Development*. Richard Robinson tr. Oxford, 1948.

Jaeger, Werner ed. *Aristotelis Metaphysica*. Oxford, 1957.

Kirwan, C. A. *Aristotle: Metaphysics Books Γ, Δ, and E*. Second Edition. Oxford, 1971.

Leszl, Walter. *Aristotle's Conception of Ontology*. Padova, 1975.

Owen, G. E. L. *Logic, Science, and Dialectic*. Martha Nussbaum ed. Ithaca, 1986.

Owens, Joseph. 'An Ambiguity in Aristotle, EE VII 2 1236a23-4' *Apeiron*, vol. XXII, no. 2, June 1989, pp. 127-137.

Owens, Joseph. 'Is There Any Ontology in Aristotle?' *Dialogue*, vol. XXV, no. 4, Winter 1986, pp. 697-707.

Owens, Joseph. 'The Grounds of Universality in Aristotle' *American Philosophical Quarterly* vol. 3, no. 2, April 1966.

Ross, W. D. *Aristotle's Metaphysics: A Revised Text with Introduction and Commentary*. (2 vols). Oxford, 1924.

Ward, Julie K. 'Focal Reference in Aristotle's Account of Φιλία: *Eudemian Ethics VII 2*' *Apeiron*, vol. XXVIII, no. 3, September 1995, pp. 183-205.

Witt, Charlotte. *Substance and Essence in Aristotle: An Interpretation of Metaphysics VII-IX*. Ithaca, 1989.

Endnotes

1. T. H. Irwin, *Aristotle's First Principles*, p. 500, 3n8. C. A. Kirwan would disagree: "[The idea that no science can have all existing things as its subject because of the multiple senses of 'exist'] is suggested by an analogy between 'thing-that-is' and 'good' which Aristotle draws at *Nichomachean Ethics I 6.* 1096a29-34, where he argues against Platonists that different kinds of knowledge or expertise are required to discover e.g. what is good in war and what is good in medicine: there could not be such a thing as a general knowledge of what is good which would short-cut these particular studies. But it is a mistake to suppose that this analogy raises a difficulty in the way of the inquiry examined in *Metaphysics Γ*. The question about existence which parallels the Platonic question 'what is good?' is 'what exists?'; and, while it is true to say that there is no single discipline that includes answers to such questions as 'do electrons exist?' and 'does conscience exist?', metaphysics, according to Aristotle's conception of it, makes no claim to be such a discipline. It seems, then, that Aristotle was troubled by a needless anxiety. No danger lurks in his concession that the senses of 'be' are multiple, if that concession is based on the analogy between 'thing-that-is' and 'good'", *Aristotle's Metaphysics Books Γ,Λ, and E*, p. 80.
2. G. E. L. Owen, 'Aristotle on the Snares of Ontology', *Logic, Science, and Dialectic*, collected papers in Greek Philosophy by G. E. L. Owen, Martha Nussbaum, ed.
3. *Sophistici Elenchi, I.* 9, 170a20-23, Ross ed.
4. G. E. L. Owen 'Logic and Metaphysics in Some Earlier Works of Aristotle', Düring ed. *Studia Graeca et Latina Gothoburgensia*, no. 11, 1960, p. 164.
5. The privation of substance is accident, of actuality potentiality, of simplicity (i.e. intrinsic unity) multiplicity (i.e. intrinsic plurality). Privation is not part of the Divine nature.
6. For a lengthier treatment of focal meaning analysis see T.H. Irwin, 'Aristotle On Homonymy', *Review of Metaphysics*, 1981 vol. 34, pp. 523-44, and Julie K. Ward, 'Focal Reference in Aristotle's Account of φιλία: Eudemian Ethics VII 2' *Apeiron*, vol. XXVIII, no. 3, September, 1995, pp. 183-205.
7. Joseph Owens develops the concept of *primary instance universal* in 'An Ambiguity in Aristotle, EE VII 2 1236a23-4' Apeiron, vol. XXII, no. 2, June 1989, pp. 127-137.
8. I depart from Ross by reading καὶ ὢν (1071a12) as found in the commentary of Themistius, instead of ὢν <ἐνὶων>.
9. Ibid., Ross, *Comm. Arist. Metaph. II*, p. 368.
10. Irwin, Aristotle's First Principles, ch. 8.86, p. 160.

11. Cf. John Thorp 'Does Primacy Confer Universality? Logic and Theology in Aristotle' *Apeiron*, vol. XXII, no. 2, June 1989, pp. 101-125.
12. Cf. Joseph Owens 'Is There Any Ontology in Aristotle', *Dialogue*, vol. XXV, no. 4, Winter 1986, pp. 697-707. The term "ontology" originates in the seventeenth century and becomes popularized through Christian Wolff's *Ontologia sive Philosophia Prima.* This work became a standard philosophy text at German Universities in the eighteenth century. If Wolff had followed my interpretation of Aristotle he would have retitled his masterwork *"Theologia sive Philosophia Prima"*; seeing that his task was to *demonstrate* philosophical truths.
13. Ibid., Ross, *Comm. Arist. Metaph. II*, p. 369.
14. 1071b12-14 does not specifically mention an *eternal substance* as the thing κινητὸν ἢ ποιητικόν, but, if the argument is to make any sense, this must be supplied in thought from the preceding paragraph which centers around ἀίδιόν τινα οὐσίαν ἀκίνητον 1071b4-5.
15. See footnote 13.
16. The *unity* of the unmoved mover is proven later at 1074a31-38.
17. Ross on 1072a33 "τὸ δὲ ἁπλοῦν πώς ἔχον αὐτό. 'One' denotes that a thing is the measure *of something*, the unit used in counting an assemblage; 'simple' denotes that a thing is *itself* in a certain condition, i.e. unmixed", ibid., vol. 2, p. 376.
18. "That for the sake of which" 1072b2 has reference either (1) to the *person willing* it or (2) to the thing itself, i.e. the *end willed.* Aristotle's point is that the former is transitory and in the process of moving towards an end, while the end itself is a constant focal point of will and desire. "It might be thought (cf. B. 996a22, K. 1059a35)," says Ross, "that the teleological view implied in calling immaterial substance (God) the πρῶτον ὀρεκτόν is incompatible with the unchanging, eternal nature of immaterial substance (a25). Aristotle therefore proceeds to point out that τὸ οὗ ἕνεκα, the object of purposive action, may in one sense of these words be found in the realm of eternal, unchangeable entities. I.e., when we speak of the οὗ ἕνεκα of a thing we may mean (1) that the thing is good τινί, for some conscious being, or (2) that it is good τινός (ἕνεκα), for the sake of some end. The latter exists in the sphere of unchangeables (ἔστι, l. 3 = ἔστιν ἐν τοῖς ἀκινήτοις), while the former does not, since the attainment of good involves change in that which attains it" *Comm. Arist. Metaph., II*, p. 376.
19. The translations of which I have made use in this and the preceding paragraph are to be found in the Barnes edition of *Aristotle's Complete Works* (2 vols.), Princeton, 1984.
20. Contrariety pervades Aristotle's thought. Cf. J.P. Anton, "Contrariety is a first principle (ἀρχή) in the understanding of substance in so far as it is in process. Contrariety presupposes substance" *Aristotle's Theory of Contrariety*, p. 13.
21. Ibid. Ross, vol. 2, p. 376.

22. ἀλλ΄ ὅμως εἰ καὶ πολλακῶς λέγεται τὸ ἕν, πρὸς τὸ πρῶτον τἄλλα λεγθησεται καὶτὰἐναντίαόμοιως 1005a6-8, Ross ed.
23. I follow *Codex Laurentianus 87.12* in omitting καὶ διὰ τοῦτο from 1005a8 because it creates an unusually awkward anacolouthon: καὶ εἰ μὴ ἔστι τὸ ὄν ἤ τὸ ἕν καθόλου καὶ ταὐτὸ ἐπὶ πάντων ἤ χωριστόν, ὥσπερ Ἴσως οὐκ ἔστιν ἀλλὰ τὰ μέν πρὸς ἕν τὰ ςὲ τῷ ἐφεξῆς , Ross ed.

Volonté et autocausalité dans la pensée de l'Un chez Plotin

Jean-Marc Narbonne
Laval Université

Que l'on puisse se référer, dans une philosophie issue de la tradition grecque, à la divinité et au premier principe en termes de volonté et d'autocausalité, voilà une nouveauté qu'il est difficile d'apprécier à sa juste valeur et dont seuls plusieurs siècles de spéculations judéo-chrétiennes peuvent nous voiler toute la radicalité.

Ni Platon ni Aristote, c'est entendu, mais ni non plus un Zénon de Cittium et un Chrysippe ou un Épicure, n'ont l'idée, et je pourrais même dire, la *possibilité*, d'attribuer à quelque réalité, ὄντος ου θεός, un pouvoir particulier et insigne au sein de la totalité des étants. La raison en est ce qu'on peut appeler le *cosmologisme* grec, qui représente l'ensemble des êtres comme une totalité d'éléments interdépendants entre lesquels, certes, une hiérarchie peut être reconnue, mais qui interdit à l'un quelconque d'entre eux de s'affranchir complètement de son lien avec les autres, le premier terme ou le premier principe—lorsqu'il se trouve qu'il n'y en a qu'un et non pas plusieurs, le terme ou le concept même de «divin» consistant essentiellement jusqu'alors en un «Prädikatsbegriff» se référant à plusieurs objets ou domaines d'objets, plutôt qu'en un «Substanzbegriff», le premier terme dis-je, étant conçu comme le premier terme *au sein de la série* et non pas comme le premier terme *par rapport ou par-delà la série*. Dans un tel contexte, défini par ce qu'on pourrait appeler le cosmologisme, l'autocausalité et la volonté d'un premier principe pensé en quelque sorte en marge ou par-delà son lien avec les autres éléments de l'ensemble, paraît à toutes fins pratiques impossible.

C'est ce qui amena par exemple A. Faust, dans une étude sur le développement du concept de possibilité dans notre tradition, à distinguer le concept cosmologique de possibilité, des concepts ontologique et noologique de possibilité.

Le concept cosmologique, qui en gros correspond à la pensée grecque, réside en ceci que le ressort de la réalité, sa «possibilité», si l'on veut, est cherchée au sein d'une entité elle-même cosmologique, tant et si bien que la réflexion philosophique demeure nécessairement «intramondaine», liée en quelque sorte à l'ordre du cosmos.

Le caractère archaïque des spéculations présocratiques par exemple se manifeste en ceci que c'est un élément lui-même physique du monde qui doit également servir de base d'explication pour tout ce qui existe d'autre dans le monde: cela vaut évidemment pour l'*eau* chez Thalès de Milet, l'*air* chez Anaximène, le *feu* chez Héraclite, les *éléments* chez Empédocle, mais aussi pour l'*infini* d'Anaximandre, les *homéomères* d'Anaxagore et les *atomes* de Démocrite. Le possible, dans une telle perspective, présuppose toujours du *pré-existant*, il se conçoit sans cesse, en d'autres termes, comme du *préalablement présent*. Le réel en tant que donné doit trouver sa source, non pas dans un *réel de second degré*, comme on verra que c'est le cas chez Aristote, mais dans une *réalité seconde*.

Le fait de situer la possibilité dans un élément préexistant, dans une *nature préexistante*, correspond d'ailleurs au sens archaïque du terme *dynamis* qui a été lui-même très tôt rapproché du terme de nature, *physis*. Originalement, en effet, la *dynamis*[1], qui renvoyait dans le langage courant à la *force physique*, à la puissance supérieure de tel ou tel individu (et par extension, à la puissance par exemple de telle armée, de tel pays), devint l'expression de la *nature*, c'est-à-dire du *caractère distinctif*, et donc *spécifique et naturel*, de tel ou tel être[2]. Tout *pouvoir-être* dans le monde se comprenait dès lors forcément comme pouvoir *d'un* être.

La réflexion aristotélicienne marquera à cet égard un pas décisif en concevant pour la première fois la possibilité comme un «moment» à proprement parler de l'être, et c'est à juste titre que Faust voit en lui le père de toute la spéculation européenne concernant le problème de la possibilité[3]. Pour Aristote, en effet, on ne doit plus chercher la possibilité dans un être préexistant, dans une quelconque entité première, mais la comprendre comme un moment constitutif, quoique tout à fait impersonnel et abstrait, de l'être lui-même pris comme tel.

La possibilité ainsi conçue par Aristote reste cependant de type *cosmologique*, comme le rappelle Faust, parce qu'elle est étroitement liée au devenir *tel qu'il se produit dans le monde*. Dans la mesure, en effet, où le devenir est *orienté* chez Aristote, où (pour prendre un exemple typiquement aristotélicien) un homme ne peut engendrer qu'un homme[4], et où la matière première n'a d'abord le «choix» que de devenir l'une ou l'autre des quatre qualités élémentaires, la possibilité elle-même est limitée par la structure ontologique du cosmos[5].

La possibilité prend une forme purement *ontologique*, et non plus simplement *cosmologique*, dès l'instant où le donné, c'est-à-dire la réalité tout entière, l'univers dans son ensemble, est référé *pour ce qui est de sa possibilité même* à un pur possible «logique» consistant en la simple absence de contradiction interne (*«ex sola habitudine terminorum qui sibi non repugnant»*)[6]. Un nouveau concept du possible est en effet nécessaire et doit être élaboré dès lors que, dans une perspective chrétienne, le problème de la création du monde et celui de la toute puissance divine entrent en jeu. Le fondement, la possibilité intrinsèque de ce monde, n'a plus dès lors à être cherché *dans ce monde lui-même* mais dans un être qui, transcendant au monde, choisit sur la seule base de ce qui est possible, pensable, représentable, de créer l'être tel qu'il est, ou plutôt tel qu'il a voulu qu'il soit, à savoir notre univers actuel.

Cette nouvelle conception du possible qui s'élabore peu à peu à travers le moyen-âge, comme le souligne Faust, répond à un processus qu'on pourrait appeler de *dé-cosmologisation de la possibilité*, lequel exprime, plus largement, une *dé-ontologisation des conditions métaphysiques de l'être*. Le fondement reste bien encore ici ontologique, dans la mesure où c'est un être, Dieu, qui doit actualiser la possibilité à l'origine du monde, mais cette possibilité n'a plus rien en elle-même de cosmologique, elle n'est plus assujettie, en d'autres termes, aux conditions ontologiques naturelles telles qu'elles se présentent dans l'univers sensible.

Si jusqu'à saint Thomas, comme le note Faust[7], la doctrine de la création ne valait que comme *article de foi*, et n'était donc qu'un pur objet de croyance, le passage du non-être à l'être reçoit une justification essentiellement philosophique dès lors que le «possible en soi» (*«possibile in se ipsum»*), entendu comme «cohérence des termes» (*«coharentia terminorum»*), constitue désormais à lui seul un critère autonome du possible à côté de la «possibilité selon la puissance», essentiellement aristotélicienne[8].

C'est évidemment ce concept de possibilité, accordé à la seule *pensabilité*[9], qui est au fondement de la métaphysique de Leibniz par exemple, chez qui l'être divin *choisit*, entre plusieurs mondes, le meilleur des mondes possibles[10].

3) Possibilité «noologique».

D'une possibilité relative au monde, intrinsèque au monde, comme l'était la possibilité *cosmologique* des Grecs, à une possibilité indépendante du monde, extrinsèque au monde, comme l'est la possibilité *ontologique* des chrétiens, on passe ensuite à une possibilité étrangère à tout fondement ontologique et ne s'intéressant plus qu'aux *conditions conceptuelles de l'être*, telles qu'elles peuvent être déduites de l'activité intellective du sujet connaissant. Le possible n'a plus désormais à être déduit ni d'une structure objective du monde, comme chez Aristote, ni d'une possibilité abstraite *réalisée* par un être transcendant, comme dans la Scolastique, mais de la seule activité transcendantale du sujet connaissant, comme cela se rencontre particulièrement chez Kant et chez Fichte. La question n'est plus alors «Qu'est-ce qui rend possible la réalité actuelle du monde?», ou encore «Qu'est-ce qui rend possible ce monde lui-même pris comme tel dans sa globalité?», mais bien: «Qu'est-ce qui rend possible la *connaissance* que j'ai de ce monde, le fait propre qu'il y ait un monde *pour moi*?» À la question de la *possibilité* de l'*esse*, du fondement de l'être comme possible, se substitue donc progressivement la question du *cognoscibile esse*, c'est-à-dire de l'être comme *pouvant-être-connu*, de l'être comme *cognoscibile*.

C'est dans un tel cadre et à la lumière de ces trois types de possibilité rapidement esquissés, que je voudrais interroger l'autocausalité et la volonté de l'Un que Plotin thématise dans les *Ennéades*. Plotin présente-t-il un cas de possibilité cosmologique, de possibilité ontologique, ou encore un amalgame des deux? C'est ce que je tenterai de déterminer.

Prenons d'abord la question de l'autocausalité, affirmée de l'Un dans l'exceptionnel traité *Sur la liberté et la volonté de l'Un* (VI, 8 [39]). Si l'on cherche des antécédents de cette doctrine dans la pensée classique, force est d'avouer que l'on n'en trouve point. Mieux, l'on trouve plutôt une objection de principe à son endroit, quand par exemple Aristote note dans la *Métaphysique*: «Se demander le pourquoi, c'est toujours se demander pourquoi un attribut appartient à un sujet... Or chercher pourquoi une chose est elle-même, c'est ne rien chercher du tout. Il faut en effet que le fait ou l'existence de la chose soit déjà connu» (1041 a 9 ss.). Ce qui transparaît à l'évidence dans ce passage, c'est qu'on ne peut pas, pour Aristote, rendre raison de l'existence de ce qui est, de l'évidence cosmologique, pourrait-on dire; ce qui «est» est un donné premier, dont la primauté ne saurait être remise en doute, d'où la conclusion qui suivra ailleurs: «aucune chose n'est antérieure à soi-même» (*Mouv. des anim.*, 700 b 3), ou encore, «rien ne s'engendre soi-même» (*Gén. des animaux*, 735 a 13).

H. J. Krämer a pu parler, s'agissant des subtiles recherches de Plotin sur le mode d'être de l'Un comme *causa sui*, d'un *radikalen Neuansatz*, d'un commencement absolu (IUrsprung, p. 395, 401). À y regarder de plus près, l'on constate toutefois que les réflexions de Plotin à cet égard s'inscrivent dans un courant de pensée, une atmosphère pourrait-on dire, se développant autour de la naissance de notre ère, dans des spéculations de tradition néopythagoricienne, gnostique et hermétique, comme si la question du départ absolu, de l'origine radicale des choses, gagnaient alors peu à peu le devant de la scène. Je ne puis reprendre ici l'analyse de ces textes que J. Whittaker a bien mis en évidence, mais je citerai à titre d'exemple cette déclaration d'Aelius Aristide (2e siècle ap. J.C.): «Zeus a produit toutes choses et il est aussi grand que tout ce qui a été fait, ... mais il s'est produit d'abord lui-même (πρῶτος αὐτὸς ἑαυτόν); (...) il est le premier et le plus ancien et le premier auteur de toutes choses, s'étant engendré à partir de lui-même (...); mais lui-même est opposé à la totalité des choses, initiée à partir de lui»[11]. Krämer lui-même, tout en soulignant l'originalité de Plotin, reconnaît la proximité de sa pensée avec les spéculations néo-pythagoriciennes: «La monade pythagoricienne est non seulement principe, élément et puissance, comme l'Un plotinien, mais elle s'engendre par surcroît elle-même» (p. 401).

Si l'on s'interroge maintenant pour savoir ce qui, chez Plotin lui-même, a pu provoquer l'irruption du vocabulaire de la *causa sui* (l'argument n'est en effet détectable que dans un seul traité de Plotin), l'on se rend compte que l'argument est avancé en réponse à un discours que Plotin nous rapporte et qu'il qualifie lui-même de provocant, osé, téméaire ou impudent: c'est le fameux τολμηρὸς λογος, discours venu d'ailleurs qui affirme que «puisque la nature du Bien est par hasard (ὡς τυχοῦσα) ce qu'elle est, puisqu'elle n'est pas souveraine (κυρία) sur sa propre essence, que cette essence n'est pas ce qu'elle est *par elle-même* (παρ' αὐτης), elle ne possède alors ni la liberté ni l'autodétermination, compte tenu qu'elle fait ou ne fait pas ce qu'elle est contrainte (ἠνάγκασται) de faire ou de ne pas faire»[12]

La nature du Bien, de l'Un, selon cette thèse, existe donc *par hasard* dans la mesure exacte où elle n'existe pas par elle-même (παρ' αὐτῆς) c'est-à-dire n'est pas pleinement *responsable, maîtresse* (κυρία), de ce qu'elle est.

Il n'est pas bien difficile d'imaginer que la nouvelle théologie de l'Un proposée dans le traité VI, 8 [39] est en fait une tentative de réponse à ce «discours téméraire» dénoncé par Plotin comme absurde et qu'il a dû ressentir comme une provocation.

Ce «discours téméraire» a ceci de particulier qu'il conclut du caractère hasardeux de l'Un à sa *non-liberté* selon une opposition qui interdit par avance tout refuge du côté de la nécessité. Ce qui se produit par hasard, c'est-à-dire tantôt d'une manière, tantôt d'une autre, ne s'oppose pas seulement à ce qui se produit nécessairement, c'est-à-dire toujours invariablement, mais aussi à ce qui se produit *par notre concours*, ce qui *dépend de nous*[13]. Opposer purement et simplement la nécessité de l'Un à son état «hasardeux» laissait donc parfaitement intact le préjudice de sa *dépendance* ou de sa *sujétion*. Dit autrement, dès lors que l'existence de l'Un était déclarée nécessaire et non plus le résultat du hasard, celui-ci abandonnait l'ordre du contingent et perdait du même coup le privilège de la liberté qui y est étroitement rattaché.

Or Plotin n'était pas davantage intéressé par une nécessité qui transformait l'Un en esclave, que par une liberté qui le rendait contingent, c'est-à-dire changeant, sujet à l'indétermination. Devant donc retrancher à la fois de la liberté de l'Un, toute idée de mutabilité, et de sa nécessité, toute idée de contrainte, sa théologie ne pouvait proposer qu'une problématique *libre-nécessité* de l'Un, niant à la fois qu'il fût contingent, parce que libre, et lié, contraint, parce que nécessaire.

Le «discours téméraire» amena ainsi Plotin à vouloir fonder ce qui *est* et n'a pas besoin de fondement, c'est-à-dire à remonter depuis l'existence, la réalité fondamentale et première de l'Un, à la condition de possibilité même de cet Un. Or, en tant que premier, l'Un ne pouvait trouver sa possibilité en aucune entité antérieure à lui. Il fallut donc, en un geste parfaitement anti-aristotélicien, trouver en l'Un lui-même, la raison même de ce qu'il était.

L'Un, répond en substance Plotin, n'est pas lui-même esclave de cette nécessité qu'il communique à toutes choses, puisqu'en lui, la nécessité même émane de la libre volonté qu'il a d'être ce qu'il est.

L'Un est un, mais dans cette unité *en acte*, la *puissance active* de l'Un est comme la cause d'un acte qui n'est pas à venir, mais est toujours déjà pleinement réalisé. La cause de l'Un ne réside nullement dans quelque chose d'antérieur à lui, mais en une instance qui, en lui, n'est nullement distincte de lui. Ce qui est nécessité pour tout le reste se nomme dès lors en l'Un liberté. L'Un devient ainsi *causa sui* en vertu d'une volonté qui transcende sa situation ontologique propre et qui le rend souverain par rapport à sa propre nature cosmologique donnée. Ce n'est plus la volonté qui dépend de l'être donné, mais l'être donné lui-même qui est fondé dans une volonté première et originaire, et l'on peut maintenant répéter avec Plotin «qu'il ne faut pas craindre de poser un acte premier sans substance, mais qu'il faut poser cet acte même, pour ainsi dire, comme son existence» (VI, 8 [39], 20, 9-11).

Il n'est pas impossible que le «discours téméraire» émane de la gnose proprement dite, comme l'a cru Bréhier[14]. Il suppose quoi qu'il en soit, comme le note G. Leroux, «l'arrière-plan philosophique d'une doctrine de la liberté divine [qui] appartient au milieu hétérogène de la pensée grecque déjà ouverte aux contacts du judaïsme, du christianisme et de la gnose»[15].

L'idée même d'introduire le hasard au sein du premier principe pour en conclure à sa non-liberté[16] est étrangère à l'esprit grec classique. On n'imagine ni un platonicien, ni un aristotélicien, ni non plus un stoïcien objecter: «puisque la nature du Bien est par hasard ce qu'elle est...» elle n'est au fond nullement libre. Un tel discours suppose la présence d'une opposition ou tout au moins d'une dénivellation, au sein du premier principe, entre l'être et la volonté, la nature et la puissance (sur-naturelle), normale dans un contexte chrétien où il s'agit de combattre la nécessité de la création, mais étrangère à la métaphysique grecque.

C'est sur cette circonstance qu'il nous paraît maintenant crucial d'insister. Quelle que soit sa provenance réelle—gnostique, chrétienne ou autre—le «discours téméraire» a forcé Plotin à redéfinir sa pensée de l'Un en des termes qui n'étaient pas originalement les siens, c'est-à-dire à se “repositionner” dans une conceptualité étrangère à la sienne. À partir de là, l'origine de toutes choses à nom de *volonté*, et non plus d'*étantité*.

C'est surtout par cet aspect que Plotin s'éloigne du paradigme classique et opère un déplacement par rapport au cosmologisme grec. Pour Aristote, on l'a montré[17], il y a des possibilités *dans* le cosmos, mais il n'y a pas de possibilité *du* cosmos. Avec Plotin, c'est la possibilité *du* cosmos lui-même, par l'intermédiaire de la volonté originelle de l'Un de s'engendrer lui-même, de s'*hypostasier lui-même*, c'est-à-dire de *réaliser sa propre possibilité*, qui surgit pour la première fois dans l'horizon grec de l'être. Et dans la mesure où le cosmologisme grec encadre et détermine toute la conception grecque de l'être, on peut conclure que l'ontologie plotinienne effectue une véritable percée et fait éclater, par l'adjonction de concepts hétérogènes, le cadre métaphysique traditionnel grec.

Dans l'histoire des idées, Plotin représente ainsi le moment charnière entre la possibilité de type *cosmologique* et la possibilité de type *ontologique*. C'est le caractère de principe de l'être lui-même, dans sa fonction cosmologique, qui passe au second rang et qui doit lui-même trouver son fondement dans une possibilité plus haute, celle du vouloir de l'Un transcendant. Mais le pouvoir et la liberté de l'Un, tant s'en faut, ne sont pas pour autant l'équivalent de ce qu'ils deviendront dans la tradition chrétienne. L'Un pour Plotin n'est nullement libre de créer ou non tel ou tel monde; c'est plutôt que la nécessité de la production (éternelle et se produisant par paliers) de toutes choses, peut désormais à partir de lui s'interpréter en termes de volonté; la liberté de l'Un est encore à ce stade unidimensionnelle ou unidirectionnelle, mais elle ouvre néanmoins, et de manière définitive pourrait-on dire, la systématique grecque à la volonté plurielle chrétienne.

Cependent par rapport à la tradition ultérieure, il va de soi que:

Premièrement l'émanation plotinienne se produit par paliers, dans un processus en quelque sorte *scalaire*, où chaque réalité nouvellement engendrée produit à son tour la réalité suivante, l'Un engendrant l'Intelligence, celle-ci à son tour l'Ame, et cette dernière ultimement (et *éventuellement*) la matière. Dieu ne produit donc pas *directement* tout l'être, comme dans la tradition chrétienne, mais de manière médiate, si bien qu'on trouve chez Plotin plusieurs principes générateurs de l'être à côté de l'Un[18]. Deuxièmement, le monde est pour Plotin éternel, ce qu'il n'est pas pour les chrétiens, si bien que le rapport de dépendance institué entre les différentes réalités de son système est purement logique[19], et qu'il n'y a pas de *rupture*, si l'on peut dire, entre l'éternité du créateur et la temporalité du créé[20]. Troisièmement, la création chrétienne est une libre création de Dieu, ce qu'elle n'est pas, ou pas tout à fait[21], chez Plotin lui-même.

Dans ces trois registres, la coupure est moins franche entre Dieu et le reste des choses chez Plotin. Sa pensée est encore à cet égard fortement marquée par le *cosmologisme* grec, la liberté limitée de l'Un ne pouvant rivaliser avec la liberté du Dieu chrétien. Néanmoins, même si elle est prononcée avec hésitation, même si elle n'introduit pas une rupture aussi nette que celle revendiquée par le christianisme, la génération de la matière par l'Un représente déjà une infraction réelle par rapport au cosmologisme classique grec, puisqu'elle rend la réalité entière tributaire du pouvoir originel de l'Un[22].

Une nouvelle conception de l'être, de sa puissance, voilà donc une des contributions essentielles de Plotin à l'histoire de la pensée, et plus particulièrement, à la tradition de la métaphysique.

Endnotes

[1] Sur le sens et l'évolution du concept de *dynamis* dans la littérature grecque, cf. l'ouvrage ancien de J. Souilhé, *Etude sur le terme ΔΥΝΑΜΙΣ dans les dialogues de Platon,* Paris, 1919.
[2] «Dans les traités de la collection hippocratique», note ainsi Souilhé, «dans ceux où l'influence des idées cosmologiques des premiers physiciens est particulièrement manifeste, le terme δύναμις désigne la propriété caractéristique des corps, leur côté extérieur et sensible, celui qui permet de les déterminer et de les spécifier. Grâce à la δύναμις, la φύσις mystérieuse, l'εἶδος substantiel, ou élément primordial, se fait connaître, et se fait connaître par son action. On comprend dès lors comment, surtout dans la suite, on a pu passer du connu à l'inconnu, de l'apparence à la réalité, et combien il a été facile d'établir entre φύσις et δύναμις une équation parfaite. Dire la nature d'un être ou dire sa propriété revient au même, puisque l'une n'est évidente que par l'autre (...). Aussi parfois la nuance de sens est imperceptible entre les deux mots, et la synonymie presque parfaite» (p. 55-56).
[3] *Op. cit.*, p. 65.
[4] *Phys.*, 193 b 8; *Mét.*, 1032 a 25.
[5] C'est pourquoi Aristote prend soin de préciser que la puissance requiert certaines conditions pour être à même de s'exercer: «Un être, en effet, a la puissance dans la mesure où celle-ci est un pouvoir d'agir, *pouvoir non pas absolu*, mais soumis à certaines conditions» (*Mét.*, 1048 a 17-19); «Quant aux êtres qui ont en eux mêmes le principe de leur actualisation [*i.e.* les êtres naturels], ils seront puissance d'autre chose en vertu de leur nature propre, si rien d'extérieur n'y met empêchement. Par exemple, la semance n'est pas encore l'homme en puissance: il faut qu'elle soit déposée dans un autre être et qu'elle subisse un changement. (...) c'est ainsi que la terre n'est pas encore statue en puissance, car elle doit auparavant subir un changement pour devenir airain» (*ibid.*, 1049 a 13-18).
[6] Saint Thomas, *Summa Theologica*, I, 46, l, ad l.
[7] *Op. cit.*, t. II, p. 212.
[8] C'est ce qui permettra notamment à saint Thomas de dire que, avant que le monde ne soit créé, il était déjà possible qu'il soit «non certes selon une puissance passive, qui est la matière, mais selon la puissance active de Dieu. Et aussi selon quoi quelque chose est dit possible absolument, non selon une puissance quelconque, mais à partir de la seule disposition des termes qui ne s'opposent pas entre eux», *Summa Theologica* (Marietti) I, 46, l, ad l. Thomas ajoute du reste en note *ad locum* que c'est cette dernière possibilité «que les philosophes d'aujourd'hui appellent la possibilité *intrinsèque*».
[9] "J'appelle" possible, écrit ainsi Leibniz, "tout ce qui est parfaitement concevable, et qui a par conséquent une essence, une idée: sans considérer, si le

reste des choses lui permet de devenir existant". Lettre à Bourguet de décembre 1714, III, p. 572-574 Gerhardt.

[10] "Il y a des représentations, non seulement de ce qui arrive, mais encore de tout ce qui est possible; et Jupiter en ayant fait la revue avant le commencement du monde existant, a *digéré les possibilités en mondes*, et a fait le choix du meilleur de tous". Cf. la fable de "Laurentius Valla" dans *Essai de théodicée*, VI, p. 362 Gerhardt.

[11] *Or.* XLIII 7 ss., p. 340, 14 ss. Keil, cf. Whittaker, «The historical Backgroung of Proclus Doctrine of the Authupostata», *De Jamblique à Proclus*, éd. par H. Dörrie, 1975, p. 203.

[12] VI, 8 [39], 7, 11-15 (trad. Leroux).

[13] Selon le schéma:

nécessité	vs.	hasard (ordre contingent)
nécessité	vs.	liberté (ordre contingent)

Ce qui *dépend de nous*, ce qui est *en notre pouvoir*, se distingue non seulement du nécessaire, mais également d'un ordre contingent qui ne laisserait aucune place à l'initiative humaine. C'est ce qui amenait notamment Aristote à préciser que l'on délibère sur ce qui à la fois "*arrive par nous* et dont le résultat n'est pas toujours le même", *Éthique à Nicomaque*, III, 5, 1ll2 b 3.

[14] Cf. la Notice du traité VI, 8 [39] dans *Plotin, Ennéades VI* [2], Paris, 1931, p. 119 ss. Sur les réserves de G. Leroux vis-à-vis le cette thèse, voir son commentaire, *op. cit.*, p. 111 ss.

[15] *Op. cit.*, p. 115. Leroux reprend cette idée de A.H. Armstrong développée dans deux essais: «Negative Theology, Myth and Incarnation», *Néoplatonisme*, Ecole Normale Supérieure de Fontenay-aux-Roses, Mélanges J. Trouillard, 1981, p. 47-62: «Two Views of Freedom. A christian Objection in Plotinus, *Enneads*, VI, 8 [39], 7, 11-15?», *Studia Patristica*, XVIII, 1982, p. 397-406.

[16] Cf. le développement plus haut, p. 21 ss.

[17] Cf. plus haut, p. 6 ss.

[18] Dans la tradition néoplatonicienne postérieure à Plotin, la matière est engendrée *directement* par l'Un (*cf.* plus loin p. 000 n. 321). Or même si Plotin défendait lui aussi cette doctrine (*cf.* l'Appendice), il y aurait chez lui, comme du reste chez les autres Néoplatoniciens, *plusieurs principes générateurs à côté du Premier* (à savoir minimalement l'Intelligence et l'Ame), ce qui n'est pas le cas dans la tradition chrétienne où Dieu est l'unique créateur.

[19] Cf. plus haut, note 245.

[20] Sur l'opposition entre la création néoplatonicienne et la création chrétienne, voir I. Hadot, *op. cit.*, p. 84 ss., notamment p. 87-88: «le fait qu'Hiéroclès conçoit, *ainsi que tous les Néoplatoniciens*, l'acte de la création du démiurge comme éternel (ἐξ ἀϊδίου), c'est-à-dire datant de toute éternité et n'ayant ni commencement ni fin, va à l'encontre des Chrétiens orthodoxes; ceux-ci insistent particulièrement sur le fait que Dieu [qui est éternel] crée à un moment

du temps le cosmos à partir du néant comme quelque chose qui n'a pas existé avant et qui doit un jour disparaître dans le néant».

[21] Selon K. Kremer (*op. cit.*, p. 446), la libre création est contenue au moins en germe «Keimhaft» dans les propositions de Plotin (voir à ce sujet du même auteur l'article cité note 43). Mais en dépit de similitudes certaines entre l'émanation plotinienne et la création chrétienne, on peut encore soutenir avec E. von Ivanka, *Plato Christianus. La réception critique du platonisme chez les Pères de l'Eglise*, (tr. française), Paris, 1990, que le schéma néoplatonicien «exclut... un concept de Dieu que l'on pouvait admettre d'un point de vue chrétien, à savoir l'idée d'un Dieu personnel, réellement transcendant et créant librement» (p. 77).

[22] En ce sens, on peut déjà parler pour Plotin d'une *creatio ex nihilo*, puisque créer *à partir de rien*, comme le rappelle justement K. Kremer, signifie créer sans le secours d'une matière ou d'un substrat préexistant (cf. *Die neuplatonische Seinsphilosophie und ihre Wirkung auf Thomas von Aquin*, Leiden, 1966, p. 12 et 419).

II.

THEOLOGY

The Task of Theology

Helmut Kohlenberger
University of Salzburg

I.

Cur Deus homo? Eröffnung einer Frage

Aus England oder sonstwoher sind wir dem Heiligen Anselm ins Exil gefolgt, nach Rom. Nicht gleich in den Lateran zwar, wo Anselm in diesen Tagen vor neunhundert Jahren als *alterius orbis apostolicus et patriarcha* residierte (1). Was Anselm eigentlich wollte, erreichte er nicht. Nicht wurde er von seinerm hohen Amt entbunden. Dafür wurde ihm aufgetragen, in Bari die lateinische Auffassung *De processione spiritus sancti* zu vertreten. Seitdem Anselm Bec verliess, verliess ihn nicht das Exil. In Sclavia und Capua erlebte Anselm Alltag im Exil, politische direkte Konfrontation. Inmitten der Fährnisse des Irdischen, die jäh die *lectio divina* und das *officium divinum* unterbrechen, steht er in der Notwendigkeit des Sprechens, das über die Mauern des mönchischen Lebens hinausdringt. Kein Engel ist der Mensch. Das hat Anselm im *Cur Deus homo* bestätigt. Ein schmerzvolles Einsehen für die, die sich der *vita angelica* weihen. Auch heisst dies: der Mensch ist nicht Zahl. Ins Leere geht die kosmologische Faszination der vollkommenen Zahl (*Cur Deus homo* = CDH I 18).

Nichts weiter ist von ihr bekannt als ihre unvorstellbare Qualität. Wir Sterbliche aber sind zur Sprache verurteilt. Schon in der Genesis spricht Gott zum Menschen. Ingeborg Bachmann, im freiwilligen römischen Exil, hat den kühnen Satz gefunden: Sie zeigt ein "furchtbares Geheimnis ....die Sprache ist die Strafe. In sie müssen alle Dinge eingehen und in ihr müssen sie wieder vergehen nach ihrer Schuld und dem Ausmass ihrer Schuld".(2) Nichts anderes sagt Anselm, wenn er *sola ratione* diese Verurteilung des Menschen und ihre Zurücknahme auslegt. Sprechen ist Getrenntsein von der Wirklichkeit, die der Geist, der Atem schlechthin ist.

Anselm berichtet, dass Gott selbst den Menschen aus dem Exil der Strafe, das heisst der Sprache zurückholt, indem er sich den Bedingungen dieses Exils, das heisst des Todes, unterwirft. Er nimmt den Tod an und auf.(3) Das sprengt selbstredend die Bedingungen des Sprechens. In der Sprache führt es über das Sprechen hinaus. Weil das so fasziniert, sind wir hier und sprechen. Die Strafverfallenheít des Menschen tritt uns im Bilde des den Menschen besitzenden Teufels entgegen. Der Mensch ist besessen. Nicht nur in den Medien können wir dies pausenlos konstatieren. In dem Besessensein wirkt eine rationale Eigendynamik, die Anselm seziert. Die *ratio* ist Strukturnachfolgerin des Teufels. Im Rahmen der Strafe Gottes hält sie gefangen. Ein stringentes und operativ in sich geschlossenes Reflexionsgeschehen tritt an die Stelle uralter betörender Bilder. So ist Anselms Werk die epochebildende Version des unlösbaren Zusammenhangs von Sprechen, Todesverfallenheit, Schuld und darin vorausgesetzter Freiheit.

Was ist es um dieses Schuld. In ihr treffen Schulden zusammen, die nicht zu bezahlen sind. Diese Schulden hat ein so tiefer Kenner des Menschlichen, Allzumenschlichen wie Nietzsche als Bedingung der Sinnhaftigkelt des Lebens anerkannt. Das Leben und damit das Leiden steht unter der Perspektive der Schuld. Damit war der Mensch gerettet, "er hatte einen Sinn ... er konnte nunmehr etwas wollen—gleichgültig zunächst, wohin, womit, wozu er wollte: der Wille selbst war gerettett".(4) Anselm hat dies weniger emphatisch achthundert Jahre früher aus einer ruhigen Betrachtung, die nicht im verbitterten Rückblick gefangen ist, formuliert. *Voluntas namque Deí numquam est irrationabilis.*(CDh I 8) Grosszügig übersetzen wir *ratio* mit Sinn. Umfassende Rahmenbedingung des Sprechens, nicht logisch rechnerischer Nachvollzug. Nur diese Grosszügigkeit bewahrt uns vor dem Irrationalismus im Rationalen, der im 20. Jahrhundert Millionen Menschenleben kostete. Sie wurden der Sinngebung des Sinnlosen geopfert. Schuld, Tod, Sprechen sind unlöslich miteinander verbunden.

Anselm hat die Voraussetzung der *ratio* genannt, Nietzsche ist ihm darin gefolgt. "Gott selbst sich für die Schuld des Menschen opfernd, Gott als der einzige, der vom Menschen ablösen kann, was für den Menschen selbst unablösbar geworden ist—der Gläubiger, sich für seinen Schuldner opfernd, aus Liebe (sollte man's glauben), aus Liebe zu seinem Schuldner ..."(5) Ohne diesen unüberbietbaren Glauben, Sinnlosigkeit, Tragik, Zwang. Nietzsche ist grandioser Zeuge dafür.

Schulden müssen bezahlt werden. Eine Grunderfahrung des Menschseins. Mehr noch. Sie können nicht bezahlt werden. In beiden Gedanken liegt eine Logik, die sich kreuzt. Diese Kreuzung führt in eine Verneinung, die ihre Voraussetzung nennt und einklammert—Zeitlichkeit. *Voluntas Dei numquam est irrationabilis*. Wir begegnen einem "Mehr, das mit der Sprache im Verhältnis zu allen Arbeiten und Werken gegeben ist".(6) Darin liegt nach Levinas der Unterschied zwischen dem lebenden und dem toten Menschen, zwischen äusserer Anerkennung und dem "von Angesicht zu Angesicht". Im Sprechen trete ich heraus und biete mich dar. Das Leben entsteht um den Preis des zumindest symbolischen Todes.

Dies sprengt jeden Rahmen der Betrachtung in den Kategorien von Gerechtigkeit und Liebe. Die neuere theologische Literatur zu Anselm hat diese von Paulus herrührende Bewegung gesehen.(7) Darin ist sie frei von den Ressentiments, die noch in den 70er Jahren eine angemessene Rezeption des *Cur Deus homo* verhindern.(8) Über Missverständnisse des Äquivalenzdenkens, über die Selbstreflektion des Denkens im *quo maius cogitari nequit* hinaus führt uns Anselm zu der unheimlichen Ahnung, dass Gottmenschentum tödlich ist. In der Kreuzung stellt sich sofort der Abstand wieder her. Es ist daran zu erinnern, dass im Kreuz der Widerspruch geschieht.(9) In diesem Sinne ist Goethe recht zu geben gegen ihn selbst, wenn er sagt: "Denn da Gott Mensch geworden ist ..., so muss man sich vor nichts mehr hüten, als ihn wieder zu Gott zu machen.".(10) Von einem Opfer ist bei Anselm nicht die Rede. Opfer ist bei Anselm mit dem Gebet, dem geängsteten Geist, von dem der Beter der Psalmen spricht, eng verbunden (11). Mit der rationalen Durchdringung des zentralen Christusereignisses geht die Verlagerung der geistlichen Dimension ins Private einher. Davon zeugen Anselms Innovationen in der Gebetsliteratur. Dies ist ein Vorgang, dessen andere Seite die Entäusserung des Kultgeschehens ist. An die Stelle des kultischen Selbstopfers der Gemeinde mit Christus tritt verstärkt seit den Kluniazensern die priesterliche Stellvertretung, die für die Bittenden und Sühnenden in vielen variierenden Anliegen eintritt. In diesem Sinne wird die Messe privatisiert, honoriert und kommerzialisiert.(12) Derselben Tendenz zur Entäusserung gehorcht auch die Dogmatisierung im Sinne der Realpräsenz, die direkt zur Reformation führt.(13) Diese Entwicklungen zeigen sich bereits deutlich zu Anselms Zeiten. Anselms Werk ist direkt eine Ortsbestimmung angesichts dieser Tendenzen. Zugleich weist es auf eine Dimension, die von diesen Tendenzen nicht berührt wird. Der Ort, der mit der Formel *quo maius* ... mehr beschworen als gedacht wird: Das bezeugt *nolens volens* Karl Barth mit seiner an sich unverständlichen Insistenz darauf, das *quo maius* ... sei bei Anselm der Gottesname. Dieser Ort ist bei Anselm mit der Stellungnahme zur *processio spiritus sancti* verbunden. Mehr gedrängt als enthusiastisch hat Anselm als prominenter Redner die westliche Sezession aus dem gemeinsamen *Credo* der Kirche verteidigt. Möglich war ihm dies, weil in der Tat Anselm selbst in seiner eigenen Sprache der Rationalisierung des Westens auf der Spur war.

Ist es ein Zufall, dass der Name des entfernten Bergortes Sclavia, seit 1860 im Zuge des *risorgimento Liberi* genannt, just dem grossen Thema des *Cur Deus homo* entspricht. Die politische Freiheit, die 1860 kam, sagt etwas über die Grenzen des Freiseins.

In diesem Sommerort oberhalb dieses schon von Horaz gerühmten Capua, wird Anselm zum Retter: Eadmer berichtet von der Quelle, die nach Gebeten Anselms gefunden wurde (14). Die Anwesenheit von Papst Urban II und Anselm bei der 40 tägigen Belagerung Capuas, an der hauptsächlich arabische Kämpfer teilnahmen, und der Herrschaftskonsolidierung nach dem Ende der oströmischen Verwaltung in Süditalien diente, spricht ihre eigene Sprache. Auch die Tatsache, dass der Heerführer keine Missionierung seiner Soldaten wünschte.(15) Mitten in den Wirren der Zeit gibt es plötzlich eine Quelle und einen Text, der eine Dimension berührt, die von der Zeitlichkeit nicht getrübt ist.

Anmerkungen:

1. Eadmer, *Vita* S. *Anselmi* cap. 29, ed. R. W. Southern (Th.Nelson, London etc. 1962), S. 105.
2. Malina, in: Ingeborg Bachmann, Werke Bd 2 (Piper, München—Zürich 1978, S. 97.
3. vgl. R. Brague.
4. *Genealogie der Moral*, 111,28 (*Werke*, hg.. K. Schlechta, München 6. Aufl. 1969, Bd. 2, S. 899f
5. Ebd. 11,2, *Werke* 2, S. 832f
6. *Totalität und Unendlichkeit*, (Alber, Freiburg, 2. Aufl. 1993, S. 266.
7. vgl. Alain Badiou, Saint Paul (puf Paris 1997). Neuere Literatur: R. Schwager, Logik der Freiheit und des Naturwollens. Zur Erlösungslehre Anselms von Canterburry, in: Zeitschrift für katholische Theologie 105 (1983) S. 125—155. H. Steindl, Genugtuung (Universitätsverlag Freiburg, Schweiz 1980). G. Gäde: Eine andere Barmherzigkeit (Echter, Würzburg 1989). G. Plasger, Die Notwendigkeit der Gerechtigkeit (Aschendorff, Münster 1993).
8. vgl. J. Ratzinger, *Einführung in das Christentum* (1968) S. 188 u. S. 23 1. H. Kessler, *Die theologische Bedeutung des Todes, Jesu* (Patmos, Düsseldorf 1970).
9. Vgl.N. Luhmann, *Die Gesellschaft der Gesellschaft* (Suhrkamp, Frankfurt a.M. 1997), S. 61 f L. beschreibt die Kreativität des Kreuzens, in der die Unterscheidung als solche einen Schnitt in die Welt reisst.
10. Goethe, *Werke*, Hamburger Ausgabe in 14 Bänden, hg.v.E. Trunz (München 1981), Bd. 12,S.231, zit. J. Hörisch, *Brot und Wein* (Suhrkamp, Frankfurt a.M. 1992), S. 159.
11. Vgl. *Oratio* 2 (laudes et preces offerre), *Ep. 10* (sacrificium orationis), *Ep.65* (sacrificium spiritus contribulati).
12. Dazu A.Angenendt, Missa specialis, in: Bd.1(1983)S.153ff. ds., *Religiosität im Mittelalter* (Wiss. Buchgesellschaft, Darmstadt 1997),S. 448T H. B. Meyer, Art. *Abendmahlfeier*, in: *Theol. Realenzyke*. Bd. I (1977) S. 278ff.
13. Dazu neuerdings J. Hörisch, *Brot und Wein* (1992), S. 71 ff
14. Eadmer, *Vita S. Anselmi* cap. 31, a. a. 0., S. 107 ff.
15. Ebd. cap. 33, S. 112.

II.

Sola ratione - Sola fide: Rationalisierungsfolgen im Mittelalter

Die uns gewohnten Trennungen im gesellschaftlichen und intelektuellen Leben unterlaufen die meist vorbewusste Einheit in der Atmosphäre einer vorgegebenen Kultur. Vermutlich war die Ausgangslage im 11./12. Jhd, in dem viele Konturen der europäischen Lebensform hervortreten, die letzte Epoche, in der eine Tradition mit universellem Anspruch in vorreflexiver Form Einheit vorgab, Missionseifer befluegelte und bestehende Trennungen wie z. B. Stammeszugehörigkeit und soziale Unterscheidung im Dunkel der Sprachlosigkeit beliess.

1. Mit demVersuch, diese Einheit unter der Forderung der *ratio* zu formulieren, der sich im Zuge der Stadtkultur und der interkulturellen Konfrontation mit Juden und Muslim aufdrängte, treten neue Problemstellungen auf. Diese legen sich auf die Selbstverständlichkeit der Tradition und unterbrechen die Kontinuität der *lectio divina*, die der tages—und jahresrhythmisch gefeierten Liturgie entsprach.

In beängstigendem Ausmasse nimmt das Schuldbewusstsein zu. Inmitten der monastischen Welt bricht Unheilvolles auf, wie Leben und Werk des Heiligen Bernhard von Clairvaux zeigen. Die Stille der gewohnten Lebensform weicht der Notwendigkeit, individuelle Lebenskonzepte zu entwickeln.(I). Ein letztes Mal hatte Anselm von Canterbury versucht, die Einheit der seit Augustinus atmosphärisch wirkenden Kirchenrhetorik auf der Ebene der *ratio* zusammensufassen. Mit dieser neuen Ebene sollten nicht nur Gläubige, sondern auch die infideles erreicht werden. Das setzt Vertrauen voraus, dass die *ratio* Basis eines universellen Dialoges sein kann. In einem heute noch beeindruckenden Ausmass ist es Anselm gelungen, eine Balanc zwischen der rationalen Diskussion und der Wahrung des Geheimnisses des Göttlichen zu finden. Sie liegt im Negativen der entscheidenden Aussagen, in der Begrenzung der Fragestellung. Diese ist im Proslogion mit der bekannten Formulierung "*id quo maius cogitari nequit*" gegeben, mit der die Denknotwendigkeit des göttlichen Seins gedacht wird.

Voraussetzung der Argumentation ist der Unterschied zwischen dem, was ist, und dem, was *in intellectu* ist. Zum anderen, dass die wirkliche Existenz grösser als die vorgestellte Existenz ist. Damit ist der

Bereich der *ratio* gegeben: Grössenunterscheidungen und die Unterscheidung von Gegebensein und Nichtgegebensein.

2. Rationales Argumentieren und seine Kompetenz werden ständig erweitert und ausgefächert. Bei Thomas von Aquin zeigt sich bereits eine Bandbreite von Unterscheidungen, die vom Seelenvermögen und Begriff bis zur *computatio*, Rechnung reicht (2). Es kommt zu einer regelrechten Terminologisierung und Schematisierung in der scholastischen Disputation. Für die Erörterung grundlegender zumal theologischer Fragen erweisen sich diese Argumentationsweisen als wenig hilfreich. Gegen Ende des Weges der scholastischen Disputation kapituliert Nikolaus von Kues vor der Gottesfrage. Für Gott findet sich kein adäquater Name. Alle Charakterisierungen stammen aus der uns bekannten Wirklichkeit. Wenn man Gott als "Einer und alles" bezeichnet, geht man über die *ratio* hinaus. "*Quoniam autem ratio contradictoria transilire nequit, hinc non est nomen, cui aliud non opponatur secundurn motum rationis*" (3). So bleibt im Entscheidenden nur eine negative Theologie, der zufolge gilt, "dass die genaue Wahrheit im Dunkel unserer Unwissenheit in der Weise des Nichterfassens aufleuchtet" (4). Das Denken findet sich in Ungewissheit zwischen rationaler Argumentation und ihren immanenten Bedingungen (und deren oft unerhörten Subtilität) einerseits, einem mystischen Verschweben andererseits. Nicht selten charakterisiert these Unentschiedenheit einunddieselbe Person, wie zurn Beispiel den Konzilstheologen Jean Gerson (5).

3. Damit werden Gewissheitsproblematik und Methodenfrage zur bewegenden Kraft, aus der die neuen Fragestellungen erwachsen. Kusanus hat dazu vieles bedacht. Für ihn ist nichts gewisser als die Mathematik. Letztlich hängt die Gottesfrage am *Tetragrammaton*, diesem "eigentlichen und unaussprechlichen Namen" (6). Der künftige Weg ist demnach von der Mathematik (in ihrer Funktion als Forschungsleitung) einerseits, vom Studium der Heiligen Schriften andererseits bestimmt. In der Mathematik, später in den methodologischen Erörterungen (*Discours de la meethode, more geometrico*) wird die Gewissheit gesucht, die mit der zunehmenden Einsicht in die Kompetenz der *ratio* und dem Verblassen der metaphysischen Dimension zum Thema geworden war.

Der Gottesbezug wird nicht mehr in der Philosophie allgemein, sondem im Glauben formuliert. Am Ende der Geschichte der Gottesfrage, die mit Anselms "*sola ratione*" kühn genug begann, steht entscheidend und aufdringlich das reformatorische "*sola fide*". Bezeichnenderweise tritt dies in der Denktradition hervor, die in der Rationalisierung am weitesten—und damit auch am weitesten in ihrer Engführung—gegangen war. In Oxford blieb neben den subtilen methodologischen Fragestellungen schon zu Zeiten von Robert Grosseteste ein von der traditionellen *lectio divina* geprägter Schriftbezug in der Theologie wirksam. Es kam nicht zu sich verselbständigenden metaphysischen Spekulationen wie sie im Paris des 13. Jahrhunderts üblich wurden. Dies führte schliesslich zu der neuzeitbestimmenden Spaltung von mathematischer Naturwissenschaft und augustinisch inspirierter Theologie mit Schriftbezug (7). Die Formel, mit der beide verbunden gedacht werden, heisst *potentia dei absoluta.* Sie steht dem Faktischen in Natur und Geschichte gegenüber, das der *potentia Dei ordinata* entspricht. Darin zeigt sich deutlich eine Grenze der *ratio*. An die Stelle des Anselmschen Satzes "*voluntas namque Dei numquam est irrationabilis*" tritt der Satz von Gabriel Biel, dass allein Gottes Wille Gerechtlgkeit ist (8). Doch kann, wie gezeigt wurde, auch jenseits der Zuständigkeit der *ratio* vernunftmässig argumentiert werden (9).

Die Losung "sola fide" weist hin auf die Faktizität des in der Schrift Gesagten. Die Stunde der Philologie, der Interpretation, der Instrumentalisierung der Schrift hat geschlagen (10). In dieser Losung verdichtete sich das augustinische Schrift—und Kirchenverstehen zu einer strukturell autopoetischen Gestalt mit absolutem Anspruch des Gewissens, zunächst. Sie setzt sich später fort in der Vehemenz, mit der Galilei seine kosmologischen Thesen vertrat und prägte den politischen Duktus der frühen Neuzeit, für den Thomas Hobbes den Satz prägte "*Auctoritas non veritas facit legem*".

4. Seit den Eucharistiestreitigkeiten im 11. Jahrhundert zerfälltkirchliches Wirken in viele unverbundene Bereiche und entlässt kirchenunabhängiges Wirken und zugehörige Institutionen. Ein Zusammenwirken von Aussenbedingungen, in denen rationale Diskussionen insbesondere juridischer Art und ökonomische Entwicklung miteinander verbunden sind, muss angenommen werden. Ein wesentliches Beispiel ist die Herausbildung der Universitäten. Sie

werden zu einem weitgefacherten Netzwerk, in dem nicht Stammeszugehörigkeit und Herkunft zählen, sondern in der ganzen *Christianitas* rationales Argumentieren eingeübt wird. Zahlreiche Professionen entstehen. Das macht die Universitäten zu einem Machtfaktor. Insbesondere die Juristen, schon im Bologna des 13. Jahrgunderts *domini legum* genannt, prägen das neue Ansehen der Laien. Die weltliche Herrschaft wird eine ernste Konkurrenz zum Papsttum und zur Kirche. Später heissen die Juristen sogar *sacerdotes legum* (11).

Die an den Universitäten gelehrte Rationalisierung bis hin zur Staatsführung stand zunächst nicht im Auftrag von Herrschern. Sie führte aber zu einer Transformation des Herrschens. Marsilius von Padua formulierte sie in klarer Weise. Das Gesetz ist nunmehr eine anerkannte Regel, die notfalls mit Gewalt durchgesetzt werden kann(12). Damit ist *eo ipso* ein territorial begrenzter Geltungsbereich des Rechtes vorausgesetzt. Unter diesen Bedingungen wird der geistlichen universellen Herrschaft der Boden entzogen(13).

Grundsätzlich gilt: "*Quod omnes tangit, ab omnibus approbari debet.*" Das trifft nunmehr auch auf das Kirchenregiment zu. Damit erweitert sich der Personenkreis der Entscheidungsträger auch in kirchlichen Fragen. Teilnehmerschaft, Geschäftsordung und Abstimmungsmodus werden Anlass zu endlos scheinenden Discussionen. Das bedingt die Unterscheidung von Ebenen der Diskussion. An die Stelle von Kirchenprovinzen treten nunmehr auf den Konzilien von Pisa zögernd, in Konstanz ganz deutlich die nationes. Diese aus der Universitätsorganisation besonders von Paris bekannte Form des Zusammenschlusses von Studentengruppen nach der Herkunft im Sinne der Himmelsrichtungen zu Zwecken der Administration macht Schule (14). Innerkirchlich wird nunmehr die von Universitäten freigesetzte Rationalisierung wirksam. Sie stösst an Grenzen—einerseits die unsichtbar gewordene geistliche Dimension, deretwegen Hus verurteilt wurde, andererseits—bei Hus eng verbunden wie später faktisch bei Luther—die *natio*. Diese unhintergehbare Gruppenbezeichnung wird im Zuge der schriftorientierten Reformation mit ihrem absolutistischen Gewissensanspruch zur neuen entscheidenden politischen Form. In Basel scheiterte der Versuch, die Kirche insgesamt nach dem Muster der Universität zu reformieren. Stattdessen entstand die Universität Basel, die Konzilsuniversität. Die westeuropäische Entwicklung wurde im allgemeinen wie wir wissen vom absolutistischen bis totalitären Gesetzespositivismus bestimmt, der der Universitätsrationalisierung entsprang. Die römische Kirche wird zum Sonderfall von Herrschaftsausübung, konstituiert in Trient. Noch in diesem Jahrhundert konnte die Kirche vor dem Vatikanum II zu der Frage verleiten, wieviele Divisionen der Papst habe.

Anmerkungen

1. Vgl. M.B.Pranger, Bernhard of Clairvaux and the Shape of Monastic Thought (Brill, Leiden 1999, S.21 ff
2. Vgl.Hist.*Wörterbuch der Philosophie* Bd 8(1992),S.39.
3. De docta ignorantia 1,24.
4. Ebd. 1,26.
5. Vgl.H. A. *Oberman, Spätscholastik und Reformation* I (EVY Verlag Zurich 1965),S.309 ff
6. Cusanus, *De docta ign.* 1,24.
7. Vgl. R.W. Southern, *Robert Grosseteste* (Clarendon Press, Oxford 2nd ed. 1992), A.Hudson M.Wilks (eds), *From Ockham to Wyclif* (Oxford 1987). Für die Philosophie bleibt nur eine elitäre Randposition,vgl. J.Domanski, *La philosophie, théorie ou manière de vivre?* (CerfParis - Ed. Univ. de Fribourg 1996),S.89 ff
8. Vgl. Anselm, Cur Deus homo 1,8. Und G. Biel, Collect. 1,43,14, zit. bei St. Swiezawski, *Histoire de la philosophie européenne au XVe siècle* (Beauchesne, Paris 1990), S. 128 *sola voluntas divina est prima regula omnis iustitiae".*
9. Vgl. Oberman a. a. 0., S. 3 1 ff
10. Vgl. Swiezawski, a. a. 0. S. 176 ff.
11. Vgl. Swiezawsk4a.a.O.,S. 172 ff.
12. Defensor pacis 1, 10 ff.
13. Eine besondere Form und Radikalisierung der traditionellen geistlichen Herschaftskonzeption findet sich noch bei Aegidius Romanus in seiner Betonung der *perfectio*. Vgl- W. Senko, "La doctrine de la perfectio personalis et la perfectio status dans le *De ecclesiastica potestate* de Gilles de Rome", in: *Miscellanea Mediaevalia* 12/2 (Berlin 1980), S. 3 3 7 ff.
14. Dazu J.Hollnsteiner, *Studien zur Geschäftsordnung am Konstanzer Konzil* (1925), in: R. Bäumer, *Das Konstanzer Konzil* (Wiss. Buchgesellschaft 1977), S. 121 ff. Allgemein mit besonderem Gewinn zu lesen ist St. Swiezawski, *Les tribulations de l'elecclésiolgie à la fin du Moyen Age* (Beauchchesne, Paris 1997).

III.

The contemporary position of theology is precarious. Though this precarious position may have come about from the crisis of rationality or institutions which have strengthened in the last decades, in its roots it goes back to modernization in the widest sense. We attempt to outline the situation: Theology is not a presuppositionless discipline—it lives in the church. In the framework of the three-fold office of the church (priesthood; teaching; pastoral), the task of theology finds its place in the teaching office of the church. Fundamentally, we must pay attention to the balance of the task in the framework of ecclesiastical offices as a whole. That means: fundamentally theology comes from the threefold work which Christ himself introduced.

Today, the three-fold task of the church is endangered in many ways through modernization. Theology shows itself as broken in the modern world itself—as in a splintered mirror. The cultic dimension is mirrored in contemporary art, in which free interplay appears even in extreme fantasies and in no way hesitates to victimize and even sacrifice men. We are mindful that in a precise sense science understands itself as "art" and that the human race is pulled into the game of science. With the destruction of Aristotelian metaphysics by the construction of scientific method on the one hand, and by the historical critical method of biblical exegesis on the other, has the teaching dimension of theology become merely a "self-comprehension of the Christian faith". Implicit in this destruction is that the teaching of, for example, theology has become a part of the "self construction of social communication." From that self-construction comes the overwhelming occupation of theology with the contemporary world (in the sense of *aggiornamento*) and the self-questioning with and without specific connection with the church. Theology does not deal any more with the simple hearing of the word of God, but concerns itself with the correspondence (correlation) between the expressions of Christian faith and human existence. With that theology does not so concern itself to deduce the expressions of faith in certain measure from man's being. Also revelation places questions to men and places him in question, not only the reverse. This is a summary from an "Introduction to Fundamental Theology." So we see clearly: How self-evident the apparently universal occurrence of communication has become, whose outer representation we see in connection with multimedia, to a kind of last instance, which will not let itself any more be shaken from without (for example, nature, God). The third dimension of the church, the legally constituted institutional church, will be pulled into the organization of contemporary society with its diverse functions (services), which are regulated by rules. Here the maxim of contemporary society is actual, valid since the time of Hobbes: "*Auctoritas, non ueritas, facit legem*" (Authority, not truth, makes law). It is not God's authority, but the real automatic positive giving of the law, which especially in the twentieth century has not in principal excluded unethical laws.

The social atmosphere is determined through art (religious), the media, and in the positive act of law-giving. Hence the decisive historically important turning points which caused modernization and has brought theology to its present situation should be briefly indicated. As is so often the case, the present situation is the result of a very long evolution, which has become self-evident, but whose results however surprise us. Theology in the modern sense is the product of a relatively independent institutionalization of passing on knowledge, especially in the universities since the thirteenth century. This movement appeared however already in the twelfth century, especially in Paris (Peter Abelard among others). Symptomatic for the freeing of rational argument from the *lectio divina*, anchored in monastic life and liturgy, was the argument between Abelard and Bernard of Clairvaux. Bernard's efforts indicated the end of the creative strength of monasticism in all areas—from cult and art to the crusade conflict in a far-reaching figure, namely Bernard. Since that time cult passed from the center of attention, theology became a science essentially determined as Aristotelian, and canon law gained an independent quality and dynamic (in a certain sense as a kind of law as revelation). This separation of areas could be understood as a desymbolization of the church. Contemporaries of the twelfth and thirteenth centuries—from Rupert of Deutz through Joachim of Fiore to Francis of Assisi—followed this interior process of change with fear, as a widespread apocalyptic vision working within history. In any event, a chapter of an era toward modernization occurred which brought with it along side the official church, which had been led by theology as a science and a strong positive understanding of law and which finally would lead to the Church of the Council of Constance, where not only heretical movements of various kinds, but independent symbols (spiritual theater, visions, pathological excesses of every kind), became competition to liturgy and teaching. Decisive for the Reformation was that liturgical unity was sacrificed to emancipated rational argumentation (for example concerning the character of the Eucharist). At the same time Scripture was separated from tradition (*sola scriptura*) and the legal independence of the church was surrendered in favor of a state, organized on a territorial basis. In Lutheranism in fact, theology became philology, liturgy became music, and church organization a kind of state bureaucracy.

In the course of late medieval "nominalism" and the scientific method which it furthered (in empirical science, especially physics), a metaphysical basis for argumentation was weakened—a witness to this is Pascal's *Pensées*, in which a sharp break with the preceding age was formulated: There is no direct way to God from nature, "vérités divines... sont au dessous la nature." Men are directed toward God, but the corruption of nature hinders a direct connection. How this insight relates to the self-making of the scientific method (in the Cartesian sense) is a tense theme which needs further discussion. In any event, methodology is clearly separate from a living connection with divine truth. We live under the impact of this separation and the position of theology is also determined by this separation. Pascal has expressed the ultimate ground of the corruption of nature which culminated in the methodological cleavage of divine reality. He sees the corruption of nature as inseparable from love of self, possession of oneself. Implicit in the methodological certainty of science is the refined specialization of an increasing self-produced knowledge—under one's own constructed instruments. It is not too far off the mark to see in this unending process of self- certainty—which was already present in Luther's trembling question concerning justification—a circularity which closes itself to outside influence. Because this effort partially succeeded, in the end only a probability of happiness, a wager, remains as the final valid question—as is clear in Pascal.

The Lutheran philological orientation has been refined today into the subtleties of the historical-critical method. In this way theology as a whole becomes a "service to the word" (that is to say, as a preparation for preaching, [Karl Barth]). On the other hand, in Catholicism there has actually been a continual controversy between the strong Augustinian position of no distinction between philosophy and theology, and the Thomistic differentiation of the two. For the first time, the strong reception in German-speaking lands of the complete rejection of metaphysics from Kant to Heidegger has placed theology in an entirely new situation: there is no philosophy which corresponds to theology. We can not get around this state of affairs by arbitrary constructions and tricks. Increasingly must theology therefore rely on itself. To rely on itself means to rely on Scripture and the tradition of the church.

In the twelfth and thirteenth centuries, theology came out of *lectio divina* which ruled monasticism and the cathedral schools—vis-á-vis the challenges and confrontation of the crusades, and the wide reception of Aristotle connected with it. Since that time theology has been determined by the fact that the demands of truth refer not only to the inner logic of the faith (*intellectus fidei*)—but the truth must be shown by a demonstration from the neutral forum of reason. From this situation a parallel history between theology and "philosophy" results. They become increasingly independent of each other in relation to systematic and metaphysical presentation, and with regard to theological questions. Self-making (*Autopoesie*) becomes apocalyptic, it takes first place when Methodology takes over. Going out from philosophy, empirical sciences take their places, since philosophy in the strict sense becomes "fundamental ontology", (Heidegger). (I am passing over for the present the following phases of deconstruction of metaphysics: ontology, metaphysics as science [Kant], Hegel's phenomenology of spirit and logic, and Husserl's phenomenology) For theology, the relationship to Scripture (*sola scriptura*) is the standard of research, but under the new governance of method (historical-critical method, historicism, hermeneutic). The beginning point of theology in the twelfth century returns to the question of true religion: *de uera religione*. Modern theology is set in relation to Scripture, and modernization: exclusion of truth in science, ecological dangers, and the world wide web. There is no question that we are unprepared for the new situation, for we still have no appropriate language. It is even unsure whether we will ever "find" an appropriate language.

To determine appropriately the place and task of theology today, it is advisable to go back to the point in historical development when theology began to portray itself in a way universally presupposed today—the dividing line of the eleventh and twelfth century, when the West separated itself from the East and fell into an apologetic against Jew and Muslim. At this point the great "monks' theology" ended which belonged to the "Bible culture" of the previous centuries, for example as with Gregory the Great. In these centuries, in which "Europe" began to grow, the word of Scripture was deeply imprinted on its soul. There was an atmosphere which at any time could be awakened. The words of Scripture were deeply anchored in the memory through their continual use in the divine office and reading, so that the monks were a kind of living concordance of the Bible. "Sacra uerba ruminans" (chewing the sacred word) was the proverb of the monks, who were inclined toward the word.

This contemplative immersion in Holy Writ, this *otium quiet* (leisure of quiet), was the foretaste of heavenly happiness; hence monasticism derived its life from eschatological expectation which came about in the monastic social setting. In this sense, life under monastic discipline became Christian philosophy. A great arch extended from late antiquity with its unity between faith and reason, taking its form especially from Augustine, in an *intellectus fidei*, a "true philosophy," to the monks of the twelfth century. The question of an independent "theology" first comes with the demands of the cultic symbolic environment through the inappropriate application of Aristotelian categories—made stronger since Berenger, Roscelin, and Abelard. St. Anselm repeats the "true philosophy", in his short but thorough work, in a first attempt at a new theological language, corresponding to the new rational demands.

In Anselm's time, the eschatological dimension is experienced more acutely. There is no longer an unconditional contemplative monastic quiet—drawn into ever extending arguments over the *libertas ecclesiae*, over the front lines in Islam (the crusades) human life becomes an exile, in which the *miles Christi* receives in any event consolation in the friendship of like-minded comrades. The confrontational situation vis-á-vis God's energies, repeated daily in the praying of the Psalms, becomes an everyday occurrence. In the midst of the continuing daily prayer of the church, in the liturgy, comes a further need for personal prayer, in which the sinner places his hopeless situation before God. The cry of the lost who hopes in God against all hope: "*heu, quam malum est sic desperare, sic tacere! Et heu, quam uanum est sine spe clamare, sine spe conari! ... Doce me, domine, unde debeam sperare, ut possim orare.*"

As deep as affectivity in Anselm's prayer is, it does not remain there: It moves him further to a language in which the new and the unexpected, an exit from customary fife, can be reported:

> man is taken "*a patria in exilium, a uisione Dei in caecitatem nostram, a iucunditate immortalitatis in amaritudinem et horrorem mortis.*

God's absence becomes a threatening presence. Man is dragged from seeing, from seeing and willing, to the humility of the word. There arises from this an ever increasing tendency to profit from thinking. This thinking is directed along the lines of the usual classical philosophy, in the question of the ultimate cause, in differentiating various degrees of greatness. In face of the presupposed causelessness in the highest being, thinking is threatened; it threatens to sink into nothingness (see *Monologion*). There is something which does not fit into any categories and yet is not, nothing—which even must be thought of as the necessary ground of everything that exists—and in the end as the ground for thinking at all. Thinking is not grounded in itself (there is nothing more to say). That "nothing" which is registered in thinking, that denial, is coupled with the determinations, coming out of reality, of greatness and its differentiations. In this way, thinking is not without boundary. Likewise, in any event, it is presupposed that we are condemned to understand ourselves in the act of thinking. That is precisely the novelty of the situation in which Anselm sees himself placed with reference to the brothers who force him to write down his thoughts. Then this act of thinking is stamped very much with blindness—and only in prayer can the one who is sent into thinking grasp the trust, not to go wholly into error. But we are not spared, it is a sign of our situation within blindness. Then to see is only possible to him who believes and experiences already now in believing what that experience really will be.

So much does thinking dominate the explanation of the traditional theme in Anselm—*sola ratio* goes ahead without so much as a glance at Scripture, while still in its atmosphere, so *sola ratio* dominates the substantial comprehension of God, his providence, and the rectitude of the human "ought." This insight includes a traditional concept of justice, which entails God's love. But love is not something to think about. We can think only rectitude. That causes a great dilemma in Anselm—from which he comprehends not only God's activity wholly (in the Trinity), but also above all God's providence in the incarnation: *Cur deus homo*. Anselm must show the *ratio ueritatis*—without a glance at Scripture (*rernoto Christo*). He sees himself obviously as standing in a continuous tradition. Faith seems directly to further progress, if it is taken only as a gift: "*Hoc igitur ergo consideratione, licet sim homo paruae nimis scientiae, confortatus, ad eorum quae credimus rationem intuendam quantum superne gratia mihi dare dignatur, aliquantum conor assurgere.*" But in his thinking this notion is not thoroughly thought through—it remains fragmentary. That God's providence in the incarnation is determined by freedom and love stands in a unique relation to the *aliquatenus intelligere*. Although the fundamental lines of his soteriology are clear, his thought needs another dimension, which pure rationality can not give, that is freedom and love.

Anselm has summarized in exemplary fashion the tradition of *lectio divina*. He has raised it to the level demanded by *ratio*. *Veritatis ratio:* not only rational argumentation, which appears in the West *in se* and *per se*, but also the confrontation of the West with those who are not Christian demands progress from faith to insight, *fides quaerens intellectum*. This strategy has remained to the present day. But today we are in a new situation, which concerns theology stemming from reason, as it concerns the entire church.

In the beginning, we saw that the history of thought has not remained within the limits under which thinking has been placed. With Heidegger, thinking has been forced to consider being itself and thus has left the level in which Being is given implicitly in every individual being. This last step of radicalization of thinking means, with reference to the situation of man, something very decisive: the eschatological dimension given in Scripture becomes unavoidable. "Being itself is . . . eschatological in itself." Within the limits of space and time, we live the phenomena of the loss of limits in the signs of technological science and its effects on the world in which we live. In the signs of the Apostolic writings of John Paul II *Tertio millennio adueniente*, the end of time comes more strongly into view, as Joseph Cardinal Ratzinger has ascertained:

> This phase of history stands now under the consciousness that the end of history is coming near, not according to the numbering of centuries, but in this way that history is going in one direction and that with that Christ is so to say the beginning of the end and the world has distanced itself from him and yet again moves toward him.

We stand in an experiential dimension which goes beyond mankind. The surprising thing is that with modern technology, this going beyond our limits is thoroughly man-made. We are reminded that modern science stands under the sign of utopia, the sun state. Galileo reported about knowledge of a star, saw himself as "siderius nuntiu", (reporter of a star). In a grandiose attempt to depart from time and space into an artificial world, earth becomes a scientific laboratory which underlies artificially made conditions. With the rapid speed of the means of transportation and media- communication, the globalization of world interconnections comes together. At the same time as the unity of man's earth appears in atomic research, mankind threatens to become a victim of technological science. We think of the Holocaust in a world wide civil war as a clearly incomprehensible monument. In Hegel's "speculative Good Friday" and Nietszche's "God is dead" aphorism, God himself is present in this total sacrifice. The church is going to become the world. The world is no longer what it was. We are reminded of the biblical phrase: "Heaven and earth will pass away; but my words will not pass away." (Lk 21:3 1)

Clearly, "man", this modern abstraction, has fallen from the center of things. As the "West" today is determined by the religion of human rights, so this is a reflex from the process, the beginning of which Freud saw in the Copernican revolution. Different from transcendental and hermeneutical philosophy and theology which concentrates on the self, which makes itself judge—or at least correlative—of God's word, the human is not "the coming into oneself," but really the "going out of oneself". Only as the "other" is man what he is: wonderful. Levinas cites the prophets of the *Lamentations*: "He offers his cheek to him who hits him, and leaves him sated with opprobrium." In this situation in which I suffer with the other, I have not come strongly to my own decision; I have collided with it: "Passivity of the wounded, condition (or un-condition), through which being shows itself as creature."

It is time for theology to become free of the occupation by modern, so called humanistic meaning, from which the new world-utopia comes. Without doubt, such common thinking still rules our thinking. Sociologically, this thinking is directed to the One-world in which increasingly problems come to us, and with increasing control what can not be controlled increases, and the hope of lessening risk seems to lie only in the gaining of time. In many scientific questions, the idea of being able to determine a world view as a whole has been given up, but in theology there is still, as always, a dependence on the demands of the final ground from a philosophical epoch, at least in terms of a "Fundamental theology." Neither can it today come into question that theology as a science should prove itself still, to present itself in a still more refined manner as a "hearer of the word." When the stones cry out, we do not need a circumstantial consideration about whether "listening to a commandment of God belongs to the inner constitution of a man." It is necessary to recognize the signs of the times in the sense of discerning the Spirit. Many questions come as a result of that, first of all the question whether we are prepared to hear God's word. In the parable of the seed, Christ speaks that the soil is not necessarily prepared. We stand in a time of pre-evangelization which corresponds to a widely observed collapse of civilized custom.

We are captured in the situation in which we find ourselves in a continuing crass contemporary erosion of culture (for example, as in Albania). In the technical world created in this very century, we have come under the globalized media, for example CNN, which calls into question not only our customs, but also our way of life in a very broad sense. Pure outbreak of violence is possible at any time, and only God himself becomes pure presence.

The decisive step toward conversion is becoming conscious of those departments in which human life is meaningful. To that belongs the difference between God and man, God and creation, gender differences, the differences between God and the media, of church and world. He is converted who endures being an alien on earth. He is a witness according to John 1: 10: "He was in the world and the world was made through him and the world did not comprehend him."

(Translated from the German by Frederick Van Fleteren)

Nicholas of Cusa's Conjectural Neoplatonism

Donald F. Duclow
Gwynedd-Mercy College

"*Coniectura igitur est positiva assertio in alteritate, veritatem uti est, participans.*"[1]

It is common—and for a fifteenth-century thinker, perhaps beyond dispute—to describe Nicholas of Cusa (1401-1464) as standing at the threshold between the medieval and the modern eras. He has sometimes been viewed as looking back, so that Hans Blumenberg describes Cusa as attempting to "save the Middle Ages."[2] But more often—as in the classic studies of Koyré, Cassirer and Jaspers—he is thought to anticipate modern developments in cosmology and theory of knowledge.[3]

One sign of Nicholas' medieval identity is his use of Neoplatonic sources. His writings are rich with references to Proclus, Pseudo-Dionysius the Areopagite, John Scotus Eriugena, Thierry of Chartres and Meister Eckhart.[4] As we shall see, Nicholas' *De principio* offers detailed analysis of key terms from Proclus. Similarly, in the dialogue *De li non aliud* Cusa acts as spokesman for Dionysius, while his friends Johannes Andreas and Petrus Balbus cite Proclus' *Parmenides* commentary and *Platonic Theology* at length. Books from Nicholas' personal library confirm his reading of Neoplatonic texts, with extensive marginalia in his own hand to manuscripts of Proclus, Eriugena, Eckhart, and Albert the Great's commentaries on Dionysius.[5] Cusa neatly places himself in these thinkers' company when, in a marginal comment to the *Platonic Theology*, he notes Proclus' reference to "*nostra familia.*"[6]

Yet Nicholas' role within the Neoplatonic tradition was complex. For he entered this tradition amid the turmoil of the late Middle Ages, when scholastic certainties were yielding to the critical forces of nominalism and humanism. "Learned ignorance" and "conjecture" may be seen as Cusa's response to the era's uncertainties. He could scarcely avoid recognizing knowledge's limits, and in response developed a "conjectural" view of inquiry as provisional and approximative. For Cassirer, this view of knowledge—coupled with a "new version of mathematical logic"—marks Cusa as "the first modern thinker."[7] Similarly, Cusa's self-conscious doctrine and use of symbolism attracted Jaspers.

The play between Cusa's Neoplatonic sources and his conjectural view of knowledge thus brings into focus his place at the boundary of the medieval and modern eras. This essay will explore how Nicholas' approach to knowledge shaped his use of Neoplatonic texts and themes—specifically, how he integrates conjecture with the unity metaphysics of Proclus and Dionysius.

Conjecture And The Mind's Unities

Coniectura is part of Nicholas' view of humanity as made in God's image. He emphasizes the creativity of the human and divine minds: as God creates the world of beings, our mind produces a "conjectural world" of rational entities (*rationalia*).[8] The human mind is the "form" of this conjectural world, as God's mind is the form of the created world. By creating mathematics, language and culture, we simultaneously construct a human world and reflect the creative activity of God. As Cusa says, "Man has an intellect which, in creating, is the likeness of the divine intellect."[9]

Among our creations, mathematics holds a privileged place. Indeed, for Nicholas it defines the mind itself. He derives the term "mind/*mens*" from "measuring/*mensurando*," since "the mind is that from which comes the limit and measure of all things."[10] Breaking with the Platonic view of mathematics as dealing with eternal realities, Cusa sees the human mind constructing numbers and geometric figures.[11] Number, he tells us, is "reason unfolded" and the condition for knowledge.[12] In so doing, the mind unfolds its own powers for measuring. Since mathematics alone yields certain knowledge,[13] it provides both a standard for all inquiry and a vehicle for our conjectures about God and the natural world.

For example, in *De docta ignorantia* Nicholas describes the human mind's relation to truth in a geometrical image. He says, "The intellect, which is not truth, never comprehends truth so precisely that truth cannot be comprehended infinitely more precisely. For the intellect is to truth as [an inscribed] polygon is to [the inscribing] circle."[14] This image brings several of Nicholas' major themes into play.

First there is a negative claim: since our intellect is not truth, it can never grasp truth as it is. Cusanus sees a radical disproportion between the infinite and the finite. The finite is marked by gradations of more and less, which the mind compares and measures in order to attain knowledge. But the infinite—whether mathematical or metaphysical—stands beyond the whole process of comparison. On this view, human knowledge as certainty disappears. For since no finite intellect can measure the infinite, theological and metaphysical knowledge of the ultimate becomes "conjectural". And since within the finite realm we can always find clearer, more precise comparisons and measures, knowledge of the natural world also becomes provisional and incomplete. Indeed, the impossibility of knowing the infinite undercuts claims to certainty regarding the finite. Because the infinite God is the cause and truth of finite things, these too cannot be known with precision. By thus recollecting the limits of knowledge, Cusa develops his learned ignorance.

Yet he also makes positive claims: progress—indeed, infinite progress—is possible in knowledge. For the intellect can approach truth indefinitely, just as the multiplying sides and angles of a polygon approach the circle without end. The approach is asymptotic: always on the way, yet never quite there. Both parts of this relation are basic for Cusa. The circle directs the multiplying process as its goal or *telos*, but can never be attained through this process. Similarly, the mind comes to know truth, but only approximately and never precisely. Hence Nicholas defines '*coniectura*' as "a positive assertion that in otherness participates in truth as it is."[15] His conjectures are thus not simply guesses that may or may not be verified; they rather express truth partially and in ways that can always be improved upon.[16] While truth "as it is" remains beyond our grasp, we can approach it through the "otherness" of concepts, language and symbols. Conjecture thus involves both ineradicable difference and on-going approximation. As Wilhelm Dupré has commented, "What matters is, first of all, the idea that the truth we presuppose and project in and beyond conjectural forms is actually out of reach; and secondly, that we are aware of this truth within the context of conjectural actuality."[17] This actuality involves the human mind discovering its own structure and being as it forms ever new conjectures to express its relation to truth.

To highlight this actuality, Nicholas places conjecture in an anthropological context. He distinguishes "four mental unities": 1) the "highest and most simple unity," which is called divine or God; 2) intelligence or intellect, which emerges as the first unity turns toward otherness or alterity (*alteritas*); 3) soul or reason, where intelligence unfolds further into otherness; and 4) the sensible or bodily unity, which is closest to sheer alterity.[18] In this progression we recognize a familiar Neoplatonic pattern—the three hypostases of the One, Intellect and Soul, plus matter or body. With this ancestry in view, commentators have generally analyzed these unities as "metaphysical". Yet for Cusa they are first of all psychological, since all four occur *within* the human mind. It is in and through these mental unities and their mathematical representations that Nicholas forms his conjectures about the universe and God.[19]

Like "the One within us" of Proclus or the divine spark and *apex mentis* of Eckhart, the first unity most clearly marks humanity as God's image. For it is the reflection or concept of God within us. Nicholas asks us to "contemplate this unity of your mind by removing all plurality"; we shall then see it as the "most precise certitude" that illumines the lower unities yet in itself remains invisible.[20] Intelligence discerns itself and everything intelligible only within this unity's truth, but "can see this infinite unity only in intellectual otherness (*alteritate*)." Hence, intelligence contemplates the divine unity "not as it is in itself, but as it is humanly understood."[21] As such, the mind's first, infinite unity transcends all multiplicity and is the source and goal of the other, differentiated unities. We have the idea of totality—expressed symbolically as one and the point—which we "unfold" in lower unities' concepts of number and extension in space. As the "most precise certitude" through which the mind unfolds and measures everything, this first unity provides a regulative idea that guides all the mind's activity. In virtue of this unity, we can conceive of truth as the circle which the mind approaches without limit.

With the second unity, difference or otherness emerges, since intelligence involves a "composition out of the one and the other." Yet this intellectual unity remains above the distinctions and contrasts of reason and sense, since it is the unifying "root" of the opposites that these lower unities will unfold.[22] Opposites thus coincide in the unity of intelligence.

The third unity of soul or reason mediates between the intellectual and sensible unities. It is the number, "word" or image where intellect shines forth,[23] and also the body's source or "root." Here contrasts and opposites become explicit, as reason distinguishes both among it own terms and constructs, and among the senses and their objects.

The fourth or sensible unity concludes the mind's descending movement. Approaching pure alterity, its three-dimensional solidity yields no further number.[24] The senses also lack their own discriminating power, and require descending reason to distinguish white from black or hot from cold.[25]

But if body thus concludes the mind's unfolding into otherness, it also begins a reversal toward unity. For sense turns toward reason as its unity and discriminating power, as reason turns to intelligence, and intelligence to the first, divine unity. Nicholas describes the circular movement among the unities as follows: "In a wonderful and reciprocal progression, the divine and absolute unity descends step by step into intelligence and reason, while the contracted, sensible [unity] ascends through reason into intelligence, and the mind in like manner (*pariterque*) distinguishes and connects all things."[26] Here too Nicholas makes psychological use of a Neoplatonic scheme, as this dynamic, interlocking relationship reflects the Neoplatonic pattern of procession and return.

In addition, he notes that each unity has its own "rules of speaking."[27] Reason and its logic of non-contradiction are appropriate in the third region, as well as for judging and measuring the fourth, bodily unity. Here Cusa ackowledges the effectiveness of the Aristotelians' and nominalists' logic, which distinguishes opposites, genera and species with discursive reason. Significantly, he also confines this logic's validity to the third and fourth unities. How, then, are we to speak and think of the higher unities? Cusa develops the coincidence of opposites to articulate the intellectual unity, and devises strategies to speak of the divine unity above opposition, coincidence and all that can be said. Conjecture requires a dialectic among the unities, their various rules and ways of speaking and not-speaking.

Nicholas' teaching on the mind's unities thus raises basic methodological issues. He criticizes theologians who would confine God within the limits of reason. He says, "When we rational men speak of God, we subject God to the rules of reason, so that we affirm one thing of God, deny another, and apply contradictory opposites [to God] disjunctively. And this is the method of nearly all modern theologians who speak of God rationally." Refusing to move from reason to the mind's higher unities, these thinkers err by saying things "which we know are to be denied concerning the region of simple unity."[28] Specifically, they miss the shift to the mind's second unity, which sees opposites enfolded in unity.[29]

Especially obtuse on this issue is the "Aristotelian sect," which refuses to admit the intellect's coincidence of opposites.[30] As if to confirm Nicholas' critique, the Heidelberg theologian Johannes Wenck judged him poorly educated in logic, and condemned the coincidence of opposites because it "destroys all scientific procedure and all inference—destroying, as well, all opposition and the law of contradiction."[31] In his reply, Cusa prays, "Lord, deliver us from logicians."[32] Yet far from abandoning dialectic, Nicholas simply distinguishes between non-contradiction and coincidence as the logics appropriate to reason and intelligence.[33] He clarifies three points: 1) that reason's distinctions apply to finite concepts and creatures; 2) that the creature is not identical to the creator; but 3) that opposites do coincide *within* God.

While Cusa's teaching on coincidence has been widely commented upon, less frequently noted has been his claim that it too is inadequate to the mind's divine unity. Having criticized other thinkers for confining themselves to reason's logic, he goes on to criticize *De docta ignorantia*, where he himself had mistakenly spoken of God from the perspective of intellect rather than the mind's divine unity.[34] In the earlier work he had spoken of God *as* the coincidence of opposites—e. g., the maximum and minimum. But from *De coniecturis* onwards, Cusa says that God is *above* the coincidence of opposites, which provides a way toward the vision of God above all opposition and coincidence.

To speak of the mind's first, divine unity, Nicholas combines an a priori method with negation. Discursive reason poses questions in such a way that we must either affirm or deny one answer or another. But this method collapses when applied to the mind's absolute unity, which—transcending and embracing all contrasts—is precisely the certainty that every question presupposes. Hence, in replying to questions about this unity, Nicholas advises that we "repeat their absolute presupposition." If asked whether it exists, we should say that it is being-ness (*entitas*), which existence (*esse*) presupposes; concerning what it is, say that it is whatness (*quidditas*); and so forth.[35] Here conjecture probes the presuppositions of thought and language, because these bring to light the mind's divine unity. Yet Cusa does not rest with this presuppositional or a priori method. For like every affirmation, its positive claims can be set against their negations. Since the first unity precedes all opposition, the "truest conjecture" concerning it must not oppose affirmations to negations. Nicholas therefore makes a further dialectical move. Because the negation of opposites is higher than their joint affirmation in coincidence, he casts off pairs of opposites in both disjunction and union. For example, asked whether God exists, he says that God "neither exists *nor* does not exist, and that neither does he both exist *and* not exist (*quod ipse nec est nec non est, atque quod ipse nec est et non est*)."[36] Cusa considers this reply "a higher, simpler and more absolute (*absolutior*) answer concerning the first, simplest and ineffable being (*entitas*)." Pleased as Nicholas is with this response, he emphasizes that it too is "conjectural because the most precise remains ineffable and unattainable to reason as well as intellect." If the mind's highest unity "as it is" remains concealed, conjecture nevertheless expresses it through the "otherness" of reason and intellect. Nicholas thus plays at the outermost edges of language and logic.

In this way, he develops a broader unity metaphysics that engages Neoplatonic texts and themes. For a fuller view of these developments, let us look at two of Cusa's later works: *De principio*, and the dialogue *De li non aliud.*

De Principio: Cusanus And Proclus

In 1459 Cusa wrote *De principio*, a treatise that began as a sermon on a puzzling Gospel text. In the Gospel of John, we are told that the Jews asked, "'*Tu quis es*, Who are you?' And Jesus replied, 'The principle who speaks to you'."[37] Nicholas quickly connects this text with another, from Proclus' *Parmenides* commentary on Plato's claim that "this world has been brought into being from an older (*senior*) cause." Proclus describes this cause as "*per se subsistens sive authypostaton*, subsisting by itself or self-constituted."[38]

Nicholas is pleased with "*per se subsistens*" as a description of the first principle, because self-constitution suggests an identity between making and being made, generating and being generated.[39] With this coincidence, the principle owes nothing to any source outside itself. Citing the authority of both the Gospel and Proclus, Cusa thus sees '*authypostaton*' as describing the one necessary cause, prior to all difference and multiplicity.[40] Lest there be any doubt about this principle's identity, Nicholas returns to his biblical text and tells us that Proclus' term describes Christ, the divine Word, because "Only what subsists by itself can truly say, 'I am'." [41]

Yet Cusanus still considers the expression '*per se subsistens*' to be conjectural because it does not adequately name the principle in itself. He again echoes Proclus' *Parmenides* commentary, and notes that Plato, "separating and taking away all things from the one, saw the one in itself and absolute. And as it is thus seen, it is neither being nor not-being, nor is it, nor does it subsist; it is neither something subsisting, nor subsisting through itself (*per se subsistens*); it is not a principle, nor even the one."[42] Here, in a series of negations, the names 'principle,' '*autypostaton*' and 'one' give way because they are inadequate to the ultimate. At this point in his *Commentary*, Proclus distinguishes between "the existing One"—i.e., the "monad of beings" which proceeds from the One—and "the One alone which is prior to existence." Concerning the latter, he says that "The very word 'is' is wrong, for it transcends even Being."[43] In his turn, Cusa explains this point in terms of language. He says, "The expression, 'The one is one' is not appropriate (*apta*), because the copula 'is' does not suit the one; nor would saying 'the one one' without the copula be an appropriate expression, since every expression which cannot be uttered without otherness and duality does not suit the one."[44] Yet naming and language presuppose difference and multiplicity,[45] so that the term 'one' suggests 'other' or at least 'not-one'—and thereby fails to name the ultimate precisely. Seeking the "unnameable principle" prior to diversity, Cusa finds that no statement involving contradictories can "attain that which precedes everything sayable."[46] The best we can do is to form a "concept of likenesses" for the one principle, although this concept inevitably falls short of "precision."[47]

With these limits in view, Cusa then restores a comparative—and thus conjectural—value to Proclus' '*authypostaton / per se subsistens*.' If we consider the ultimate not in itself, but in its causal relation to contingent being, the expression has some adequacy. For it describes the ultimate more truly than it does anything else—e. g., those things that subsist not on their own, but through another. As Nicholas says, "'To subsist by itself' suits nothing more truly (*verius*) than that which is the cause of all subsisting things."[48] Through a consideration of language and causality, Cusa thus reaffirms the conjectural truth of Proclus' description of the ultimate principle as "*per se subsistens sive authypostaton*."

In *De principio* Cusa thus uses Proclus to comment on a Gospel passage, and proceeds to write a Neoplatonic treatise. His use of Proclus' *Parmenides Commentary* is direct, and can be traced in his marginal glosses to his own manuscript of the text. *De principio* rarely disagrees with Proclus, and occasionally even gives him authority on a par with the Gospels. Yet we may note two points of disagreement. First, Cusa says that Plato saw the Ideas "within himself conceptually," rather than in the existing order—that is, Plato invented the Ideas. Consistent with his conjectural view of the mind's activity, Nicholas rejects the Ideas' independent reality. As the "principle of concepts or rational beings," our mind forms ideas as "likenesses of real things," and then sees the creator's mind acting as though on ideas of its own fashioning.[49] Second, Nicholas rejects Proclus' claim that there are many co-eternal self-constituting principles; there can be only one eternal principle and its Trinitarian expression, because "the eternal and eternity are the same and cannot be multiplied any more than the one."[50] By paring away Plato's Ideas and Proclus' eternal henads, Nicholas drastically simplifies the Neoplatonic universe. Indeed, as F. Edward Cranz has noted, Proclus' entire hierarchically mediated cosmos disappears.[51] What remains is what fascinated Nicholas most in the Neoplatonic tradition: its dialectical account of the infinite principle in both its transcendence and its intimate connections with the finite. And this too he modifies by highlighting the role of the human mind and language. In this way, all that we think and say about the ultimate becomes "conjectural."

De Li Non Aliud[52]

Conjecture works within the tension between truth's simple unity and the otherness of concept and language. In 1462 Nicholas addressed this problem in one of his most original—and strangest—works, *De li non aliud (On Not Other)*. A peculiar grammatical construct, his definition of the *non-aliud* appears circular: "Not-other is not other than the Not-other, *non-aliud est non aliud quam non aliud*."[53] The very circularity of this word play renders it attractive to Cusa, who comments, "I see that *Not-other* defines itself and, hence, all nameable things."[54] As the coincidence of defining and defined, the *non-aliud* expresses the precision of definition itself. For in the polarity of other and not-other, the *non-aliud* defines not only itself, but everything else as well. As Nicholas asks, "What would you answer if someone asked you, 'What is *other*?' Would you not reply, 'Not other than other'? Likewise, if someone asked you 'What is the sky?' you would reply, 'Not other than the sky.'"[55] The *non-aliud* thus provides a rule for definition—namely, that "A is not other than A."

This definition's self-evidence may not be quite as simple as it appears. For the term '*non-aliud*' conceals an internal dialectic between otherness or difference and its negation. Reason and language distinguish objects and names from one another, and therefore proceed under the conditions of the *aliud*. Definition first calls this otherness into play, as the indefinite pronoun '*aliud*' sets the object under consideration among any number of objects. The sky, for instance, is other than the earth, fire, humanity, etc. As Dangelmayr comments, "The *aliud* therefore erects the absolute, indefinite-infinite horizon of 'others' and places the sky within the series of *alia et alia*."[56] But the negative '*non*' immediately restricts this horizon to the object's own identity: "The sky is not other than the sky." Negation is implicated within the very structure of definition. The circularity of the *non-aliud* is no mere tautology, since through the reciprocal expansion toward otherness and its restriction in negation, the *non-aliud* expresses not only the logical form of definition, but also the mind's dynamics in the act of defining.

Further, as self-defining, the *non-aliud* transcends every particular definition. For the negativity of the *non-aliud* undercuts language's proper mode of operation—the *aliud*. Considered in itself, the *non-aliud* remains prior to otherness and difference; it is essentially *not* the other. By pointing beyond all names and definitions, the *non-aliud* signifies a unity prior to reason and language. Yet this negation and prior unity also make possible all propositions and names. For just as colors can only be seen in light, so concepts can be distinguished only in light of their principle, the *non-aliud*.[57] Here alone, Nicholas says, "negation is not opposed to affirmation. For the *non-aliud* is not opposed to the *aliud*, because it defines and precedes it."[58] It is therefore not one concept among others, but the defining, constituting ground of concepts—what Cusa calls "the absolute concept."[59] The *non-aliud* thus expresses the presupposition of thought and language, that is, what *De coniecturis* describes as the mind's first unity.

In and through this first unity, Nicholas also seeks the "unnameable name of God." With his usual caution, Nicholas insists that the *non-aliud* is not this proper name of God. Rather, he says, "through 'Not-other' I disclose to you the name of my concept of the First. There does not occur to me any more precise name which expresses my concept of the Unnameable."[60] Once again Cusa emphasizes thought's mediating function, and hence the conjectural character of the *non-aliud*. While it may name our "absolute concept" or idea of infinite unity, the *non-aliud* remains strictly conjectural with regard to the divine itself. And yet Nicholas considers it a remarkably good conjecture—so good that he uses the theme to revise the Neoplatonic pre-eminence of the One. Citing Plato's *Parmenides* and Dionysius, he acknowledges the One's proximity to the *non-aliud*, yet notes their difference as follows: "Since one is nothing other than one, it is *other* than Not-other."[61] Cusa gives the *non-aliud* priority over the one, as well as over being, truth and goodness, because the *non-aliud* defines all of these divine names. Since every definition derives from the *non-aliud* which alone defines itself, it directs the mind's contemplation toward God, whose unity likewise grounds and transcends all created otherness and difference.

More clearly than *De principio*, Cusanus' dialogue *De li non aliud* marks out a conjectural Neoplatonism. By exploring a self-defining rather than a self-constituting principle, Nicholas emphasizes the psychological dynamics of conjecture. He expresses special satisfaction with the *non-aliud* because it yields what he had long sought by means of the intellect's logic of coincidence: a self-defining rule that is prior to the very opposition of affirmation and negation.[62] The *non-aliud* thus expresses the mind's first, divine unity—and thereby provides a symbol for God's name as well. The dialogue also includes extensive comparisons and source work for the *non-aliud* theme in Plato's *Parmenides*,[63] Proclus and Pseudo-Dionysius. But in a rare move for Cusanus, he claims the *non-aliud* as his original insight, although he credits Dionysius with having come closest to it.[64] Nicholas' originality here may consist less in his terminological innovation than in how *De li non aliud* clarifies his conjectural program. For here the analysis of definition, thought and language sustains a metaphysical vision that engages the deepest themes of the Neoplatonic tradition.

Conclusions

Neoplatonism, I would suggest, lends itself to Cusanus' conjectural approach. For this tradition's emphasis on the One's transcendence introduces a disruptive force that undermines ultimate truth claims, and reminds us that all metaphysical constructs are partial and provisional at best. In the fashionable terms of deconstruction, this negativity of the One marks an irreducible *différence*, an absence that cannot be overcome.[65] Yet as such, it also opens an infinite play of conjectures at the boundaries of thought and language. For since none can ever be precise, we need constant attempts at truer, more precise statements of these very boundaries.

Another feature of Neoplatonism shapes Cusa's approach. Since Plotinus' three hypostases—the One, Intellect and Soul—derive from human psychology rather than from a physical account of beings and substances, the Neoplatonic tradition's core may be described more accurately as a metapsychology than a metaphysic. Hence, when Nicholas works out the mind's four unities and their circling activity, he simply returns Neoplatonic categories to their original, central place. Cusa's difference from his predecessors may lie in the self-consciousness with which he first detaches and then realigns human psychology with knowledge of the ultimate. He underlines the mind's mediating and constructive activity in working out his unity-metaphysics. In going "beyond being"—the standard Neoplatonic gesture—Cusa moves not directly to the One itself, but first to the human mind with its "absolute concept," and our struggle to express this concept in language and dialectic.[66]

We may therefore say that Cusa gives us a conjectural view of Neoplatonism when he highlights the tradition's limits and the human mind's role in constructing its categories. This self-conscious view of inquiry and knowledge has understandably struck commentators like Cassirer and Jaspers as "modern." Yet we should notice two points. First, Nicholas proclaims no break with his past, but rather uses conjecture to continue and modify the Neoplatonic tradition in the ways we have seen. Second, his view of conjecture is itself deeply Neoplatonic. He defines 'conjecture' in terms of the relation between "truth as it is" and the "otherness" of the mind's concepts and assertions. By describing this relation with the loaded term 'participation,' Nicholas secures both truth's ultimate concealment—since nothing can express it "as it is"—and a confidence that our conjectures have value as approximations.[67] Although they cannot attain truth itself, they can nevertheless always be truer (*verior*). For Hans Blumenberg these factors keep Cusa on the medieval side of the divide between the medieval and modern epochs. And Louis Dupré suggestively decribes Nicholas' historical role: he "succeeded in bridging the gap that nominalist thought had opened up between nature and its transcendent source. Cusanus was probably the last thinker to reunite the theocentric and anthropocentric forces that had begun to pull the medieval synthesis apart."[68]

Finally, Cusanus reminds us of the rich diversity within late medieval and Renaissance thought. For in his work we recognize that the late Middle Ages offered more alternatives than a limited rationality on the one hand and a foundational faith on the other—the familiar division between nominalism and Reformation-style faith.[69] In the Neoplatonic tradition Cusanus found the resources for a dialectic that leads beyond reason to intellect and the divine.[70] He has given us a conjectural project whose "modern" features serve a goal that he shares with Proclus and Dionysius: a vision of the unknowable God.

Endnotes

[1]*DC* 1,11, n. 57. Nicholas of Cusa's works will generally be cited from the Heidelberg Academy's edition of his *Opera omnia* published by F. Meiner (Leipzig/Hamburg, 1932-). This edition will be cited as "h", with appropriate book, chapter and section numbers ("n.") References will use the following abbreviations and translations:

Ap Apologia doctae ignorantiae, h 2, ed. R. Klibansky (1932); trans. in Jasper Hopkins, *Nicholas of Cusa's Debate with John Wenck* (Minneapolis: Banning, 1981).

Be De beryllo, h 11, ed. H. G. Senger & C. Bormann (1988).

DC De coniecturis, h 3, ed. J. Koch, C. Bormann & H. G. Senger (1972); my translations.

DI De docta ignorantia, h 1, ed. E. Hoffmann & R. Klibansky (1932); trans. J. Hopkins, *Nicholas of Cusa on Learned Ignorance* (Minneapolis: Banning, 1981).

IM Idiota de mente, h 5, ed. R. Steiger (1983); trans. M. L. Führer, *The Layman on Wisdom and the Mind* (Ottowa: Dovehouse, 1989).

NA De li non aliud, ed. & trans. in J. Hopkins, *Nicholas of Cusa on God as Not-other* (Minneapolis: Banning, 1987; 3rd ed); Hopkins corrects the edition of L. Baur & P. Wilpert in h 13 (1944), and gives section numbers from P. Wilpert's German translation, *Vom Nichtanderen* (Hamburg: Meiner, 1976; 2nd ed).

Po De Possest, h 11, ed. R. Steiger (1973); trans. in J. Hopkins, *A Concise Introduction to the Philosophy of Nicholas of Cusa* (Minneapolis: University of Minnestota, 1978).

Pr De principio, h 10, fasc. 2b, ed. C. Bormann & A. D. Riemann (1988); my translations.

VS De venatione sapientiae, h 12, ed. R. Klibansky & H. G. Senger (1982).

[2]Hans Blumenberg, *The Legitimacy of the Modern Age*, tr. R. M. Wallace (Cambridge, MA: MIT Press, 1983), pp. 484 & 502. In *Nicholas of Cusa's Dialectical Mysticism* (Minneapolis: Banning, 1985), J. Hopkins criticizes Blumenberg's view of Cusanus and concludes, "This first modern philosopher neither breaks with the medieval world nor attempts to save it" (p. 93). See also Elizabeth Brient, *The Immanence of the Infinite: A Response to Blumenberg's Reading of Modernity* (Ph.D. dissertation, Yale University, 1995; Ann Arbor: UMI Dissertation Services, 1997), pp. 167-178 & 314-328.

[3]See Alexandre Koyré, *From the Closed World to the Infinite Universe* (Baltimore: Johns Hopkins, 1957), pp. 5-27; Ernst Cassirer, *The Individual and the Cosmos in Renaissance Philosophy* (Oxford: Blackwell, 1963); and Karl Jaspers, *Anselm and Nicholas of Cusa* (from *The Great Philosophers*, vol. 2; New York: Harcourt Brace Jovanovich, 1966).

[4]For example, see *Ap* nn. 17-21 concerning Dionysius, nn. 22-26 for Eckhart, and the catalogue at nn. 29-30.

[5]For Proclus, see *Cusanus-Texte* III. *Marginalien,* 2.1 *Theologia Platonis, Elementatio theologica,* ed. H. G. Senger, and 2.2 *Expositio in Parmenidem Platonis*, ed. K. Bormann (Heidelberg: C. Winter, 1986). Nicholas' marginalia to Book I of Eriugena's *Periphyseon* appear in "Kritisches Verzeichnis der Londoner Handschriften aus dem Besitz des Nikolaus von Kues," *Mitteilungen und Forschungsbeiträge der Cusanus-Gesellschaft* 3 (1963): 85-100. Ludwig Bauer has published Cusanus' marginalia to his copy of Albert the Great's Dionysius commentaries in *Nicolaus Cusanus und Ps. Dionysius im Lichte der Zitate und Randbemerkungen des Cusanus, Sitzungsberichte der Heidelberger Akademie der Wissenschaft*, 1940-41, pp. 93-113. The editors of Meister Eckhart's Latin *Opera* include Cusanus' marginalia in the critical apparatus (Stuttgart: Kohlhammer, 1936-).

[6]Senger, *Marginalien*, 2.1, p. 24 and marg. n. 23.

[7]Cassirer, *Individual and Cosmos*, pp. 14 & 10; see p. 40 concerning Nicholas' "new version of the theory of knowledge."

[8]*DC* 1,1, n. 5. See Pauline M. Watts, *Nicolaus Cusanus: A Fifteenth-Century Vision of Man* (Leiden: Brill, 1982), pp. 91-92; and C. L. Miller, "Nicholas of Cusa's *On Conjectures (De coniecturis)*," in *Nicholas of Cusa: In Search of God and Wisdom*, ed. G. Christianson & T. Izbicki (Leiden: Brill, 1991), p. 122.

[9]*Be* n. 7: "Ideo homo habet intellectum, qui est similitudo divini intellectus in creando."

[10]*IM* 1, n. 57; *Layman*, p. 57: "Mentem quidem a mensurando dici conicio." See also *IM* 9, nn. 123-124. Cusa's mathematical focus belongs to his "quadrivial theology"; see Werner Schulze, *Zahl—Proportion—Analogie* (Münster: Aschendorff, 1978), especially pp. 97-121; and M. L. Führer, "The Evolution of the Quadrivial Modes of Theology in Nicholas of Cusa's Analysis of the Soul," *American Benedictine Review* 36 (1985): 325-342.

[11] See Vittorio Hösle, "Platonism and Anti-Platonism in Nicholas of Cusa's Philosophy of Mathematics," *Graduate Faculty Philosophy Journal*, New School for Social Research, 13, 2 (1990): 79-112.

[12]*DC* 1,2, n. 7: "Nec est aliud numerus quam ratio explicata."

[13]See *Po* n. 44; *DI* 1,11-12, n. 31-33; *DC* 2,1, n. 77; Miller, "Cusa's *On Conjectures*," p. 126; and Helmut Meinhardt, "Exaktheit und Mutmassungscharakter der Erkenntnis," in *Nikolaus von Kues: Einführung in sein philosophisches Denken*, ed. K. Jacobi (Freiburg: K. Albert, 1979), pp. 109-110.

[14]*DI* 1,3, n. 10; *Learned Ignorance*, p. 52.

[15]*DC* 1,11, n. 57.

[16]See Miller, "Cusa's *On Conjectures*," p. 120; and Brient, *Immanence of the Infinite*, pp. 289-291.

[17]Wilhem Dupré, "Absolute Truth and Conjectural Insight," in *Nicholas of Cusa on Christ and the Church*, ed. G. Christianson & T. Izbicki (Leiden: Brill, 1996), pp. 326-327.
[18]*DC* 1,4, nn. 14-15. These unities are not separate "faculties", but rather as Watts describes them, "kinds of mental activity" (*Nicolaus Cusanus*, p. 98). *DC*'s editors find the immediate sources for Cusa's four unities in Proclus and Eckhart; see pp. 193-194.
[19] While Josef Koch describes the four unities as "metaphysical principles," he also notes that the whole scheme begins with the mind's self-reflection, and correlates the unities with ways of knowing, degrees of certainty and modes of expression. See Koch, *Die Ars coniecturalis des Nikolaus von Kues* (Köln: Westdeutscher Verlag, 1956), especially pp. 16-17. C. L. Miller writes that the four numerical 'unities' "can be applied conjecturally to the four 'mental unities,' our conceptions of the metaphysical realms that comprise all reality" ("Cusa's *On Conjectures*," pp. 127-128).
[20]*DC* 1,5, n. 19. Here Nicholas explicitly places the first unity within the human mind: "Contemplare igitur mentis tuae unitatem."
[21]*DC* 2,16, n. 167.
[22]*DC* 1,6, n. 23: "Intellectualis illa unitas radix quaedam complicativa oppositorum in eius explicatione incompatibilium exsistit."
[23]*DC* 1,6-7, nn. 25-27.
[24]*DC* 1,8, n. 30.
[25]*DC* 1,8, n. 32.
[26]*DC* 1,4, n. 16; see *DC* 1,8, n. 36: "*regressionis progressiones*". At *Be* n. 40, and *IM* 14, nn. 152-153, Nicholas uses a similar pattern to reconcile Plato and Aristotle.
[27]See Koch, *Ars coniecturalis*, pp. 44-45; and H. G. Senger, "Die Sprache der Metaphysik," im *Nikolaus von Kues*, ed. Jacobi, pp. 85-95.
[28]*DC* 1,8, n. 34.
[29]*DC* 1,10, n. 53.
[30]*Ap* n. 6; *Debate*, p. 46; see also *Be* n. 40.
[31]J. Wenck, *De ignota litteratura*, ed. & trans. by J. Hopkins in *Cusa's Debate with Wenck*, pp. 25 & 30, nn. 24 & 29. Somewhat perversely, Wenck claims that Nicholas' "*paucitas instructionis logicae*" leads him to think that logic yields him "*adaequatam et praecisam ad Deum proportionem*" (p. 102, n. 24).
[32]*Ap* n. 21; *Cusa's Debate with Wenck*, p. 56. Nicholas attributes this prayer to Ambrose.
[33]See Wilhelm Dupré, "Die Idee einer neuen Logik bei Nikolaus von Kues," *Mitteilungen und Forschungsbeiträge der Cusanus-Gesellschaft* 4 (1964): 357-374, especially 363-364.
[34]*DC* 1,6, n. 24. See F. Edward Cranz, "The *De aequalitate* and the *De principio* of Nicholas of Cusa," in *Nicholas of Cusa on Christ and the Church*, pp. 272-273.

[35]*DC* 1,5, n. 20.
[36]*DC* 1,5, n. 21.
[37]John 8:25, following the Vulgate text, as interpreted by Augustine, *In Iohannis Evangelium* 38, 11; *CCSL* 36, pp. 344-345. In contrast to Cusa's metaphysical view of this verse, Augustine sees Christ as the "*principium*" of faith.
[38]*Pr* n. 2; citing Proclus, *In Platonis Parmenidem* 785-786; see Nicholas' marg. 116-118 in Senger, *Marginalien* 2.2. G. R. Morrow & J. M. Dillon have translated *Proclus' Commentary on Plato's Parmenides* (Princeton: Princeton University Press, 1987). In contrast to Cusa's first references, Proclus argues that "the self-consituted must exist, but posterior to the First Principle" (*Elements of Theology*, ed. & trans. E. R. Dodds [Oxford, 2nd ed, 1963], prop. 40, p. 43); see Dodds' note at pp. 223-224, and *In Parm* 1150-1151. See also John Whittaker, "The Historical Background of Proclus' Doctrine of the AUTUPOSTATA," in *De Jamblique à Proclus, Entretiens sur l'antiquité classique* 21 (1975): 193-230, especially pp. 217-219.
[39]*Pr* n. 3.
[40]*Pr* n. 6.
[41]*Pr* n. 18: "Solum per se subsistens veraciter dicere potest: ego sum"; citing Jn 8:28, and echoing Ex 3:14.
[42]*Pr* n. 19; see *Im Parm* 1239-1240.
[43]*In Parm* 1239-1241, trans. Morrow & Dillon.
[44]*Pr* n. 19.
[45]*Pr* n. 35.
[46]*Pr* n. 19.
[47]*Pr* n.39: "Sic de uno principio, quantum nostra capacitas nobis suffragatur, conceptum facimus similitudinarium aliqualiter, licet valde praecisionem"; see also *Pr* n. 26, about naming the principle '*unum*' from our concept of unity.
[48]*Pr* n. 20; Cusa then generalizes, "For to what can all words signifying something (*omnia vocabula aliquid significantia*) more truly apply than to that from which all things have what they are and are named? What is more truly substance than that which gives substantial being to every substance, although it is greater than every nameable substance?"
[49]*Pr* n. 21.
[50]*Pr* n. 25.
[51]F. Edward Cranz, "The Late Works of Nicholas of Cusa," in *Nicholas of Cusa: In Search of God and Wisdom*, pp. 147-148; and "*De aequalitate* and *De principio* of Cusa," p. 279.
[52]This section has been adapted from D. F. Duclow, "The Analogy of the Word: Nicholas of Cusa's Theory of Language," *Bijdragen* 38 (1977): 282-299.
[53]*NA* 1, n. 4; p. 35.
[54]*NA* 5, n. 16; p. 51; Hopkins' emphasis. As Werner Beierwaltes comments, the

formula "*non aliud quam...*" indicates a metaphysical or ontological motion of definition as well as a logical one; Beierwaltes, *Identität und Differenz* (Frankfurt: Klostermann, 1980), p. 114. See also Gerhard Schneider, *Gott—das Nichtandere* (Munster: Aschendorff, 1970), pp. 104ff.
[55]*NA* 1, n. 5; p. 35.

[56]Siegfried Dangelmayr, *Gotteserkenntnis und Gottesbegriff in den philosophischen Schriften des Nikolaus von Kues* (Meisenheim am Glan: A. Hain, 1969), p. 247.
[57]*NA* 3, nn. 8-10; pp. 39-43.
[58]*VS* 14, n. 41.
[59]*NA* 20, n. 94; p. 139: "Vocetur igitur ipsum non-aliud conceptus absolutus, qui videtur quidem mente, ceterum non concipitur." See also *Po*, n. 40. Werner Beierwaltes places the "absolute concept" within Cusanus' Trinitarian theology as articulating the divine Word (*Indentität und Differenz*, pp. 127-128).
[60]*NA* 22, n. 99; p. 145: "Sed de ipso primo conceptus mei nomen per 'ipsum non-aliud' tibi patefacio. Neque mihi praecisius occurrit conceptum meum exprimens nomen de innominabili." See Robert L. Scharlemann, "God as Not-Other: Nicholas of Cusa's *De li non aliud*," in *Naming God*, ed. R. Scharlemann (New York: Paragon House, 1985), pp. 116-132.
[61]*NA* 4, n. 13; p. 47 This interpretation resembles Proclus' *Theologia Platonis*; see Senger, *Marginalien* 2.1, p. 25, and marg. 143: "vnum est nichil aliud quam vnum."
[62]*NA* 4, n. 12; p. 45.
[63]Cusanus commissioned the first Latin translation of the *Parmenides* from George of Trapezunt; see Raymond Klibansky, "Plato's *Parmenides* in the Middle Ages and Renaissance," published with a new preface in *The Continuity of the Platonic Tradition* (Munich: Kraus, 1981), pp.v-ix, 9-13, & 24-30.
[64]*NA* 1, n. 5; p. 35, referring to Dionysius' *Mystical Theology*, ch. 5 (*PG* 3, 1048A-B) which affirms the creator to be "neque quidquam nominabile, neque aliud quid."
[65]For Jacques Derrida's engaged critique of Neoplatonism and negative theology, see his essay on Dionysius the Areopagite, "How to Avoid Speaking: Denials," in *Derrida and Negative Theology*, ed. H. Coward & T. Foshay (Albany: SUNY Press, 1992), pp. 75-142; and John D. Caputo, *The Prayers and Tears of Jacques Derrida* (Bloomington: Indiana University Press, 1997), pp. 1-68.
[66]See Dupré, "Apriorismus und Kausaldenken nach der Cusanischen Auffasung von Gotteserkenntnis?" *Mitteilungen und Forschungsbieträge der Cusanus-Gesellschaft* 11 (1975): 180-181. Cranz describes Cusa's progressive shift from a metaphysics of being to one of intention and meaning ("Late Works," pp. 148-149).
[67]See W. Beierwaltes, "Cusanus and Eriugena," *Dionysius* 13 (1989): 144-146.
[68]Louis Dupré, *Passage to Modernity* (New Haven: Yale University Press, 1993),

p.186; Cusanus does so by "retheologizing nature" and conceiving "of God's immanence in a more intimate way than later Scholasticism had done" (p. 58). In *Immanence of the Infinite*, Brient develops this point at length (pp. 228-313).

[69]For a more nominalist and fideist reading of Cusanus' Neoplatonism, see William J. Hoye, "The Meaning of Neoplatonism in the Thought of Nicholas of Cusa," *Downside Review* 104 (1986): 10-18.

[70]Brient notes that Blumenberg ignores the Neoplatonic tradition and its role in Cusanus' thought (*Immanence of the Infinite*, pp. 321-322).

Toward a Whiteheadian Doctrine of God

James E. Caraway
Dowling College

John Cobb's attempts to understand God's being and relationship to the world entirely in terms of the principles of Whitehead's own philosophical system. He asserts that "Whitehead's philosophical reasons for affirming God and his attempt to show that God is not an exception to all the categories appears. . .philosophically responsible and even necessary" (CNT, 176). Yet, Cobb's thesis is that Whitehead was not successful in his attempt to show that God is not an exception to the categories descriptive of reality. According to Cobb, Whitehead's God, conceived as an actual entity, does not always act in a way characteristic of the activity of other actual entities. He becomes an exception, and incoherence is thereby introduced. Cobb undertakes, therefore, "to develop a doctrine of God more coherent with Whitehead's general cosmology and metaphysics than are some aspects of his doctrine" (CNT, 176). Although Cobb affirms that Whitehead did go far toward overcoming this incoherence, he nevertheless stresses that "one can go and therefore should go, further yet" (CNT, 177). In attempting to make Whitehead's system more coherent, Cobb focuses around five areas of concern, namely: God as Actual Entity, God and Time, God and Space, God and Eternal Objects, and God and Creativity.

Consider in the first place Cobb's criticism of Whitehead's development of God as an actual entity. It is Cobb's contention that Whitehead deals too often with the consequent and primordial nature of God as if they were genuinely separable entities or as if God were merely an addition of these two natures. But, is this in fact the case with Whitehead? Whitehead himself seemed to realize the danger of God's being so considered that he would appear to be an instance of two dichotomized natures. He cautioned time and again that God is an actual entity, and as such, is a unity any one aspect of which cannot be "actual" in and of itself. That is to say, Whitehead's insistence that God is an actual entity is an insistence on the unity of God. No one aspect of God considered alone is actual, for only actual entities are fully actual and "there is no going behind actual entities to find anything more real" (PR,

27-28). That Whitehead emphasized the unity of God as actual entity is clearly seen in several important passages.

> To sum up: God's primordial nature is abstracted from his commerce with 'particulars,' and is therefore devoid of those 'impure' intellectual cogitations which involve propositions. It is God in abstraction, alone with himself. As such it is mere factor in God, deficient in actuality (PR, 50).

It is well to note that this observation comes early in *Process and Reality*, so that one who reads of the primordial nature of God subsequently, regardless of how many pages are expended in such a delineation, will know that he is reading about an abstracted aspect of one unitary entity. Of this observation, Professor Leclerc, says: "The last point in the previous quotation is highly important. God is not to be identified with his 'primordial nature'; that is, God is not to be conceived as wholly constituted by a primordial conceptual valuation of pure abstract eternal objects" (WM, 203). Or another of Leclerc's observations notes: "The primordial nature is only one aspect of God. We must be clear that in considering the primordial nature we are making an abstraction from God's complete actuality" (WM, 203). That Whitehead does not intend for God to be viewed as two dichotomized natures is also to be seen when he emphasizes that God considered in this abstraction "as primordial" is deficiently actual in two ways:

> His feelings are only conceptual and so lack the fullness of actuality. Secondly conceptual feelings apart from complex integration with physical feelings, are devoid of consciousness in their subjective forms (PR, 521).

It is to be noted that in this quotation Whitehead speaks of the primordial nature of God as an abstraction but also that he talks of this aspect as being "deficiently actual." Such caution should be adequate to convince one that the primordial nature of God is not a genuinely separable entity. This point is likewise emphasized in Sherburne's interpretation of Whitehead's doctrine. Of the primordial nature of God he says: ". . . when we make a distinction of reason, and consider God in the abstraction of a primordial actuality, we must ascribe to him neither fullness of feeling, nor consciousness" (KWPR, 180). Noteworthy in this passage are the phrases with reference to the primordial nature as "a distinction of reason" and "an abstraction." Schubert Ogden, too, observes that Cobb's criticism of Whitehead's dichotomizing God's primordial and consequent natures is unwarranted. Of Cobb's position he says,

> His claim . . . that Whitehead associates God's aim 'exclusively with the primordial nature' (p. 183) ignores Whitehead's statement that 'the process, of finite history is essential for the ordering of the basic vision, other. wise mere confusion' (Essays in Science and Philosophy, pp. 89ff) (CA, IX, 18, 12).

Finally, not unimportant is Cobb's observation that "It is always the actual entity that acts, not one of its poles as such, although in many of its functions one pole or another may be primarily relevant" (CNT, 178). Of importance with reference to this observation of Cobb is Cobb's concession that Whitehead "must certainly have meant to say this also about God" (CNT, 178). It has been observed that there are instances in which Whitehead himself explicitly did say this about God, and it has been noted that three of his interpreters viewed his thought as exemplifying this unitary view. Add to these considerations Cobb's own recognition that this was in fact what Whitehead "meant to say," and it seems reasonable to assume that this is in fact what he did say, thus leaving unwarranted Cobb's criticism that Whitehead dichotomizes the two natures of God in such a way that they are presented as genuinely separable entities.

Yet, Cobb assumes that this criticism is warranted, and retaining this assumption, views Whitehead's system as incoherent insofar as it entails "arbitrary disconnection of first principles" (CNT, 177, *PR*, 9). That is to say, the four ultimate elements of his system, actual entities, God, eternal objects and creativity are arbitrarily disconnected. Cobb stresses that any such dichotomizing results in arbitrary disconnection, for any attempt to analyze an actual entity merely in terms of the addition of the analyzation of the two poles taken individually omits the subjective unity, concrete satisfaction, the power of decision and self-creation requisite of an actual entity (CNT, 198). Hence, since Cobb finds the dichotomizing of God's nature in Whitehead, he feels it necessary to explain, more adequately than did Whitehead, how God is related to actual occasions, eternal objects and creativity. Yet, if one accepts Whitehead's delineation as being that of presenting God as a unified actual entity, then the disconnection of which Cobb speaks is not present, and Whitehead's system is adequate, in this respect at least, without Cobb's proposed alternative. That is to say, if the criticism that Whitehead dichotomizes God's two natures is not warranted, then Cobb's revision of Whitehead's system to explain "how the eternally unchanging primordial nature of God can provide different initial aims to every occasion" is unwarranted or at least unnecessary (CNT, 179-180).

For our next consideration, Cobb introduces the thesis that the simplest way to understand Whitehead's description of God—the non-temporal, ever-lasting actual entity—is "to regard God, like human persons, as a living person" (CNT, 188). Cobb advances this thesis in an effort to make the Whiteheadian doctrine more coherent than did Whitehead himself. Two areas of concern must be dealt with here. In the first place it must be considered whether regarding God as a living person is warranted by the Whiteheadian system. A second necessary consideration is Cobb's contention that "the view that God is a living person. . .makes the doctrine of God more coherent, and no serious new difficulties are raised" (CNT, 192).

Cobb observes that for Whitehead God as actual entity differs from all other actual entities in that he is non-temporal and everlasting. Yet, God's being non-temporal does not entail the absence of process in God. Cobb contends that Whitehead has made the difference between God and other actual entities a radical difference, and that a consideration of God as a person would make the system more coherent. He argues that Whitehead's attribution to God of mere internal process raises several problems. First, if the process attributed to God is merely internal process, then God cannot directly affect the world, so Cobb maintains. Secondly, internal process alone cannot account for the fact that God provides the initial aim for each occasion. Thirdly, mere internal process raises problems regarding God's satisfaction. If God is a single entity never to be completed, he can never know satisfaction; yet, Whitehead explicitly refers to God's satisfaction. To overcome these problems, Cobb suggests that God be considered as a person rather than an actual entity.

The alternative which Cobb suggests at this point may serve to settle the problem of the possibility of satisfaction on the part of God and the problem of God's ability to prehend other occasions, but even if this is granted, doesn't the alternative also offer grave problems? In his consideration of God as a person, Cobb agrees with the Whiteheadian understanding of person when he says: "A living person is a succession of moments of experience with special continuity" (CNT, 188, PR, 531). As long as one is speaking of temporal persons this definition of a person offers no great problem. One may ask the question regarding the ground of the succession of the moments of experience. That is, the question of the unifying agency could be asked, for there is no purely internal reason why the various moments of experience should constitute "special continuity" (CNT, 188) or "with some peculiar completeness sum up their predecessors" (PR, 531). But with the Whiteheadian system, the answer is forthcoming in terms of prehensions which can be traced to the initial aim whose origin is traceable to God (IWM, 322-330, 334-336). However, if God is considered to be a person, that is, if God is viewed as a route of successive occasions in which the successors with some completeness—except in God's case the "some completeness" would be absolute completeness—sum up their predecessors then the question of the ground of the unity of succession is also applicable to God. So long as God is considered an actual entity, then the question of unity is not raised. If, however, God becomes a series of ontologically discrete units of actualization, the question of the ground of his unity cannot be answered within the system.

Cobb's notes further that there are systematic reasons why Whitehead prefers to speak of God as an actual entity rather than a person. While persons experience lack of self-identity through time and loss of what is past, Whitehead wants to deny both of these limitations of God. Cobb contends that both self-identity through time and no loss of what is past can be maintained of God even if God is considered as a living person rather than an actual entity. Yet, such a person would have to be a unique person indeed. This leads to a consideration of the systematic advantages accrued when God is considered as a person rather than an actual entity. In the case of a human person there was a time when he was not, and he faces a time when he will be no more. This is true of temporal actual entities also. But God, considered by Whitehead as the non-temporal actual entity and by Cobb as a person, is different insofar as he is eternal—there never was a time when he was not—and everlasting—there never will be a time when he will not be. This can be said neither of ordinary actual entities (IWM, 192-193) nor of ordinary persons. Moreover, in both ordinary actual entities and in ordinary persons, the passage of time entails loss. Yet, this is not so with God, who, according to Cobb, "vividly and consciously remembers in every new occasion all the occasions of the past. His experience grows by addition to the past, but loses nothing" (CNT, 191). There is no loss in God either through his facing of a time when he will be more, or through fragmentary reenactment of the past in the present. Yet, all other persons experience this loss. That is to say, Cobb's God, who is a person, is indeed a unique person, even as is Whitehead's God as an actual entity a unique actual entity. Cobb's contention is that Whitehead's system which calls for a non-temporal, everlasting actual entity is incoherent. Yet, is Cobb's alternative which calls for a non-temporal, everlasting person who experiences no loss through time any more coherent? This is not to agree with Cobb and say that Whitehead's system is incoherent. It is merely to assert that if Whitehead's system is incoherent, Cobb's alternative is likewise incoherent. In other words, even if Cobb can say that in his consideration of God as person "no serious new difficulties are raised," he cannot say that he has alleviated the old difficulties which he sees (IWM, 300-301) in Whitehead's delineation.

Whitehead's reluctance to speak of God as a person is discussed by Christian in *An Interpretation of Whitehead's Metaphysics*. He notes that personality is not one of Whitehead's systematic categories, and observes that in Whitehead's system human persons are interpreted as highly complex societies of actual occasions, and that God, being an actual entity, "clearly . . .is not a person in this systematic sense" (IWM, 409410). According to Whitehead's theory, God—who is an actuality which enjoys everlasting existence with no loss of immediacy has a unity which is a continuing unity within an individual immediacy rather than a unity characterized by a persistent pattern of definiteness with a continuity between individual immediacies. In an effort to avoid ambiguities, Whitehead is reluctant to speak of God as a person even in a presystematic way. His reluctances stems from the fact that traditional views of God as a person are related too easily with unreflective supernaturalism, a position which Whitehead wants to avoid (IWM, 410).

While attempting to avoid the simple attribution of personality to God, Whitehead also wants to avoid the opposite extreme of conceiving God as "sheer infinity" (PANW, 675) or as "the impersonal order of the universe" (RM, 150). Hence, "he proposes his theory as a view that avoids both these extremes" (IWM, 410). Even when, in more interpretative passages, he uses personal images (e.g., PR, 525, 527, 532) in reference to God, he stresses that such images are symbolic, interpretative and unsystematic (IIVM, 410).

Whitehead realizes that the God, who is an actual entity, is a unique actual entity, but his contention is that the facts of our experience require such a unique entity (WM, 192-195). By the fact that God is unique one cannot expect all statements about God to be univocally applicable both to God and to other actual entities. Yet, Cobb seems to feel that coherence demands this. However, can statements about God who is a unique person be univocally made in reference to other persons? Does coherence demand such univocity? Or rather, is Whitehead's system, and Cobb's, coherent insofar as God, whether conceived as an actual entity or a person, does not negate, supplant or supersede the activity of other actual entities, but rather supplements and enhances the real individuality and the influence of actual occasions (IWM, 301, 336, 381)

Moreover, Whitehead stressed that the really real was to be understood as an actual entity. He found that an adequate description of the really real required the admission of a unique actual entity, God, who was to be the chief exemplification of all the categories, not a principle invoked to save their collapse (PR, 521). Cobb accepts this approach, too, as being the only adequate way in which God is admissible. Yet, he maintains that the Whiteheadian system is coherent only if God is considered as a person rather than an actual entity. Given Cobb's assertion that God is a person, should not Cobb reconstruct Whitehead's philosophy by describing how God as a person is related to all other actualities which themselves are to be considered as essentially personal. That is to say, Whitehead's requirement is that the ultimate "should disclose the same general principles of reality which we dimly discern as stretching away into regions beyond our explicit powers of discernment" (SMIV, 135). Cobb contends that the ultimate should be considered as a person. Yet, his suggestions for alteration of the Whiteheadian system which consist in every instance of considerations of God as an actual entity in relation to other actual entities is merely to engage in a discussion utilizing the concept of God which he has already rejected. If Cobb is to be consistent he should consider the problem on the basis of how God as a person relates to all other actualities. This, too, offers problems however, for Whitehead's demand is that God "should disclose the same general principles of reality" as all other entities. Does this not entail that if God is considered to be a person rather than an actual entity, then all other actualities are to be considered somehow as individual persons rather than individual actual entities? Consequently, the relationship which Cobb should describe is not the relationship between God, a person, and other actual entities, but rather between God as a person and other actualities who themselves are considered as individual persons.

Another area in which Cobb understands Whitehead's system to involve incoherence is Whitehead's doctrine of God's relation to the eternal objects. Cobb's contention is that Whitehead's doctrine affirms that God alone is to be responsible for the ordering of eternal objects. However, the doctrine can be coherent, he maintains, only if the possibility of temporal occasions responsibility for some ordering of eternal objects is admitted. Cobb's altered Whiteheadian doctrine would assert that while God orders *all* eternal objects, it is also possible for temporal occasions to order an infinitesimal selection of eternal objects (CNT, 201). It is to be noted that Cobb alters the role of God with regard to his relation to the eternal objects, just as he alters it with regard to his function as sole provider of the initial aim. He rejects God's role as that of being *solely* responsible for ordering the eternal objects, just as he rejects God's function as *sole* provider of the initial aim. He makes God more like other occasions by admitting that other actual entities contribute to the initial aim of a becoming entity and also have the ability of ordering eternal objects. These considerations serve to indicate that Cobb's alterations in both cases have imposed limitations upon God which Whitehead himself does not impose. When Cobb turns to Whitehead's doctrine of creativity, however, he takes a different stand and demands that Whitehead must give to God a more radical role in creation (CNT, 1971).

As has been shown, part of Cobb's rendering of the Whiteheadian system more coherent consisted of his attempt to show that God functioned in a way not radically different from that of other actual entities. The difference was to be alleviated by rejecting Whitehead's doctrine that God was unique in that he was solely responsible for the provision of the initial aim. Secondly, Cobb rejected attribution of uniqueness to God insofar as God alone is purported to have an unmediated relation to eternal objects while all other actual entities have a mediated relation (CNT, 197). His contention was that God should not be unique in the sense that he alone envisaged directly the eternal objects and provided the initial aim that "Whitehead should not preclude in principle the possibility that a temporal occasion may have toward some eternal objects the kind of relation God has toward all;" (CNT, 203). It is to be noted that the initial aim and the eternal objects as pure possibilities for becoming are fundamental in the role of creation. Whitehead has found it necessary to attribute to God a role unique from that of all other actual entities in relation to both the initial aim and the envisagement of the eternal objects. Cobb, as has been shown, questions this attribution of uniqueness to God and takes steps to make God function in a way not radically different from that of other actual entities. He has made God's function in relation to the initial aim and the eternal objects—both of which are fundamental in God's role in relation to creativity less radical. Yet, he criticizes Whitehead for failing to have a radical doctrine of creation, and attempts "the attribution to God of a more decisive role in creation than Whitehead himself intended" (CNT, 204).

In his attempt to give God a more radical role in creation than did Whitehead, of what does Cobb's proposed reconstruction of the Whiteheadian system consist? As we have noted, Cobb showed that Whitehead did have a doctrine of creation in that God functioned to establish the initial aim of each occasion and that God also envisaged all the eternal objects, the pure possibilities for becoming. However, Cobb pointed out that even though God's role in creation was significant in Whitehead's thought, Whitehead nevertheless placed restrictions upon his creative role. These limitations may be summarized as follows: First, although God is the sole initiator of the initial aim, this aim must always be given in consideration of the actual situation of the world. Secondly, although the initial aim profoundly influences the outcome of an actual entity, it is not wholly determinative. Third, God does not create the eternal objects, the pure possibilities for becoming. Finally, Whitehead has no doctrine of *creatio ex nihilo*.

Cobb concludes that Whitehead's concept of creativity is fundamentally intelligible even though it can only be pointed at and hoped that it will be intuitively grasped (CNT, 210). Yet, Cobb considers the big question to be whether Whitehead's principle of creativity can answer the question as to why there is anything at all. Cobb's answer is that it cannot. Therefore, his alteration consists in an explanation of the limitations of Whitehead's concept of creativity insofar as it cannot answer the question *why*. He says. "My contention is that 'creativity' can not go even as far in the direction of an answer as did 'prime matter'" (CNT, 210). However, Cobb should have no quarrel with Whitehead at this point for Whitehead's ontological principle affirms that the only "reasons" for occurrences are to be given in terms of actual entities (PR, 28).

Cobb has viewed his task as that of giving God a more radical role in creation than did Whitehead himself. The results of Cobb's proposed alteration may be summarized as follows. First, the only "reasons" for occurrences are to be given in terms of the decisions of actual occasions. Second, the actual occasions occur and find their limitation by reason of God's establishment of their subjective aim. Finally, "creativity," not being an actual entity, cannot be the reason for their occurrence. Creativity itself provides no reason, while God is the reason for the being as well as the form of actual entities (CNT, 214).

This doctrine, Cobb alleges, is a more radical doctrine of creation than that which Whitehead himself espouses. Yet, how does it differ from that of Whitehead, or how is it more radical? Whitehead sums up his whole philosophy by pointing out that there are four creative phases in which the universe accomplishes the actuality. It will be noted that God is central in each phase of this accomplishment. First, there is the phase of conceptual origination, which is deficient in actuality, "but infinite in its adjustment of valuation" (PR, 532). This is God's primordial nature. Second, there is the temporal phase of physical origination giving rise to the multiplicity of actualities. This is directed by God's establishing subjective aims. Third, is the phase of perfected actuality, "in which the many are one everlastingly, without the qualification of any loss either of individual identity or of completeness of unity" (PR, 532). God functions as the ground of this phase, as the principle of limitation and concretion which directs by his lure for feeling. In the fourth phase of creativity the creative action completes itself. This is accomplished by God's "infinite patience" and "tender care that nothing be lost" (PR, 525).

Moreover, it must be noted that Cobb's "radical" doctrine of creation entails the incorporation of elements in Whitehead's system which Cobb has already rejected or at least mitigated. This "radical" doctrine of creation includes affirmations that God is the provider of the subjective aim and the reason for the being as well as the form of actual entities. Previously, however, Cobb had wanted to attribute these functions in some respects to actual entities other than God.

What has the foregoing noted? On the one hand, Cobb has been interested in making God function in a way precisely like that of all other actual entities. He has done this by making other actual entities to function in their relation to creativity in a way not different from the way in which God functions. Hence, God is not to have a unique function as provider of the initial aim and envisager of the eternal objects. In this manner, Cobb contends, coherence is maintained. On the other hand, Cobb contends that God must have a more decisive role in creation than that assigned by Whitehead's system. Two questions immediately arise. First, does not the maintenance of coherence require that God function in his creative role in a way not radically different from that of other actual entities? Yet, Cobb, who has argued for the similarity, suddenly wants the difference stressed. Second, if Cobb wants to maintain for God a more decisive role in creation than Whitehead's system allows, why did he attempt to alleviate God's unique function as establisher of the initial aim and the envisager of eternal objects? That is to say, Cobb, in the defense of his understanding of coherence has rejected the points in Whitehead's system in which God plays a decisive creative role. He has attempted to show that other actual entities can function in the provision of the initial aim and the envisagement of the eternal objects. It is true that Cobb stresses that God entertains all possibilities of becoming while other actual occasions entertain only an infinitesimal number. However, a particular becoming actual entity does not require more than the actualization of an infinitesimal number of eternal objects in order for it to become. If entities other than God in a particular becoming entity's past can provide for that entity its initial aim, and if the entity in concrescence can envisage the number of eternal objects requisite for its becoming, however infinitesimal that number may be—then God need not have any role in that entity's becoming. Hence, the thesis emerges: Instead of making God's role in creation more radical, Cobb has rather presented a situation in which God need not be considered as necessary at all—even though he may at one time have been necessary—in the role of creation. Although he may still function in the creative role, the possibility that he need not do so has been introduced. An entity could become, independent of God's activity, a possibility which Whitehead's "non-radical" doctrine would never admit. Instead of making God's role in creation more radical, Cobb has at least taken a step in the opposite direction toward a deistic position or the position of Sherburne's "Whitehead Without God."

Works Cited

CNT —John B. Cobb, *A Christian Natural Theology*
PR —Alfred North Whitehead, *Process and Reality*
RM —Alfred North Whitehead, *Religion in the Making*
SWM —Alfred North Whitehead, *Science and the Modern World*
IWM —William A. Chriatian, *The Interpretation of Whitehead's Metaphysics*
KWPR —Donald W. Sherburne, *A Key to Whitehead's Process and Reality*
CA —Schubert Ogden, "A Christian Natural Theology," *The Christian Advocate*, IX, 18, pp. 11-12
WM —Ivor Leclere, *Whitehead's Metaphysics*
PANW —Paul A. Schilpp, *The Philosophy of Alfred North Whitehead*

III.

AESTHETICS

Wine, Song, And The Magico-Medicinal In The Homeric *Hymn To Dionysos*

Linda Ardito
Dowling College

Introduction

The cultivation of the vine and the development of song are two important factors in the greater 'cultivation' and flowering of civilization itself. At the same time, both wine and song were highly valued as potent agents of the magico-medicinal, of 'mystical' transcendence beyond the rational self, and of inspiration. Both were thus instrumental in psychagogic religious rites of the remote past where, typically combined with dance, they would overcome the 'pollution' that resulted from illness of the body, mind, and/or soul. Among the Greek healer deities honored in such rites is Dionysos[1] who, in addition to other attributes and functions, was, himself, a symbol of wine, musical inspiration, and transformation. The objective of those who participated in the *chorus*, or danced hymn of the peasantry called the *dithyramb*,[2] was that of catharsis and spiritual transformation. Archaic choral lyric and ritual[3] is widely held to be the fundamental basis for the development of tragedy;[4] cult lyric not infrequently venerated Dionysos as symbol of the vital connection between wine and song, particularly with respect to their function as magico-medicinal agents of transformation. Celebrations honoring the gods were each typically accompanied by a new choral hymn and Homeric Hymns introduced the festal recitations of the rhapsodes. In this paper I explore symbolic dimensions of wine and song in the context of the Homeric *Hymn to Dionysos* (hereafter referred to as the *Hymn*), the popular tale of the god's abduction by pirates. First, however, to underscore the importance of wine and song in the ancient Greek world and to better contextualize their meaning in the *Hymn*, I shall provide a brief overview of their widely recognized affinity and purported medicinal efficacy.

Part One

As long as you live, [shine forth[5]]; let nothing grieve you. For life is short, and time claims its tribute.[6]

Authored by Seikilos in about the first century CE,[7] these verses and their supporting musical notation,[8] are inscribed on a tombstone found at Tralles (Aïdin) in Western Asia Minor and constitute a type of *skolion* or ancient Greek drinking song.[9] The song's brevity, a characteristic feature of *skolia*, is well suited to its message of the certain and relatively swift passage from life to death. This simple and perhaps somewhat grim reminder of the paradoxical constancy of change and of time's ultimate authority is most aptly given a musical setting in that, *time*—a concept of meter and measure—is, of course, a musical element. Moreover, it was the predominant influence in the pronunciation of language as well as the basis of the poetical rhythm of song.[10] Thus, in general, the sung music of ancient Greece was subject to the primacy of poetry—a relationship which naturally resulted in an emphasis upon the linear, temporal dimension of melody over the vertical, spacial dimension of 'harmony.'[11]

Perhaps, in part, to enhance the effects of wine-drinking and to ease the burdens associated with one's sense of linear time, *skolia* and other forms of music, sometimes accompanied by dance,[12] were often introduced at symposia,[13] the earliest models of which derive from the Homeric warrior feast and symposium.[14] In such settings, wine and song were indeed highly valued for their pleasing effects. In the *Odyssey*, for example, Odysseus, attending a banquet given by the Phaiakians in his honor, is moved by the singing of the blind Demodokos, saying:

> 'O great Alkinoös, pre-eminent among all people, surely indeed it is a good thing to listen to a singer such as this one before us, who is like the gods in his singing; for I think there is no occasion accomplished that is more pleasant than when festivity holds sway among all the populace, and the feasters up and down the houses are sitting in order and listening to the singer, and beside them the tables are loaded with bread and meats, and from the mixing bowl the wine steward draws the wine and carries it about and fills the cups. This seems to my own mind to be the best of occasions...'[15]

To break the bonds of linear time altogether, narcotic herbs were sometimes added (usually by the Symposiarch) to the customary mix of wine and water. Intoxicative drinks, it was believed, provided mortals the opportunity to experience a sense of the timelessness of the divine, where past, present, and future are one eternity. In Plato's *Republic*, for example, we find reference to Musaeus' song which tells of a symposium of saints in Hades who are in a perpetual state of intoxication as a reward for their virtue:

> ...Musaeus and his son have a more excellent song than these of the blessings that the gods bestow on the righteous. For they conduct them to the house of Hades in their tale and arrange a symposium of the saints, where, reclined on couches and crowned with wreaths, they entertain the time henceforth with wine, as if the fairest meed of virtue were an everlasting drunk.[16]

Guests at symposia often drank to each other's health.[17] In this setting, drinking songs or *skolia* were sung. Such customs undoubtedly relate to much older medical associations between wine and song. Indeed, there is little question of the affinity of wine and song, to say nothing of other forms of music, including incantations. A wealth of ancient 'medicinal' recipes mention wine[18] and/or music. Furthermore, ancient Greek vases often depict these combined themes which likely echo traditions rooted in the remote past.

Wine and music were so frequently combined in practice that, in the context of a theory of education at large, the Athenian in Plato's *Laws* says:

> ...a really sound theory on [drinking] cannot be surely and adequately expounded apart from a true theory of music...[19]

In a sense, it may even be said that a variety of peasant songs were, and still are in some regions, partly responsible for wine's very existence. These include, for example, the 'dirge-like' tunes sung to honor the death of the grape during its harvest[20] and the song of the *lenos* (wine press) that accompanied the dance of crushing grape underfoot.[21] These activities may be thought of as an integral part of the cycle of life, death, and transformation associated with wine-making; for the grape seed gives birth to the vine which bears fruit. Song accompanies the grape harvest. Its power then combines with that of dance to extract the fruit's life blood so that, through the transformative process of fermentation, it will become wine. The life-giving rhythms of song and dance now accompany the drinking of wine in connection with various religious rites, dramas, social and civic ceremonies, banquets, and symposia. Upon ingesting wine, the cyclic process continues as this divine liquid, it was believed, impacts and transforms body, mind, and soul.

It is not generally held that wine originated with the Greeks.[22] Even so, it was infused with divine essence by the apotheosis of Dionysos who, it is believed, has pre-Archaic roots, venerated, perhaps, some nine-thousand years ago as child of the earth-mother.[23] Literary reference to Dionysos in connection with wine and with song, however, is found in the Homeric Hymns.[24] The word *hymnos* (hymn) is a musical term that denotes a kind of devotional song to a deity.[25] In the first of the Homeric hymns dedicated to Dionysos, it is said that only those who honor the deity "may call holy song to mind."[26] In another of his hymns, he is praised as "god of abundant clusters!"[27] These references to wine and song symbolize Dionysos' divine life energy, a power responsible for vegetative growth and the inspiration of song. The remaining pages of this paper are dedicated to an exploration of this symbolism within the context of the *Hymn*, the story of Dionysos' abduction by pirates.

Part Two

Let us briefly review the story. Dionysos appeared on a bluff by the sea. He is youthful, with dark, wind-blown hair. Symbolic of his divinity as god of wine, he wears a purple robe draped over his shoulders. Suddenly there appeared a ship filled with Tyrrhenian pirates who, thinking Dionysos the son of a king, signaled one another and seized him in the hope of securing a large ransom. The ropes intended to bind the smiling, dark-eyed Dionysos, however, fell from his arms and legs. Seeing this, the helmsman cried out to the men:

> Madmen! What god is this whom you have taken and bind, strong that he is? Not even the well-built ship can carry him. Surely this is either Zeus or Apollo...or Poseidon, for he looks not like mortal men but like

> the gods who dwell on Olympus. Come, then, let us set him free upon the dark shore at once: do not lay hands on him, lest he grow angry and stir up dangerous winds and heavy squalls.[28]

The captain, however, yelled back at the helmsman:

> Madman, mark the wind and help hoist sail on the ship: catch all the sheets. As for this fellow we men will see to him: I reckon he is bound for Egypt or for Cyprus or [for] the Hyperboreans or further still. But in the end he will speak out and tell us his friends and all his wealth and his brothers, now that providence has thrown him in our way.[29]

Mast and sail were hoisted on the ship and wind began to fill the sail. Shortly thereafter, however, strange events were witnessed among them. A stream of aromatic wine was suddenly flowing throughout the ship. Then, a vine with many clusters spontaneously appeared along the top of both sides of the sail. Ivy, filled with flowers and berries, coiled the mast and garland covered the oar-locks. Upon seeing these things the pirates cried out to the helmsman to bring the ship to land. Dionysos, however, had suddenly transformed himself into a fierce lion. A bear also suddenly appeared. The roaring lion and ravening bear naturally caused even greater panick among the sailors who fled towards the stern, near the helmsman. The lion then sprang forth and seized the captain. To escape such a fate the sailors jumped ship and were transformed into dolphins. Dionysos held back the helmsman, however, and said:

> Take courage...you have found favour with my heart. I am loud-crying Dionysos whom Cadmus' daughter Semele bare of union with Zeus.[30]

The *Hymn* closes with these words:

> Hail, child of fair-faced Semele! He who forgets you can in no wise order sweet song.[31]

Though the scope and aim of this paper does not permit an account of the many facets of this tale's complex symbolism, I shall discuss two of its basic themes, with focus upon the symbolism of wine and song as magico-medicinal agents. These include the themes of *transformation* and *belief*. Let us begin with the former. There is little question that the *Hymn* is a story of transformation. Moreover, it is about *exoteric* and *esoteric* aspects of transformation, both of which are symbolized by the god Dionysos. Instances of exoteric transformation include the visible metamorphoses of Dionysos into a fierce lion and the crew into dolphins. Esoteric transformation in the context of the *Hymn* relates to hidden changes of the *psyche* and to an aspect of Dionysian power that explains various stages of change, growth, and transformation. The Dionysian-influenced human life cycle is symbolized by the crew. Indeed, the tale leaves us with a living helmsman, a dead captain, and a transformed crew. These are obvious metaphors for the respective stages of life, death, and transformation.

Agents of this Dionysian cycle of transformation include the vine and song, both of which are, themselves, subject to this same basic process. Dimensions of the vine symbol, for example, include all stages of the cycle for wine-making. The seed is symbolized by the presence of Dionysos. He also symbolizes the power that promotes the vine's growth and yields its fruit. In the *Hymn*, Dionysos' power of transformation, via wine and its aromatic essence, permeates the ship. His divinity is underscored in the tale in that the stages of vegetative growth aboard the ship are not subject to the normal patterns associated with linear time. So escalated and intense are Dionysos' generative powers that ivy, replete with berries and flowers, and a cluster-filled vine appear instantaneously. Moreover, wine flows aboard the ship even before the appearance of the vine. Contact with this divine liquid sets the pirates' cycle of transformation in motion.

The symbol of song is somewhat analogous to that of the vine in that it, too, refers to a Dionysian cycle of transformation. The final line of the *Hymn* directly addresses Dionysos, saying: "He who forgets you can in no wise order sweet song."[32] Unlike the vine which eventually yields 'sweet wine,' however, 'sweet song' in the *Hymn* is mentioned only as a formulaic afterthought. This afterthought, however, makes clear that harmony is nonetheless the goal. Perhaps the journey towards harmony in the *Hymn* falls just short of any mention of song within the context of the story as a reminder that mortals can never fully participate in song's divine, Dionysian nature. Even so, song is the medium through which the entire story of the *Hymn* unfolds and the singer would have at least aimed at a 'harmonious' performance.

The cycle of song in the tale, unlike that of the vine, unfolds in a more gradual, temporal manner and is best understood when the sequence of events related to its progress is considered comprehensively. In broad terms, therefore, the cycle constitutes a sequence of communication that intensifies over the course of the tale, with 'harmony' mentioned only after the most extreme point of intensified communication. So let us consider the cycle of language that eventually makes 'sweet song' possible. The tale opens with the silent signaling gestures of the pirates. As the *Hymn* tells us, "...they made signs to one another" (line 7); this is what initiates the cycle. To advance and intensify this cycle, the helmsman, realizing that they have actually abducted a god, cries out to captain and crew: "Madmen! what god is this whom you have taken...?" (line 14). The captain yells back with "taunting words," calling the helmsman a "madman" (line 25). This is followed by the subsequent cries of the crew who finally plead with the helmsman to bring the ship to land (line 43-45). The pirates' initial signaling gestures are later answered by the more intensified and wild animal gestures of the Dionysian lion which "glar[ed] fiercely with scowling brows" and of the "shaggy" bear which "stood up ravening" (line 47-8). Moreover, the Dionysian sounds of the roaring lion and ravening bear are an intensifed replacement of the yells among helmsman, captain, and crew. This is the last step in the cycle, with its augmentation of both physical gesture and sound. It is only after this step that Dionysos provides the missing link of moderate speech, telling the helmsman, who is now the only remaining person aboard ship, that he has "found favor" with his "heart" (lines 55-6). After Dionysos' short speech we are given the formulaic final line in which 'harmony' is mentioned. Thus, just as all stages of the wine-making cycle are present in the *Hymn*, all of the basic auditory and visual ingredients for a musico-dramatic performance are present. This performance 'recipe' includes obvious pointed references to gesture, silence, word, and sound. Furthermore, the *Hymn* reveals that the Dionysian events of the tale are an exaggerated reflection of mortal activity. For example, the pirates' signaling gestures, followed by yells, set in motion a more intensified, Dionysian cycle of gesture and sound which now merge. Thus it is in the *Hymn* that the deeds of mortals are reflected back to them, sometimes with Dionysian vengeance. Recognizing this 'truth,' as symbolized by the transformative power of wine and divine sound, is crucial if harmony is the goal.

Motion and the implied energy waves that cause it are also symbols which underscore Dionysos' transformative power. Examples include the wild gestures of both lion and bear and the sound waves of the god's inharmonious roar as lion. With respect to the latter, let us consider an animal's roar in terms of the physics of acoustics. Unlike the identifiable frequencies associated with the tones of a song, such sound phenomena would be described solely in terms of its power spectrum. The wild and threatening gestures and elemental sounds of the roaring lion and ravening bear are catalysts in the crew's process of transformation as the men flee in the direction of the helmsman. Also implicit in the *Hymn* is the wave energy behind more apparent types of motion—the instantaneous growth of ivy and of the vine which spring forth from Dionysos' implied solar light waves, the waves of air that breath life into the ship's sail and propel its motion, and the water waves beneath the ship. As with Dionysos' roar, the random waves on the surface of the sea would also be described in terms of their power spectrum. Moreover, the waves of this amniotic and 'baptismal' sea are intersected not only by the interruptive gliding motion of the ship but by the crew who frantically dives into its depths. Just as the Dionysian cycle of transformation continues after the ingestion of wine, affecting body, mind, and 'soul,' it likewise continues as the crew is submerged into the depths of the sea and become dolphins.

Let us reflect upon yet another symbolic dimension of Dionysos. As god of the vine and of vegetation in general, he is related to the earth, an exoteric symbol of the mean between that which lay above and below its surface. In drinking the material substance of wine, one partakes of the non-material soul of Dionysos. Thus the deity also occupies the more esoteric realm of the soul, a symbol of the mean between the lower physical body and the higher spirit. In this sense, Dionysos is as much a catalyst for transformation towards the spiritual realm as he is master of the material world. Indeed, it may be said that he occupies a vital but neutral position, representing not only the irrational, wild, counter-god to Apollo, as popularly portrayed, but a god who makes transformation possible in either direction of, and to any degree within, the so-called Apollonian/Dionysian spectrum.

In the mythical realm, however, man's involutional processes, which are understood to block movement toward harmony, are reversed through discordant intervention and purging. In the *Hymn*, it is important to note the opposites that merge to bring about harmony. Lunar symbols of water[33] and bear,[34] for example, juxtapose the more popular contrasting solar symbols of wine and lion. Indeed, water—a passive, rational, cool, and sober drink—mixes with the active, fiery energy of intoxicative wine. The vine and ivy symbols aboard ship may be similarly compared. The seasonal vine flourishes in the sun while ivy, an evergreen, thrives in cooler, shaded areas. Also, recall the more gradual movement towards harmony that, in the *Hymn*, would result in 'sweet song' through the unfolding cycle of communication whereby gesture and sound increasingly intensify.

Let us now consider our second theme, namely, that of *belief*. In the context of the tale, transformation and movement toward harmony is contingent upon a kind of belief that extends beyond the rational. Recall that the captain calls the helmsman a "madman" (line 26) for his fear that their abductee is actually a god. In going about the usual business of being a captain, he instead instructs the helmsman to "...mark the wind[,] help hoist [the] sail...[and] catch all the sheets" (lines 26-7). Thus, the captain, believing in nothing greater than his own authority aboard ship, demonstrates a moral blindness. Moreover, his deific posture costs him his life, with wine symbolizing his sacrificial blood.[35] Intoxication from the divine wine of Dionysos would have resulted in a suspension of the captain's will. Instead, his will is reinforced since he is swimmingly drunk, not on the wine of Dionysos, but, rather, on his own arrogance. He thus heeds not the warning of the helmsman and may be regarded as an archetypal figure of self-destruction. Similar moral warnings are found throughout the ancient literature. Pindar's fifth Isthmian Ode, for example, warns:

> Do not seek to become Zeus; you have all there is, if a share of those blessings should come to you.[36]

In the Gospel of *Mark*, Christ cautions:

> Whosoever shall not receive the kingdom of God as a little child... shall not enter therein."[37]

Let us consider the latter quote with respect to some basic characteristics associated with small children. Broadly speaking, it may be said of a child's nature that it is trusting and believing. Also among their traits is the ability to easily engage in great flights of fancy and to become completely filled with wonderment and inspiration. By comparison, the captain's characteristics are antithetical. Indeed, the captain personifies the so-called 'mature' adult who is tempered by self-identification, guided largely by rationality, and confident that he/she is in total command of his/her surroundings. Indeed the captain wrongly surmises that his abductee is "bound for Egypt or for Cyprus or to the Hyperboreans..." (lines 28-9). Thus, though the ship is actually under the complete and indestructible influence of the god Dionysos, the so-called 'captain' has no knowledge or understanding of this. It never occurs to him that there may be a greater reality than the one he has constructed with his limited, reasoning, and mortal mind. Thus, perhaps one of the *Hymn's* deeper messages extends beyond a consideration of the characters within the context of the story, being instead an invitational message intended for the very real persons either participating in, or subjected to, its actual performance: to fully appreciate and participate in the fantastic journey and the lessons of the *Hymn*, one must suspend rational judgement and instead believe; to put it another way, one must not take up the position of the captain but, rather, that of the helmsman. Indeed, the men aboard ship are transformed, each commensurate with their ability to access Dionysos. Thus, listeners, too, upon hearing the Dionysian tones of the *Hymn*, would be comparably affected.

We are perhaps given yet another message, this time from the captain's demise: when the limited reasoning of mortals is the sole dictate of belief, Dionysos' magico-medicinal power is inaccessible. In general, the contingency of belief in accessing powers of healing is a widespread idea rooted in pre-history. Belief in a shaman's ability to communicate with the dead and with 'nature spirits,' for example, is understood to be an essential requirement for healing. Belief is also the contingency for healing in *Mark* 16:16-18, whereby Christ says:

> He that believeth and is baptized shall be saved; but he that believeth not shall be damned.
>
> And these signs shall follow them that believe; In my name shall they cast out devils; they shall speak with new tongues;

> They shall take up serpents; and if they drink any deadly thing, it shall not hurt them; they shall lay hands on the sick, and they shall recover.[38]

In the *Hymn*, belief in Dionysos is an obvious contingency in accessing the god's favorable power. Without it, one suffers the fate of the captain. Symbols of Dionysos' magico-medicinal power abound. Let us first consider the water symbol. The story unfolds at sea, a powerful symbol of purification and initiation. Indeed, as Burkert points out:

> The most widespread means of purification is water, and in Greek purification rituals contact with water is fundamental.[39]

The pirates, by jumping ship, are 'baptized' and thus transformed, albeit into dolphins. They thus "escape" from the "miserable fate" of the captain (line 52). The ship's ivy-coiled mast is symbolic of Dionysos' powerful thyrsos. Indeed, his staff may be said to be analogous to any number of magico-medicinal rods including, the staff of Asclepius, the magical caduceus of Hermes, and the shepherd's staff of Apollo, to name a few. It is interesting to note that herbalists preserved their medicinal plants within the *narthex*, that is, the fennel stalk of the *thyrsos*. But the *thyrsos* was more than a container of medicines. The ivy that coiled the *thyrsos*—as it does the mast of the ship in the *Hymn*—was a known intoxicant, as were its berries.[40] In fact, the plant was known to be curative but also potentially fatal. Moreover, the crowning pine cone of the *thyrsos* came from a tree whose fermented resin is an intoxicant.

Another of the *Hymn's* medicine symbols is the healing lattise structure of the flourishing, cluster-filled vine that spans the sail above the mast of the ship. This symbol calls to mind ancient tree sanctuaries which were typically located out of doors and far from everyday existence. Cult scenes at such sanctuaries occurred beneath a single large and distinctive tree that had been chosen as sacred. Of such trees, Burkert points out that they…

> …are not found on mountains and are not likely in the palace complexes. The shrines must therefore have lain in the open countryside.[41]

The vine symbolism aboard ship may also refer to the routine practice of healthful eating and drinking beneath a vine trellis or tree, both of which are protective with respect to the sun and to conditions of weather and temperature. In the tale, beneath the cover of the vine, wine works its purgative and transformative action. First, the core of the moral disease, namely, the captain, is purged of all existence. Next, the crew's physical contact with the divine wine of Dionysos, as it flows aboard ship, causes their minds to be filled with fear and panic. Finally, the wine penetrates their souls as it mixes with sea-water and transforms them.

With respect to song, this pattern of influence would have been understood to occur in the reverse order—first impacting the soul, then the mind and, lastly, the body. Song, however, is but one aspect within the sound spectrum of Dionysos. The more elemental sound of the lion's roar and, in another of the *Hymns* to Dionysos, the "outcry" of the Nymphs who follow in his train, may also be regarded as part of this divine spectrum. In this sense, any form of sound may be intoxicative, serving an almost identical purpose to that of wine—namely, to pave the way towards self-forgetfulness, purification, spiritual transcendence, and ecstacy.

So what are we to make of this short tale of wonder? First, it is clear that Dionysos caused all aboard ship to experience a fate commensurate with their position in the process of life's journey. The arrogant captain was killed, the fearful crew was transformed, and the believing helmsman was spared. To effectively commune with the essence of Dionysos, the crew, who needed more convincing than the helmsman, required submersion in the broad expanse of medicinal sea-water and wine. In the *Hymn*, the dominant presence of both of these liquids is a likely metaphor for the actual practice of mixing them together. Water and wine were usually mixed in the proportion of 2 or 3 parts water to one part wine,[42] though this varied on different occasions. Indeed, drinking unmixed wine was generally considered barbaric and even injurious to one's physical and mental health. Honey, spices, and/or narcotic herbs were also added at times.

As with the symbolism of mixing wine with water in the *Hymn*, the ship's ivy-coiled mast, which recalls Dionysos' drug-containing fennel stalk or *thyrsos*, may be understood to symbolize the actual practice of adding herbal intoxicants to wine. With or without herbal additives, however, wine was almost invariably mixed with water. Furthermore, although it may seem a bit odd to us, sea-water was not infrequently added to wine. Indeed, '*oinos thalassikos*' (sea-water wine) was, as William Younger put it, "not only tolerated, but even admired."[43] Moreover, salt-water, being a common preservative, was added to wine so it could be stored and sealed in large amphorae for transport throughout the Mediterranean. It is therefore not unlikely that the recognized medicinal properties of wine in the ancient world were also partly attributed to its salt-water content. The fact is, unlike fresh waters which are slightly acid, sea-water is always slightly alkaline due mostly to the presence of several alkaline earth minerals, principally sodium, calcium, magnesium and potassium.[44] To neutralize any acid that might be formed in wines, particularly those of lesser quality and with a lower alcohol content, sea-water was the principal *conditurae* used in wine.[45] Similarly, for optimum human health, we know today that the pH of the body's internal fluids should, in fact, be slightly alkaline. This would indicate a healthy reserve of essentially those same minerals found in sea-water. Without expressing it in these terms, the ancient Greeks knew that the proper mix of sea-water and wine was a kind of medicine. Indeed, not only was salt added to wine as a flavoring, it was used as a preventative or corrective for wine, and, by extension, as a health tonic for the human body as well.

In the *Hymn*, to symbolize the magnitude and influence of Dionysos' medicinal power, the mixture of wine and sea-water takes place in a seemingly infinite expanse of the sea itself. As the wine-drenched and suddenly god-fearing crew is submerged into its depths, they are 'baptized' into the realm of belief, transformed, and healed. Indeed, we may say that, in the *Hymn*, the way of truth and of harmony lies in the ever-present power of belief and that wine and divine sound are its catalysts. In them lie the omnipotent life-force of the god Dionysos. In closing, as the formulaic final line of the *Hymn* tells us, none forgetting Dionysos will know the way to composing 'sweet song.' So, in the spirit of the ancient Greeks, let us remember Dionysos and raise the wine cup with a toast to song, then sing a song that honors wine.

Endnotes

[1] The early formation of the cult of Dionysos appears to be the result of broad cross-cultural contacts. Thus, as with most, if not all, 'Greek' gods, the figure of Dionysos likely represents non-Greek and wider Mediterranean influences.

[2] Scholars do not agree as to its origin. We do know, however, that the early *dithyramb* was a choral song, typically in honor of Dionysos. It usually accompanied dance and its original theme was the god's birth. '*Dithyrambos*' was also one of the names of Dionysos himself. After the period between the sixth and fourth centuries BCE, there were modifications to the 'genre,' including solo performance and accompaniment by the aulos.

[3] As Burkert points out, "...almost all archaic choral lyric is cult lyric..." Walter Burkert, *Greek Religion*, trans. John Raffan (Cambridge, MA: Harvard University Press, 1985), 4.

[4] Aristotle, in his *Poetics*, says that tragedy developed from the *dithyramb*; Aristotle, *Poetics*, 1449a7-11. Finley asserts that what emerged from this influence "...was neither ritual dance nor choral celebration of the god nor a straightforward pairing of the two, but something new and different, namely, theatre"; M.I. Finley, *The Ancient Greeks* (New York, NY: Penguin Books, 1977), 100. For Burkert, the theory of the ritual origin of tragedy advanced by Gilbert Murray and Francis Macdonald Cornford, respectively, was to "have a profound and stimulating effect not only on the study of antiquity but on literary and philosophical culture in general." Burkert, *op. cit.*, 3.

[5] Davison and Apel's translation from the 1949 revised edition of their *Historical Anthology of Music*, the source of the present translation, includes the reading "be cheerful" (*euphrainou*) which is here replaced by Warren D. Anderson's reading of "shine forth" (*phaínou*); as stated by Anderson, the former reading, also found in notes to the Halaris 1992 compact disc, has no textual basis. Anderson's full translation of Seikilos' skolion reads: "While you live, shine forth: don't be sad at all. We have only a little while to live; time demands the end [of life] (Anderson's insertion) in repayment." See Warren D. Anderson, *Music and Musicians in Ancient Greece* (Ithaca, NY: Cornell University Press, 1994), 223, 239; Archibald T. Davison and Willi Apel, "Oriental, Medieval, and Renaissance Music," *Historical Anthology of Music*, revised edn., 2 Vols., (Cambridge, MA: Harvard University Press, 1949), Vol. 1, 239; Compact disc: *Music of Ancient Greece*, Christodoulos Halaris and instrumental ensemble, vocal soloists, Orata Orangm 2013, 1992.

[6] English translation in Archibald T. Davison and Willi Apel, *op. cit.*, 239.

[7] Though this work has been dated variously from the second century BCE to the first century CE, most scholars now agree that epigraphical evidence suggests the first century CE.

[8] Seikilos' notated skolion is rare in that Greek music was largely improvised. Moreover, of the more than forty extant papyri or inscriptions that contain Greek musical notation, this song is exceptional in that it combines precise rhythmic and pitch notation. It is not known when musical notation was first used by the Greeks. The oldest known fragment of Greek music is the Leiden papyrus which dates from the first half of the third century BCE. It consists of two excerpt settings of Euripides' tragedy *Iphigenia in Aulis*. Anderson gives some measure of support to the claim that these settings indeed comprise the earliest surviving annotated text; Warren D. Anderson, *op. cit.*, 214.

[9] Though from a relatively late period, Seikilos' song is among the earliest surviving examples of ancient Greek music. In the strictest sense, its status as Greek music has been called into question by some scholars. According to Anderson, Beaton makes a strong case that "the affiliations of Seikilos' song lie with Turkish popular melodies." The work nonetheless exhibits general characteristics associated with *skolia*. *Skolia* are short patriotic or moralizing poems—often consisting of no more than four lines—that were sung at symposia. The term 'skolion' meant 'crooked' or 'zigzag' and refers to either the more specific pattern in which the lyre was passed from one singer to another on opposing sides of the banquet table or to the more random manner in which these songs went around the table. In the latter, one of the party would improvise a strophe or stanza and then pass the lyre or myrtle-branch to any guest of his choosing whereby that person was obliged to improvise a stanza matching the same subject. Persons selected at 'random' were usually quite skillful musicians. Skolia were also passed on to succeeding generations and it is believed that the same melody was applied to different texts. The social activity of performing skolia was also considered "a mark of culture." See Anderson, *op. cit.*, 106, 125, 226-27; Roderick Beaton, "Modes and roads: Factors of change and continuity in Greek musical tradition," *British School of Athens*, 1980, 75:1-11.

[10] It is generally believed that, compared to our modern day systems, language and music shared a much closer relationship. The two were often nearly indistinguishable as is evident in terminology associated with a variety of poetic "genres" such as *lyric* poetry (sung to the lyre) and *tragedy* ("*tragoedi*" is partly derived from the noun d , meaning "the art of singing"). Some ancient musico-poetic "genres" for chorus include the *hymnos* (typically sung in honor of a deity), the *paian* (usually sung in honor of Apollo), the *dithyrambos* (often sung in honor of Dionysos or otherwise possessing a Dionysian aesthetic), the *hymenaios* (a wedding song), and the *threnos* (a funeral song).

[11] 'Harmony' is here referred to in its modern sense, as tones sounded simultaneously. It does not to refer to the varied ways in which the term *harmoniai* was understood by the ancient Greeks. Aristoxenus' (b. ca. 365 BCE) *Elements of Harmony* defines *harmoniai* as tunings; that is, as the adjustments of notes produced by a particular instrument. To the *tonoi*, he ascribes the names Dorian, Phrygian, Lydian, etc. Plato and Aristotle, however, ascribe these same ethnic names to the *harmoniai*. It is thought, therefore, that the *harmoniai* differed tonally based upon considerations of ethos. *Harmoniai* also has the broader meaning of 'fitting together,' though this still has a musical application in that tuning is a kind of 'fitting together' of notes. For an informative discussion of the *harmoniai*, see Andrew Barker, "Appendix A: the *harmoniai*," in *Greek Musical Writings: The Musician and his Art*, 2 Vols., Andrew Barker, ed., (Cambridge: Cambridge University Press, 1984), Vol. 1, 163-68.

[12] A great many ancient vases and drinking vessels depict scenes of women dancing and playing the aulos and the kithara at symposia.

[13] According to Plato, men of "gentle breeding and culture" had no need for "childish" and "nonsensical" music at symposia since, in the best sense, such gatherings were designed to encourage philosophic thought. Nonetheless, *skolia* and music of kithara and aulos, were frequently introduced at symposia. Moreover, Xenophon, in his *Symposium*, says that Socrates appreciated the mimetic dancing and other skills performed during such occasions.

[14] Wine and song share a combined history rooted in a period well before the fifth-century banquet and symposium. Both were commonplace at dinners held between soldiers and their chief. In the *Iliad*, Agamemnon refers to wine in the context of such feasts as he sings the praises of the Cretan captain Idomeneus; Homer, *Iliad*, IV, 293-97.

[15] Richmond Lattimore, trans., *The Odyssey of Homer* (New York: Harper Collins, 1965), IX.2-11.

[16] Plato, *Republic*, trans. Paul Shorey, from *The Collected Dialogues of Plato*, ed. Edith Hamilton and Huntington Cairns, Bollingen Series LXXI (Princeton, NJ: Princeton University Press, 1961), II.363d. For an interesting thesis and informative study on the whole question of intoxication in the ancient Greek world, see Wasson, R. Gordon, Carl A.P. Ruck, and Albert Hofmann. *The Road to Eleusis: Unveiling the Secret of the Mysteries*, Ethno-mycological Studies No. 4. New York: Harcourt Brace Jovanovich, 1978.

[17] A guest in possession of the wine cup would typically toast the health of the person to whom he would pass the cup (the cup was usually passed around the table from left to right, in the same order as much of the activities on such occasions). Theramenes' toast to Critias, who led the tyrants against him and caused him to be put to death in 404 BCE, is a jestful reference to this custom. As recounted by Cicero, "[Theramenes] was flung into prison by order of the

thirty tyrants and when he had swallowed the poison like a thirsty man he tossed the remainder out of the cup to make a splash, and with a laugh at the sound it made, 'I drink this,' said he, 'to the health of fair Critias,' the man who had treated him abominably." Cicero adds that "... at their banquets the Greeks make a practice of naming the guest to whom they are going to pass the cup." Cicero. *Tusculan Disputations*, trans. J.E. King, 28 Vols., (Cambridge, MA: Harvard University Press, 1989; first published 1927), Vol. XVIII, I.xl.96-7.

[18] The vast majority of recorded remedies that comprise the Hippocratic Corpus mention wine. One passage relates that "It is better to be full of drink than full of food." See John Chadwick and W.N. Mann, "Aphorisms," in *The Medical Works of Hippocrates* (Charles C. Thomas Publisher, 1950), II.11.

[19] Plato, *Laws*, trans. A.E. Taylor from *The Collected Dialogues of Plato*, eds. Edith Hamilton and Huntington Cairns, I.642a.

[20] This was a widespread tradition in the ancient world. Kerényi comments that "the note of lamentation in Homer's song on the grape harvest is understandable if so sad a thing as the [symbolic] dismemberment of [Dionysos] was involved." He adds that "Cornutus, the tutor of the Roman poet Persius, tells us that the wine treaders invoked the god by various names, such as '*Bakchos*' and '*Euios*.' Reference to these scenes was made at the Second Council of Constantinople, the Trullianum, in the year 691 [CE]. Until that date the wine treaders still cried out 'Dionysos,' but this was now forbidden. The council ordered that instead, whenever a load of grapes was brought in, the treaders should cry "Kyrie eleison." He also comments that "...in the Near East, as in Homer, the grape was entitled to a dirge at the time of the grape harvest." See Carl Kerényi, *Dionysos: Archetypal Image of indestructible Life*, trans. Ralph Manheim, Bollongen Series LXV.2 (Princeton NJ: Princeton University Press, 1976), 67, 257.

[21] *Sileni* or *satyrs* are 'divine' wine pressers depicted in archaic vase painting. As Kerényi points out, "...they remain the indispensable performers of this act in ancient art down to the end of antiquity—except when they are replaced by *Erotes*, or cupids, likewise divine beings." He further states that "in the Dionysian procession of Ptolemaios Philadelphos about 275 BC[E], an enormous wagon bore a *lenos* [(wine press)] in which sixty satyrs supervised by a *silenus* treaded out the grapes. The sweet juice ran out into the street and the wine pressers sang the *melos epilenion*, the song of the *lenos* ... [which], like the wine press itself, involved the dismemberment of Dionysos." He adds that "in a list of melodies played on the flute, various laments are followed by the *epilenion aulema*, the 'flute melody to the wine press.'" See Kerényi, *Ibid.*, 66-7.

[22] Wine was undoubtedly known in pre-historic times. However, it was mead (prepared from fermented honey and water) that was said to be the nectar and early drink of the ancient gods. As stated by Kerényi, Orphic doctrine placed

wine "among [Dionysos'] last gifts." William Younger, in speaking of the earliest days of Western Civilization, says, "It seems...clear that there was a fairly sudden change when, instead of beer or of mead, wine became the chosen drink of the gods." In Greece, this "fairly sudden change" may, in fact, have been largely due to changes in climate and in conditions of the terrain. André Bonnard, for example, states that "...in primitive times the Greeks had felled the trees, to build their villages or to make charcoal. The forests lost ground. By the fifth century the hills and peaks showed the same naked ridges that they do today. And Greece in her ignorance was abandoned to the sun, to violent rainstorms and naked rocks. People fought 'to get into the shadow of a donkey.' On this hard earth, under the capricious and pitiless heavens, the olive and vine were most successful; cereals, whose roots could not go deep enough to reach moisture, less so." It is also important to note Albert Leonard Jr's assertion that "...by the Late Bronze Age (ca. 1550-1150 BCE), viticulture was well established among the cultures of both the Aegean and the Levant. Whether Dionysos had been a fellow traveler during its journey to Greece cannot be proven, but there is both archaeological and philological support for his worship in the Aegean at that time." See Albert Leonard Jr., "'Canaanite Jars' and Late Bronze Age Wine Trade," in *The Origins and Ancient History of Wine*, Patrick E. McGovern, Stuart J. Fleming, Solomon H. Katz, eds., The University of Pennsylvania Museum of Archaeology and Anthropology, Philadelphia (Amsterdam, The Netherlands: Gordon and Breach Publishers, 1996), 236. See also Hesiod's *Theogony*, 642; Kerényi, *op. cit.*, 35; William Younger, *Gods, Men, and Wine* (The Wine and Food Society, Ltd., in association with World Publishing Co., Cleveland, 1966), 29; André Bonnard, *Greek Civilization, From the Iliad to the Parthenon*, 3 Vols., trans. A. Lytton Sells (New York: The Macmillan Co., 1957), Vol. 1, 25-6.

[23] The Stone Age shrines at Çatalhöyük on Turkey's Konya Plain are the source for this dating. Though the connection with Dionysos cannot be made with absolute certainty, archeological evidence of wine-making in this region dates from about 8000 BCE. This and other interesting facts, along with a lively discussion on Dionysos in the context of wine, is found in "The Drinking God," chapter 5 of *Hugh Johnson's Story of Wine* (London: Mitchell Beazley, 1989), 47-58. See also Younger, *op. cit.*, 79-150. For discussion on the shrines and deities of Çatalhöyük see Brian Fagan, *From Black Land to Fifth Sun: The Science of Sacred Sites* (Reading, MA: Helix Books, 1998), 89-99.

[24] Our first record of Dionysos by name dates from about 1250 BCE and appears on three fragmentary Linear B tablets from Pylos and Khania (Crete). Though these tablets make clear Dionysos' divinity within the Mycenaean religion, any connection he may have had with wine or with song is unknown. It is thought that one of the Pylos tablets may indicate a vague reference to Dionysos in the

context of wine and the Khania tablet refers to Zeus and Dionysos as recipients of libations of honey. Much later, in the *Iliad*, Dionysos' gift is "ecstasy, joy to mankind." Though no examples of 'extreme antiquity' survive, the Hymn is believed to be a very ancient form. The oldest of the Homeric Hymns are the *Hymn to Delian Apollo* and the *Hymn to Hermes*, both traditionally dated no later than 650 BCE. The date of the collection as we know it today is unknown. Diodorus Siculus is the first to mention such a body of poetry and, according to Hugh G. Evelyn-White, it is likely that this is essentially what has come down to us. Of the thirty-three extant Homeric Hymns, three are dedicated to Dionysos; the first is of uncertain date and consists of two fragments, the second of which makes reference to Dionysos in the context of song. The second hymn (VII) is variously dated from the seventh to the third century and identifies Dionysos with both wine and song, as does the third (XXVI) which, according to Evelyn-White, appears to have been designed for use in connection with particular religious festivals. See Hugh G. Evelyn-White, trans., G.P. Goold, ed., "Introduction," in *Hesiod, Homeric Hymns, Epic Cycle, Homerica*, The Loeb Classical Library (Cambridge, MA: Harvard University Press, 1936), xxxiv-xxxv; Homer, *Iliad*, trans. Robert Fagles, (New York, NY: Viking, 1990), 14.389.

[25] Hymns were traditionally sung at religious festivals or some other solemn event. The Homeric Hymns are distinguished from other types of hymnic poetry in that their meter is dactylic hexameter and they include formulae that begin and end each poem. The generic name for this kind of poem was *prooimia* ('preludes'). The first mention of the term in connection with its use as an introduction to Homeric epic narratives appears in Pindar's *Second Nemean Ode*. While it is believed that not all of the Homeric Hymns were used as preludes, it has been suggested that, in this context, the term *prooimion* ('prelude') may be considered somewhat analogous to the musical term 'prelude' in that it is not necessarily prefatory in nature and can be quite developed in its own right. Discussion of *prooimia* appears in various scholarly sources. See, for example, Apostolos N. Athanassakis, "Introduction," in *The Homeric Hymns*, trans. Apostolos N. Athanassakis (Baltimore, MD: The Johns Hopkins University Press, 1976), xii; Hugh G. Evelyn-White, trans., *op. cit.*; Charles Boer, trans., "Introduction," in *The Homeric Hymns*, rev. 2nd edn. (Woodstock, CT: Spring Publications, 1970), ii-iii.

[26] Hugh G. Evelyn-White, trans., Homeric Hymn I, "To Dionysos," *op. cit.*, 19-20.

[27] Hugh G. Evelyn-White, trans., Homeric Hymn XXVI, "To Dionysos," *op. cit.*, 11-14.

[28] Hugh G. Evelyn-White, trans., Homeric Hymn VII, "To Dionysos," *op.cit.*, 14-24.

[29] *Ibid.*, 25-31.
[30] *Ibid.*, 55-57.
[31] *Ibid.*, 58-59.
[32] *Ibid.*, 58-59.
[33] Though not scientifically explained, the ancients knew that the moon influenced the ebb and flow of the earth's seas. In the Homeric *Hymn to Selene*, the goddess is described as "the long-winged Moon" whose "rays beam clear, whensoever [she has] bathed her lovely body in the waters of Ocean." Hugh G. Evelyn-White, trans., Homeric Hymn XXXII, "To Selene," *op. cit.*, 2, 7-9.
[34] Bear hibernation symbolized the moon-like and Dionysian 'death and rebirth' idea. Also, the goddess Callisto was once associated with the moon goddess Artemis. She bore Zeus a son, Arcas. Zeus' jealous wife Hera turned Callisto into a bear. Arcas then killed Callisto and Zeus turned her into the constellation known as 'The Great Bear.'
[35] The association of wine and blood is, as Burkert notes, "ancient and widespread." Burkert, *op. cit.*, 164.
[36] Pindar, Isth. 5, 14-15 in *Pindar: Nemean Odes, Isthmian Odes, Fragments*, ed. and trans. William H. Race, Loeb Classical Library 2 Vols. (Cambridge: Harvard University Press, 1997), Vol. 2, 177.
[37] King James version, *Mark* 10:13.
[38] *Ibid.*, 16:16-18.
[39] Walter Burkert, *op. cit.*, 76.
[40] As Harrison remarks, the Dionysian Maenads "chewed ivy leaves for inspiration, as the Delphic prophetess chewed the bay." Jane Ellen Harrison, *Prolegomena to the Study of Greek Religion* (Princeton, NJ: Princeton University Press, 1991; first published by Cambridge University Press, 1903), 428.
[41] Burkert, *op. cit.*, 28.
[42] Though other ingredients could be added, the Greek krat r was developed for the purpose of diluting and mixing wine with water.
[43] Coan wine, regarded as a premium wine, for example, had, as one of its varieties, a white wine heavily flavoured with sea-water. Several others flavoured in this way and mentioned by Younger include Clazomenian, Ephesian and probably Erythraean wines, all from Ionia; from Caria in Asia Minor, Halicarnassian and Myndian; from the Island of Rhodes, Rhodian; and Phorinean, which is thought to derive from Attica. Athenaeus says that "Wine is sweet when sea-water is poured into it." At times the flavor of pitch-preserved wines was undesireable. Columella, in his *De Re Rustica* (1st century CE), suggests adding roasted salt to remedy this problem. Others who refer to the practice of mixing sea-water and wine include Dioscorides, Pliny, Strabo, and Theophrastus. For recent commentary on the subject see William Younger's

fine book, *op. cit.*, 130-33; Carolyn G. Koehler, "Wine Amphoras in Ancient Greek Trade," in *The Origins and Ancient History of Wine*, *op. cit.*, 328, 336 n21.

[44] When carbon dioxide from the atmosphere is dissolved in sea-water, the initial reaction, just as in fresh water, is the formation of carbonic acid. This, however, promptly reacts with the alkaline elements to form carbonates and bicarbonates, rendering the water alkaline.

[45] Other *conditurae* used individually or combined in a variety of ways included turpentine (pure or in the form of pitch), tar, resin, lime, herbs, spices, and gums.

Philosophy, Epistemology, and Hermeneutics: Plotinus On Beauty[1]

Robert M. Berchman
Dowling College

Introduction

I should like to again recall how Plato formulated the task of philosophy: "to see things together in respect of the one" or to elicit the universal eidos from the manifold appearances of things.[2] In this sense I would like to propose another *eidos*, or perspective, from which we can describe and interpret the speechless language of beauty in Plotinus.[3] The starting point for this inquiry is Ennead I.6.[1].[4] Not only is it the earliest of Plotinus' treatises on beauty but more importantly its primary focus is on "sensible" beauty.[5] The intention of this study is to ask how was beauty as a property of things understood by Plotinus? Some preliminary remarks are apposite before this larger question can be addressed, however.

I. Philosophy, Epistemology and Hermeneutics

Two of the more forceful and controversial figures in contemporary philosophy are Richard Rorty and Alasdair MacIntyre.[6] Their critiques offer some valuable insights which may help us frame our questions about Plotinus on the experience of beauty. They ask why philosophers engage in the language games they do. The answer to this question requires a genealogical unmasking where we become aware of the historical accidents and contingencies that shape what we take to be intuitive and self-evident in the history of philosophy. Rorty's and MacIntyre's understandings of how philosophy moves by fits and starts are not be uncritically accepted for our purposes. There is much to criticize in the specific genealogies they elaborate. Their forays into the history of philosophy do uncover prejudgments and prejudices that should be avoided. Nonetheless, to understand Plotinus we must uncover the metaphors, distinctions, and problems that characterize his own form of inquiry. This requires historical digging into how and why he built upon Platonism in the way that he did.

Hence Rorty and Gadamer are heuristically useful.[7] The dominating notion of epistemology is that to be rational we need to be able to find agreement with other human beings. Rorty claims we are epistemological "where we understand perfectly well what is happening but want to codify it in order to extend, or strengthen, or teach, or ground it." Hence, to construct an epistemology is to find the maximum amount of common ground with others. Sometimes this common ground is seen to lie in the realm of Being or the Ideas, which both guide inquiry and are its goal. That is to say, epistemology proceeds on the assumption that all contributions to a given discourse are foundational and commensurable. Inquiry here is implicit conversation.

Hermeneutics is largely a struggle against such assumptions.[8] As Gadamer suggests, to construct a hermeneutics is to be willing to refrain from epistemology, from thinking that there is a special set of terms or a maximum amount of common ground with others. There is no foundation or matrix that unites thinkers. There are only relations among various discourses or strands in possible conversation. We are hermeneutical where "we do not understand what is happening but are honest enough to admit it". Inquiry here is routine conversation.[9]

The transition from Rorty to Gadamer is an easy and natural one. Briefly, Gadamer defends the centrality of tradition and rightful authority in all hermeneutical understanding. We are always shaped by and shaping the traditions that form us. Tradition is not a repository of truth, and in dialogical conversation with tradition our task is to find new better, more fruitful ways of speaking and expressing ourselves.[10] For example, all understanding for Gadamer involves appropriation (and this is what he seeks to do with Aristotle's texts). Appropriation requires what Gadamer claims Aristotle called *phronesis* rather than *episteme*, where knowledge is not detached from our being but is determinative of what we are in the process of becoming. Hence, hermeneutical understanding is for Gadamer a form of *phronesis*, a judgmental mediation or conversation, not *episteme*, a pursuit of metaphysical foundations.[11]

Use of terms such as "epistemology" and "hermeneutics" may seem forced in a discussion of Plotinus. However, the distinction is useful. The contrast between hermeneutics and epistemology is one between a desire for edification and the desire for truth.[12] For Plotinus the only way to be edified is to realize our essences by knowing essences. Indeed, man's essence is to be a knower of essences. In this sense Plotinus is, in Rorty's words, a "systematic" philosopher not an "edifying" philosopher. He is constructive and offers arguments rather than being reactive and offering satires, parodies, or aphorisms. Plotinus, like Plato, could give reasons, argue for his views, justify his standpoints. As a systematic philosopher, he built for eternity not for his own generation.[13]

Gadamer's critical use of the history of philosophy is helpful in grasping what Plotinus was up to when he read Plato. There are many family resemblances between Gadamer's understanding of the role of narrative and tradition, especially in his appeal to Plato and Aristotle, and Plotinus' appropriation of Plato. Plotinus attempted to show continuities and affinities between an authoritative textual past and an interpretive textual present. However, Plotinus did so by communicating with Plato on common epistemological "horizons" such as—what is it that makes things beautiful or what is the experience of beauty? He was not interested in hermeneutically dissolving "horizons" as he was going beyond them.[14]

In *nuce*, a conflict between "epistemology" and "hermeneutics" underpin and explain Plotinus' treatises on beauty.[15] What resulted was a dialogical encounter between Plotinus and Plato where the student attempted to grasp the teacher's positions on beauty in the strongest possible "epistemological" light. There is a play, a to-and-fro movement in this encounter. Plotinus seeks a common ground with Plato in order to clarify, strengthen, and expand his mentor's theories of beauty.

This epistemological dialogue resulted in a novel Plotinian philosophical vocabulary of metaphors, distinctions, and problems. In this sense Plotinus is a revolutionary philosopher as well as a normal philosopher.[16] Indeed, he is a special kind of revolutionary philosopher, one who found a new school within which normal philosophy could be practiced. The fact that there is an apparent incommensurability between his new vocabulary and older ones was a temporary inconvenience. Plotinus thought that this was to be blamed on the shortcomings of his predecessors and would be overcome by the institutionalization of his own vocabulary. In time it would be seen as commensurable with Plato's own. Plotinus introduces a novel set of aesthetic metaphors, distinctions, and problems. It is to his reflections on beauty that we now turn.

II. On Beauty

In the preliminaries to his analysis of the experience of beauty in *Ennead* I.6.[1].1-6, Plotinus includes not only perceptual beauty, which is the beauty of nature and art that we see and hear, but also non-perceptual beauty, which are tied to the virtues and intellect. This opening is followed by a series of provocative questions:

> Very well then, what is it which makes us imagine [*phantazesthai*] that bodies are beautiful and attracts our hearing to sounds because of their beauty. And how are things which depend on soul beautiful. What is this principle, then, which is present in bodies? We ought to consider this first. What is it that attracts the gaze of those who look at something, and turns and draws them to it and makes them enjoy the sight? If we find this perhaps we can use it as a stepping-stone and get a sight of the rest [I.6.1.7-20].

The sheer range and detail of Plato's theory of the experience of beauty is indeed, at first sight, overwhelming. Hence, careful account needs to be taken of Plotinus' interpretation of this whole range of material if our reconstruction of his interpretation of Plato's theory is to be more than mere guesswork.

In brief, Plotinus praises Plato because he treats beauty both as a property existing in things which make them beautiful, and as a complex psychological reaction.[17] But he also tacitly corrects him: first, when he argues that beauty is not limited to sensible particulars alone but beauty is also in those particulars' intelligible archetypes; and secondly, when he reflects on the experience of beauty in the activities of judgement and imagination.

Plato's suggestion that beauty is both a property and a reaction are related theories, but they are not the same. He argues that beauty is a property of things because it participates in the form of beauty in a way similar to large things participating in the form of largeness.[18] Through such participation beautiful objects remind us of an earlier vision of the world of ideas. He also contends that the soul reacts to the presence of beauty much like the lover reacts to the beauty of his love.[19] He views this reaction as a recollection of the idea of beauty seen by the soul of the lover in a previous life. Finally, Plato suggests that mental activities such as recognition, remembrance, and desire of a higher existence underlie the aesthetic experience.[20]

Here Plotinus grasps Plato's teachings in the strongest possible epistemological light. Next, he dialogically goes beyond them. That is to say, he broadens the "horizon" of Plato's initial insights. First, for Plotinus, the soul recognizes the idea of beauty in bodies which participate in it:

> What likeness, then, is there between here and there? If there is a likeness, let us agree that they are alike. But how are both the things in that world and the things in this beautiful? We maintain that the things in this world are beautiful by participating in form.[I.6.2.13-17].

The soul does not recall just one Idea, Plotinus argues next, she grasps the whole realm of Ideas:

> So let us go back to the beginning and state what the primary beauty in bodies really is. It is something we become aware of even at the first glance: the soul speaks of it as if it understood it; recognizes and welcomes it and as it were adapts itself to it. Our explanation of this is that the soul, since it is by nature what it is and is related to the higher kind of reality in the realm of being, when it sees something akin to it or a trace of its kindred reality, is delighted and thrilled and returns to itself and remembers itself and its own possessions [I.6.2.1-12].

The soul recalls all of intelligible reality in the experience of beauty. This recollection is triggered by a reflective relation between beautiful bodies and intelligible forms. Therefore, bodies are beautiful to the extent that they participate not just in a particular Idea such as beauty, but in all Ideas. Participation in the world of Ideas is what makes bodies beautiful and what makes the soul react to them in the way she does when she recognizes Idea in them.[21]

This latter claim, in its immediate context, appears problematic. After all the range of things participating in Idea is wider than the range of beautiful things. Moreover, does not Plotinus fail to account for the specific character of beautiful things as distinguished from other formed bodies? Fortunately, for Plotinus, these ambiguities are resolved. Elsewhere in his writings he claims that beauty is everywhere in the world.[22] Because of the intelligible causal unity present in all things, beauty means being together with the cause of all things.

> Things are beautiful with their cause; since even now something is beautiful because it is everything [VI.7.3.9-10].

Indeed, even in the humblest of things nature or beauty is present because final causality, and not chance predominates.[23] This means there are degrees in the participation in Idea. Things are more or less beautiful insofar as they participate more or less in Idea.[24] Indeed, simple beauties like light and colors are matter mastered by Idea, which means that form is everything in the sense that matter is completely shaped by the form so that there is nothing unintelligible in the thing.[25]

The full implications of these suggestions are apparent in his attack on the Stoic identification of beauty with symmetry.[26] In his attack on the Stoics, Plotinus agrees that beauty consists in symmetry rather than its opposite. But if it were simply identical with symmetry, consisting of a harmony of parts neither Ideas nor incomposite material things could be beautiful. Beauty should be identified with Idea and ugliness with matter unmastered by Idea.[27]

The point is that beauty is in simple [non-composite] objects such as colors, light, gold, lightening, and individual sounds.[28] Moreover, the soul judges such simple objects as beautiful through the power of her imagination.

It is through "color blooming" on the intelligible world that the soul grasps color forming in material things quickened to life by the radiance cast upon them by the Good.[29] Such imagery is tied to Plotinus' later claim that it is not Idea but Life that one sees the essence of beauty. He argues for instance that living ill-proportioned faces have more beauty than lifeless symmetrical ones.[30] This is so because even the beauty of the Ideas would fail to stir us if they were not hastened to life by the radiance cast upon them by the Good.[31]

In brief, participating in, and becoming Idea, is to become beautiful. This is possible because Idea not only makes things beautiful. It is itself beautiful. That is to say, beauty is Idea or true being.[32] Finally, the identification of beauty with Idea and intellect leads Plotinus to assert that the One is the source of the beauty that is intellect:

> Soul is beauty through intellect. And the rest is beautiful when shaped by soul, the [beauty] in actions and pursuits. And indeed those things such as are called bodies are made by soul and are made beautiful by it, since it is divine and as if a part of beauty, when it touches and orders them, to the extent to which they can participate [I.6.6.27-33].

This claim is significant for two reasons. First, it grounds Plotinus firmly as an aestheticist. Secondly, it leads immediately to questions about the ascent of the soul to the One. The pursuit of beauty is the pursuit of true being and its source, the One or the Good. Moreover, the pursuit of beauty also allows the soul to purify herself, and to return to her original, undescended self:

> Thus when the soul is purified it becomes Idea and rational principle and altogether incorporeal and intellective and completely part of the divine, whence is the source of all beauty and all things of that kind. So when soul is brought up to intellect, it is more beautiful. But intellect and what goes with it is soul's beauty, its very own and not another's, for then is soul truly and solely itself [I.6.6.13-18].

There is a twofold movement here. In becoming beautiful oneself, soul not only approaches the source of all beauty, the One. She becomes whole and one with herself.

> Come back into yourself and look. If you do not see yourself as something beautiful, just as the sculptor, to make a beautiful statue, removes this, polishes that, making this smooth and this pure...thus should you remove what is superfluous, and straighten what is crooked, purifying what is dark, making it shine [I.6.9.7-12].

This reflects an attempt by Plotinus to expand beauty to the whole of reality and the experience of beauty to constitute a primary realm of human experience. Once the soul grasps beauty it apprehends the totality of the intelligible world, its final cause, and becomes beautiful herself. This is because the intellect or form that makes bodies beautiful is also that which constitutes the beauty of soul.

Indeed, when Plotinus says that the soul becomes one and whole with herself and when he characterizes the soul as a work of sculpture that gives birth to herself, he is adumbrating an aestheticist position. It is, as if, Plotinus characterizes reality as a work of art. There are degrees of beauty relative to the One, Mind, Soul, and Matter, and many ways of grasping beauty relative to an entity's metaphysical place or status in reality. In Ennead I.6.[1] Plotinus explains how sensible beauty is encountered and experienced from the eidos or "perspective" of soul.[33] Here Plotinus offers one of a variety of complementary [not inconsistent] views on the experience of beauty which were revolutionary, if not provocative.

Conclusion

In the first half of the third century, we find ourselves caught up in an unfolding crisis still incomplete. In a way, Plotinus had a heady impulse to "aestheticize" reality. I say "heady" because as a "systematic" yet "revolutionary" philosopher he fractured the foundations of earlier Platonic "aesthetics."[34] The results were a new, late-classical, aestheticism.

Bit by bit, the static framework of the noetic world on which Platonic metaphysics rested was dismantled. The ineffaceable character of forms and gods, which earlier Platonists saw as the ultimate justification of a mimesis between the intelligible and sensible worlds, between intelligibility and sensibility has been dissolved in the experience of beauty. Plotinus views such *mimesis* as imagining form. This usually occurs when we are confronted by the mute, yet profoundly familiar Pythagorean harmonies of form in color and sound. Beauty is present in things whenever it succeeds in representing to the soul a configuration, an order of unity in tension, perhaps a world of its own in miniature.

Aristotle said—and when do we encounter a truth in Plotinus that is not already found in Aristotle?—that a proper work is one where there is neither too little nor too much, nothing in excess and nothing missing.[35] A simple but difficult measure for beauty, which in Plotinus the soul now provides in a speechless image [*mimesis*] of beauty. To be "speechless" does not mean that beauty has nothing to say. On the contrary, the speechlessness of beauty is really a kind of speech. It is a rich, colorful, and resplendent language whose light brightly, clearly and fluently, shines out from the One which is the:

> spring and origin of beauty. [I.6.9.44] [36]

If we were to ask Plotinus to account for beauty—that "speechlessness" which addresses us so forcefully with its unique mute eloquence—his answer might be—such speechlessness is really a kind of speech for:

> no eye ever saw the sun without becoming sun-like, nor can a soul see beauty without becoming beautiful. [I.8.9.30-33]. [37]

Endnotes

1. To study Plotinus on beauty is to risk telling in one's own words a story that has often been excellently told before. In vivid works, de Keyser, Rist and D. O'Meara have brought Plotinus' theory of beauty to the attention of the historians of philosophy. cf. E. de Keyser, La Signification de l'art dans les Enneades de Plotin, Louvain: Peeters, 1955; J. Rist, Plotinus: The Road to Reality, Cambridge: Cambridge University Press, 1967; D. O'Meara, Plotinus, Oxford-London: Oxford University Press, 1995, 88-99. The patient work of Anton, Armstrong, Horn, Moreau, and Rich have increased and clarified the substantial dossier of Plotinus' philosophy of art in studies ranging from a critique of the theory of symmetry to the relation between beauty and the Good. cf. J. Anton, "Plotinus' Refutation of Beauty as Symmetry," *Journal of Aesthetics and Art Criticism*, 23 [1964-5], 233-237; "Plotinus' Conception of the Functions of the Artist," *Journal of Aesthetics and Art Criticism* 26 [1967-8], 91-101; A.H. Armstrong, "Beauty and the Discovery of Divinity in the Thought of Plotinus," in J. Mansfeld and L. de Rijk [eds.], *Kephalaion Studies*, Assen: 1975, 155-173; H.-J. Horn, "Stoische Symmetrie und Theorie des Schoenen in der Kaiserzeit, " *ANRW* 2.36.3: 1455-1471; J. Moreau, "Origine et expressions du beau suivant Plotin," *Néoplatonisme: Mélanges offert à Jean Trouillard = Cahiers de Fontenay* [Fontenay, 1981], 249-263; A. Rich, "Plotinus and the Theory of Artistic Imitation," *Mnemosyne* 13 [1960], 233-239.

2. Plato, *Phaedrus* 265d.

3. This essay continues a theme introduced in Robert M. Berchman, "A Speechless Image: Plotinus on the Experience of Beauty" in James E. Caraway [ed.] *Mediterranean Perspectives*, Dowling College Press SSIPS Binghampton: 1999.

4. On beauty also see Plotinus, *En.*, V.8.[31]; VI.7.[38]; I.3.[20].1-2; VIII.[31].13; II.9.[33].17; and III.5.[50].1

5. On the imagination [phantasia] see *En.*, IV.3.29.31.

6. R. Rorty, *Philosophy and the Mirror of Nature*, Princeton: Princeton University Press, 1979; A. MacIntyre, After Virtue, Notre Dame: University of Notre Dame Press, 1981.

7. See, H.G. Gadamer, *Truth and Method*, New York: Continuum, 1975. Rorty appropriated the expression hermeneutics from Gadamer. cf. R. Rorty, *op. cit.*, 315-356.

8. R. Rorty, *op. cit.*, 317.

9. *Ibid.*, 318.

10. For an example of this see his "conversation" with Kant on "the subjectivization of the aesthetic" in the *Critique of Judgement*, cf. H.G. Gadamer, *op. cit.*, 87.

[11] Cf. e.g., H.G. Gadamer, "Hermeneutics and Social Science," *Cultural Hermeneutics* 2 [1975], 312.
[12] *Ibid.*, 360.
[13] *Ibid.*, 368.
[14] Plotinus, *En.*, I.6.1
[15] *Ibid.*, I.6.[1], V.8 [31], and IV.7.[38]. Also see, I.3.[20]1-2; II.9.[33].17; and III.5.[50].1.
[16] Following R. Rorty, *op. cit.*, 369.
[17] Plato, *Symposium* 210ac; *Hippias major* 297e-298b.
[18] Plato, *Phaedo*, 100bd.
[19] Plato, *Symposium* 210a-211c; *Phaedrus*, 249d-252a.
[20] Plato, *Phaedrus*, 251a-256e.
[21] Plotinus, *En.*, I.6.2.13-16.
[22] *Ibid.*, V.8.8.
[23] *Ibid.*, VI.7.2.19-29.
[24] *Ibid.*, V.8.9.43-47.
[25] *Ibid.*, I.6.3.17-28.
[26] *Ibid.*, I.6.1.20-54.
[27] *Ibid.*, I.6.2-3.
[28] *Ibid.*, I.6.1.32-38. cf. Plato, *Philebus*, 51cd.
[29] *Ibid.*, V.8.10.29-30; VI.7.22.1-36.
[30] *Ibid.*, VI.7.22.24-36.
[31] *Ibid.*, VI.7.22.1-24.
[32] *Ibid.*, I.6..6.21.
[33] For the perspectives from the vantagepoint of intelligible beauty see *En.*, V.8.[31]; and from the One see *En.*, VI.7.[38].
[34] On these terms see R. Rorty, *op. cit.*, 365-372.
[35] Aristotle, *Nic. Ethics*, 1106b9.
[36] Plotinus, *En.*, I.6.9.40-45. cf. Plato, *Phaedrus*, 245c9.
[37] Cf. Plato, *Rep.*, VI 508b3; 509a1.

Neoplatonism and the Art of El Greco

Robert Meredith Helm
Wake Forest University

Dominikos Theotokopoulos was a native of Candia, the capital of the island of Crete, which since 1204 had been a possession of the Serene Republic of Venice and which accommodated a substantial number of Venetians among its inhabitants. Virtually nothing is known of his early years, and even the date of his birth, probably in the year 1542, is uncertain. From the apparent depth and scope of his education, it appears that he was a member of a family of some standing, but the earliest documented reference to him that survived is an instrument signed before a notary public in 1561 by 'Maistro Menegos Theotokopoulos, sgourafos' (Toledo Museum 15). Toward the end of that year, he offered one of his paintings for sale in a lottery. This sketchy information is all we know of his life in his native Crete.

We next hear of him in Venice, where there was a sizeable colony of Cretans. On August 18, 1658, he was making arrangements to dispatch drawings to a Candian cartographer. Two years later, he had moved on southward. A letter from John Clovis, a miniaturist, to Alessandro Farnese, written on November 15, 1570, says, "There has arrived in Rome a young man from Candia, a pupil of Titian, who, I think, is a painter of rare talent . . . He has painted a portrait of himself which is admired by all the painters in Rome. I should like him to be under the patronage of your reverend lordship without any other contribution towards his living than a room in the Farnese Palace" (*Encyclopaedia Britannica*, v. 22, 69).

Venice was a cultural link between East and West, and the art of that city at the time of the young Greek's residence there incorporated something of the spirit that would characterize the Greek's developing style. Titian, at that time in his nineties, and the grand old man of Venetian art, was a principal source of the style of painting that Theotokopoulos was to follow throughout the years of his residence in Italy. He was also strongly influenced by Tintoretto, Veronese, and Giacopo Bassano.

Non-Venetian sources of his Italian style are evident as well. Raphael's "The Healing of the Lame Man in the Temple," also known as "Peter and John at the Beautiful Gate," clearly provided some material for Theotokopoulos' small painting, "The Purification of the Temple." Executed in tempera and staged in an architectural setting representing a hodgepodge of the tricks of perspective popular at that time, it shows Raphael's influence on some of the figures in the young Greek's painting, notably those of a woman and a little naked boy bringing their offering to the temple.

More significant for an understanding of El Greco is the fact that his works of the Venetian and Roman period, conforming in many respects to the prevailing Italian Renaissance style, nevertheless give hints of an earlier influence, one that was later to reassert itself powerfully in the masterpieces that would establish the unique place he occupies in the history of art.

At about the age of thirty, having already attained some fame as an artist, Theotokopoulos left Rome. The reasons for his departure are somewhat obscure, but a story told by a seventeenth-century writer, G. Mancini, may shed some light on the matter. According to Mancini, the Greek was given the opportunity of becoming the "breeches maker" for the figures that Pope Pius considered indecent in Michelangelo's "Last Judgment" in the Sistine Chapel. Theotokopoulos suggested that it might have been better if the whole painting had been cast to the ground so that he himself might have done it with sincerity, decency, and artistic integrity. There seems little reason to doubt that such an insult to the foremost artist of the age may have raised the temperature of Rome to a point where he thought it advisable to find another place to live and practice his art.

Why he chose Spain is not known. It may have been because Philip II was building the Escorial and looking for artists to decorate it. At any rate, his choice turned out to be a felicitous one. He was obviously struck by the stark Spanish landscapes and he promptly began to incorporate in his paintings the clean and dramatic colors he found there, which must have reminded him more of those of his native Crete than of the lasher hues of Italy.

We find him in Toledo in 1577, completing a set of paintings for the rebuilt Church of Santo Domingo el Antiguo. Those works enhanced his already great reputation, and he was commissioned by the Chapter of Toledo Cathedral to paint a picture for the Sacristy. The result was "The

Stripping of Christ before the Crucifixion," in which the essential elements of the altered style that would ultimately be dominant in his work were clearly evident.

Controversy about certain aspects of the painting and a dispute over his compensation entangled him for some time after its completion, but it must have impressed King Philip, for he asked Theotokopoulos to paint an altarpiece for his church in the Escorial.

El Greco, to use the name by which he must have been generally known by that time, responded to the monarch's request with the painting of "St. Maurice and the Theban Legion," depicting the mass martyrdom of a body of third-century Roman soldiers who refused to obey orders to persecute their fellow Christians. He portrayed the event, not in the expected Spanish mode, with emphasis on the horror of the beheading, but in a way that demonstrated that he was not entirely hostile to the style known as *Maniera*, or High Mannerism, based on the paintings of Raphael and Michelangelo, but emphasizing artistic form over dramatic content. El Greco chose to place at the center of his painting an elegant Maurice, with members of his staff and a little armor-bearer, conferring courteously with an official about their impending execution and that of their comrades of the legion, who are seen in the distance lining up to have their heads cut off, a procedure which is already under way in matter-of-fact fashion, with no indication of ill feeling on either side. Meanwhile, the heavens above are an integral part of the scene, filled with a host of celestial beings preparing a reception for the prospective arrivals. Despite the religious propriety of the theme, the style so irritated Philip that he refused to have the painting installed over the altar, though it remained at the Escorial.

Quite undeterred by royal disapproval, the Greek went on with his painting, gradually developing a mode of artistic expression that eschewed earthly realism in favor of an embodiment of a philosophical and religious outlook that regarded the material world not as something ultimate in its own right, but rather as an expression of a transcendent spiritual reality.

The juxtaposition of the earthly and the heavenly became a frequent theme in El Greco's paintings. His colors, were borrowed less and less from the Venetian and Roman masters, taking on colder blues, greens, and steely grays, with accents of white, yellow, green, and wine red. All the time, his figures were becoming increasingly more sinuous and elongated, possibly owing something to such Italian painters as Tintoretto and Parmigianino, but clearly expressing something so significant for El Greco that it subordinated the influence of painterly convention to religious and philosophical influences more important to him than the more mundane concernsCmoney, high living, romance, controversy, and the likeCthat had their place in the other side of the balance of his complex nature. Those more spiritual and scholarly aspects of his character were fueled by a way of life marked by a thirst for books and an appreciation of good conversation with the *intelligentsia* of Toledo, with whom he was on the best of terms. One of those companions wrote of him, "He was a great philosopher." (Byron and Rice 183)

A thoroughly typical expression of the sort of art that ultimately became such a powerful vehicle for his philosophy is "the Opening of the Fifth Seal," one of three works executed late in the artist's life for the Tavera Hospital in Toledo. The work was inspired by a passage in the Apocalypse of St. John:

> And when he had opened the fifth seal, I saw under the altar the souls of them that were slain for the word of God, and for the testimony which they held: And they cried with a loud voice, saying, How long, O Lord, holy and true, dost thou not judge and avenge our blood on them that dwell on the earth? And white robes were given unto every one of them: and it was said unto them that they should rest yet for a little season, until their fellow-servants also and their brethren, that should be killed as they were, should be fulfilled. (*Revelation*, 6: 9-11)

Other painters of the High Renaissance had put on canvas their vision of heaven and earth, with descending angels, aspiring souls, and rejected sinners. They too had bathed their scenes in a celestial brightness that endowed the vivid, earth-based colors they employed a radiance that spoke of the presence of God in nature.

But these colors are different. They hardly seem to derive from earthly substances at all. The areas of red and yellow are muted and completely dominated by the cool and curiously other-worldly hues of the remainder of the painting. The gigantic figure of St. John on the left is enveloped in a gray-blue robe highlighted by a pure white light that must have its source in the celestial realm glimpsed behind the swirling clouds that seem to move in a line parallel to the saint's outstretched arm and of the body of the little angel floating at the upper right of the painting.

That same radiance robs the naked figures of the risen dead of any semblance of the human flesh tones with which Michelangelo in some degree and Memling in an even greater measure endowed their resuscitated saints and sinners in their depictions of the Last Judgment. In El Greco's space, the highlighted portions of the bodies gleam with the pure white illumination that streams through breaks in the dark storm clouds overhead, and the shadowed area tend toward the violet end of the spectrum.

And what are we to make of the figures themselves? Painted with consummate skill, they nevertheless defy the unwritten canon that set boundaries for even the most radical Italian masters who taught the Greek his craft. To be sure, it was not uncommon for Renaissance painters to make heads less long and bodies longer than they are generally seen in real life. Denys of Fourna, in his *Guide to Painting*, had written, "Learn O my pupil that the body of a man is nine heads in height" (Byron and Rice 94). This exaggerated proportion is especially evident in Michelangelo's frescoes on the ceiling of the Sistine Chapel. But El Greco's sinuous and elongated figures of his later Spanish period are quite unlike Michelangelo's idealized human forms. They are attenuated, fluid, unearthly, hardly seeming to be bodies at all.

How are we to account for this astounding climactic development in Renaissance art? A great deal of insightful criticism and a fair amount of nonsense have been written about El Greco in attempts to explain the characteristics that set his paintings apart form others of the era. He has been seen as a Mannerist, a reviver of Byzantine art, a madman, a proto-modernist, and, most curiously, a painter whose distinctive style can be attributed to astigmatism.

This latter theory, which enjoyed surprising popularity during the early years of the twentieth century, was presented as a plausible explanation for the figures that fill the Greek's later paintings. It is difficult to understand why it was not apparent to the critics who espoused the ophthalmic hypothesis that even if El Greco had indeed suffered from such a condition, he himself would inevitably have seen his exaggerated figures as abnormal in comparison with those who served as his models. The real explanation must lie elsewhere, and if we want to divine the reason, we must attend less to some possible visual pathology or to personal eccentricity than to the intellectual orientation that governed his artistic activity during the last years of his career.

It is astonishing that even the modern critics who defended El Greco against the charge of visual aberration were for the most part oblivious to a ground of art in which his roots were so deeply embedded.

Meier-Graefe, who, unswayed by a turn-of-the-century characterization of the Greek as a painter of "horrors," asked, "Where does he come from?" replied simply, "We do not know" (Byron and Rice, 6).

That same critic, to be sure, later found a clue to some of the mystery of El Greco's art in the mosaics of Daphne near Athens. He was not the first of the modern commentators to see Greek and Byzantine influence in Theotokopoulos' paintings, but the organic continuity between Byzantine painting and the art of El Greco was clearly recognized only when critics began to discover an affinity between Byzantine and modern art and it became apparent to some of them that El Greco was a sort of missing link. The painting and sculpture that had emerged in the Eastern empire as a consequence of its struggles against iconoclasm turned away from the naturalism of earlier centuries in favor of a mystical aspiration to express in finite works the mysteries of the eternal and immutable. The felicitous result was the great tradition of Byzantine iconography, coexisting with the sort of Aristotelian philosophy espoused by St. John Damascene, whose writings were later to have a profound influence on Eastern Scholastics (Byron and Rice, 91). In the ninth century, the Patriarch Photius sparked a revival of Platonism in Byzantium (Byron and Rice, 17). Though it did not result in a revival of the naturalistic Greek and Hellenistic art, it did humanize the iconographic representation of the Byzantine painters and breathed into the art of Christendom a spirit that would ultimately move westward and transform European art.

Two centuries after Photius, Michael Psellos, a fundamentally Neoplatonic scholar, put an indelible stamp on Byzantine culture. Psellos had an encyclopedic range of knowledge, combined with a Platonic rational mysticism. One result of his enormous influence was a form of art characterized by a warmer sort of representation of the divine, which, without sacrificing anything of the mystery, nevertheless brought a still more humanistic element to iconographic art and produced its full flowering.

In a very real sense, Psellos may be considered the progenitor not only of a revitalized Byzantine and Greek culture, but of the Italian Renaissance, though centuries were to elapse after his death before the Neoplatonic spirit of humanistic mysticism would come into full flower in the West.

The relation of that spirit to art is no accident. An understanding of the relationship between philosophy and the arts permeates the *Enneads* of

Plotinus in a somewhat less ambiguous fashion than is the case with Plato's writings. Works of art, Plotinus said, Ago back to the Reason-Principles from which Nature derives and . . . are holders of beauty and add where nature is lacking" (Plotinus *Enneads* IV. 8. 1. McKenna 422-423).

There is a real sense in which the World Soul is for the Neoplatonists an artist, acting on the bare potentiality of matter to express something of the ineffable beauty shining through *Nous* from the One. Human bodies are expressions of soul, and the individual soul shares in the nature of the ultimately real. It too can shape its own nature as an artist shapes his work.

> Withdraw into yourself and look. And if you do not find yourself beautiful yet, act as does the creator of a statue that is to be make beautiful: he cuts away here, he smoothes there, he makes this line lighter, this other purer, until a lovely face has grown upon his work. So do you also: cut away all that is excessive, straighten all that is crooked, bring light to all that is overcast, labour to make all one glow of beauty until there shall shine out on you from it the godlike splendour of virtue, until you shall see the perfect goodness established in the stainless shrine (Plotinus, *Enneads* I. 6. 9. MacKenna 63).

None of this is to deny that not only has the Platonic tradition in is entirely been a fountainhead of inspiration for great art, but that Plato himself was not insensitive to the proper role of the arts in human life. It is true that in the *Republic* he expressed doubts not only about drama but about *all* works of representative art as simulations twice removed from realityCfaulty copies of particular objects that are themselves flawed reproductions of Ideas.

His criticism of the arts, however, was far less sweeping than his *penchant* for hyperbole would make it appear, for he never condemned them on the grounds of their impotence, but rather on his conviction that they are too powerful to be trusted in the hands of those not versed in philosophy. He proposed to harness that power for good by challenging the artists to prove that they could elevate their work to a sufficient height to convey to those who contemplated it the essence of the truths that lie behind the world of phenomena. This is precisely the role that Plotinus assigned to works of art. We do not so much contemplate *them* as employ them as focusing glasses through which we see with greater understanding the more real world of *Noeta*.

In the Byzantine world, the victors in the war against the iconoclasts claimed a precisely similar function for art. "This was the chief iconodule contention," art historians Byron and Rice say, "that pictures, like statues to Plotinus, were an effective means of communication with the extra-terrestrial universe."

This was the way iconographic painting was viewed in Crete when young Domenikos Theokotopoulos was a boy there. The spirit of those vivid representations of spiritual truths followed him to Venice, where it was again alive in an uniquely Adriatic mode, and then to Rome, where it had found expression in the colossal work of Michelangelo, whom the boy from Crete first studied and then emulated and at last rejected. "Michelangelo was a good man," he was later to remark, "but he could not paint" (Byron and Rice 78).

It was not until he got to Spain and became "El Greco" that he gradually became able to to draw his nourishment from the very roots of that spirit, incorporating in his work all the skills he had learned from the Italian masters, but purifying and spiritualizing his art from sources that sprang from the rich soil of the Eastern Platonic and Neoplatonic tradition. This is not to say that at some point he discovered that he was a Platonist or Neoplatonist and decided to paint according to the canon. He was, to be sure, interested in philosophy and enjoyed talking with philosophers. He had a substantial library, though it is not known whether he ever read the writings of Plato or Plotinus. He never lectured or wrote essays on metaphysics.

Rather, his philosophy, as an expression of his soul, is in his paintings, and it is clear that he intended them to be his way of stating his profoundest convictions about the world. Like Plotinus and the Christian Neoplatonists, he saw the natural world not as inert matter, but as animate and fluid. Material objects are created and sustained by soul, and even a relatively horizontal city, in his "View of Toledo" seems to be straining upward, seeking to regain its identity with some celestial city from which it derives its nature.

As for human bodies, they are unlike even the most spiritually inspiring bodies of the Italian painters. Whatever incarnation of *Nous* and Soul is celebrated in the figures of El Greco's later works is an incarnation that has passed the point at which the Word initially becomes Flesh and revels in bone and muscle and sinew. The bodies of his saints and sometimes even of the infant Jesus are bathed in a white radiance that seems to draw them upward toward the One Reality that typically makes its presence known only through rifts in the storm clouds that must be penetrated before the aspiring souls can achieve the destiny that awaits them in the celestial realm. That realm, as seen through El Greco's painting, has a reality that transcends that of the ephemeral world beneath it, imparts to it whatever life it is capable of receiving, and draws it back toward itself. Even souls in danger of damnation in these paintings never wholly lose that touch of derivative radiance, suggesting Plotinus' conviction that in the very nature of a soul, it can never be entirely lost.

In 1577, the year El Greco moved to Toledo, St. John of the Cross was imprisoned there. Whether or not he and El Greco ever knew each other is uncertain, but much of St. John's poetry embodies the qualities that the Greek achieved in his painting, as evidenced in these lines about the ascent of the soul:

> The dreadful force of dazzling light
> Blinded me as aloft I flew,
> The greatest gain that ere I knew
> as made in blackness of the night.
> But love it was that won the day,
> Blindly, obscurely did I fly;
> I soared aloft and soared so high
> That in the end I reached my prey.
> (Myers and Copplestone 85).

The recognition of El Greco as a painter whose works embody a whole philosophy is well expressed by Byron and Price:

> . . . . for us, and in relation to us, he is always relevant and always great, great not only as a painter but as a man, one to whom the vision of his World's reality was vouchsafed and who pursued it independently of mental fashion, a cosmic figure, sustained in his own life by a profound conviction of his own magnitude. On his canvasses, the whole gamut of emotions provoked by landscape, allegory, or sitter, are co-ordinated in the expression of a grand philosophy, of the intrinsic, mystical seed of perfection contained in all terrestrial phenomena and the artist's debt thereto in his communing (Byron and Rice 3).

The grand philosophy that invested the paintings of the Greek with their enduring power to move and inspire us can have been none other in essence than the philosophy of Plotinus and the Christian Neoplatonists.

Works Cited

Byron, Robert, and Rice, David Talbot. *The Birth of Western Painting*. New York: Hacker Art Books, 1968.

Encyclopaedia Britannica. Chicago, William Benton, 1958.

Myers, Bernard S., and Copplestone, Trewin, eds. *Art Treasures in* Spain. New York: McGraw-Hill, 1969.

Plotinus. *The Enneads*. Stephen McKenna, tr. 3rd ed. London: Faber, 1962.

Revelation. Holy Bible. Authorized King James Version.. Nashville: Thomas Nelson, 1976.

Reflejo de la evolución del pensamiento político de Miguel Hernández en su obra dramática

Antonio Noguera

La íntima relación existente entre la creación literaria y la actividad política en el corpus de Miguel Hernández ha sido ampliamente estudiada y comprobada en los textos poéticos de este autor. También han sido objeto de análisis, bajo la misma óptica, sus escritos en prosa. Pero, aunque es en sus obras dramáticas donde mejor se patentiza el profundo cambio ideológico que experimentó MH en sus pocos años de vida pública, este aspecto de su teatro aún no ha recibido la atención merecida pues a pesar de que el teatro fue siempre una prioridad en la vida de Hernández, este aspecto de su creación literaria no ha sido tan estudiado como su poesía. En 1978 Florence Delay (109)[1] mantenía que "el teatro de Miguel Hernández es aún poco conocido, tal vez porque apenas ha sido representado." Este acertado juicio fue pertinente por muchos años. Al menos, eso muestra la opinión de Manfred Lentzen que en 1994 afirma que "El teatro de Miguel Hernández ha sido hasta hoy relativamente poco estudiado" (73)[2]. Como consecuencia los trabajos de Mariano de Paco, Jesucristo Riquelme, Francisco Javier Díez de Revenga, Agustín Sánchez Vidal y José Carlos Rovira, en 1996 la consideración del teatro hernandiano era ya un hecho. En esa fecha opina Serrano que, "[N]o parece admisible en el momento actual la difundida creencia de que el teatro de Miguel Hernández apenas posee interés en el conjunto de su producción" (71)[3]. Mas a pesar de haber alcanzado el reconocimiento merecido aún se siguen echando en falta estudios que se acerquen a la obra dramática de MH para tomarla como un conjunto e intentar hacer análisis temáticos de ella.

La unión de intereses políticos y literarios de forma explícita dentro del texto literario es tan antigua como la propia escritura, y tiene sus raíces asentadas en los orígenes de la cultura mediterránea. Esta fusión entre lo ético y lo estético, que se muestra de forma patente en toda la producción literaria de Miguel Hernández, tiene una particular importancia en su producción dramática, pues prácticamente todas sus obras de teatro fueron escritas en función de unos intereses circunstanciales que trascendían la mera inspiración o apetencia del autor. Por lo general MH utilizó sus textos dramáticos tanto como vehículo de promoción personal, como de difusión y propaganda de sus ideas socio-políticas.

Para la aproximación a la producción dramática de Hernández, se debe utilizar la totalidad del corpus dramático hernandiano que, por haberse truncado su vida en lo que pudo ser el comienzo de su carrera, no es demasiado extenso. Aunque toda clasificación resulta arbitraria y discutible, sus obras han sido agrupadas en tres grupos. Las dos primeras corresponden a la etapa de su primer compromiso, e incluye dos títulos: *Quién te ha visto y quién te ve y sombra de lo que eras* (1934) y *El torero más valiente* (1934). La primer obra es un auto sacramental, y la segunda está hoy felizmente recuperada después de haberse dado por perdida durante muchos años. El segundo grupo de dramas hernandianos está compuesto también por dos obras que en abierta oposición a las primeras, tienen un marcado carácter social. Los títulos que componen este grupo, *Los hijos de la piedra* (1935) y *El labrador de más aire* (1937), son lo que se han dado en llamar "las tragedias de patrono" (Riquelme 1990, 18). Dentro del tercer, y último grupo, se integran las obras más comprometidas del teatro de MH. *Teatro en la guerra* (1937), título genérico que alberga a cuatro piezas de corta duración y *El pastor de la muerte* (1938[4]), el último gran proyecto de MH y su postrera producción teatral.

Del análisis de los primeros textos dramáticos del joven MH puede establecerse que fueron éstas unas obras poco comprometidas con las ideas progresistas. En algunas ocasiones se llega, incluso, a establecer proclamas claramente reaccionarias. Mas, pronto comienza una progresiva evolución, y su teatro va mostrando un constante incremento en su compromiso político con las ideas democráticas, hasta alcanzar en sus obras finales una actitud totalmente militante.

Las razones que marcaron la evolución ideológica del joven Miguel Hernández, hay que buscarlas en el propio cambio personal del poeta, y en las circunstancias vitales que moldearon su existencia. Por eso se debe seguir su biografía, para ir marcando sus diferentes etapas productivas. En cada una de estas etapas hay un viaje que marcará un hito que ejerza una influencia clave en el proceso evolutivo del joven MH.

Hasta 1933, la etapa de formación

La patria chica de MH, su natal Orihuela donde nace en 1910, ha sido tradicionalmente un feudo de las ideas conservadoras. Quizás el hecho de ser sede arzobispal, o el poderoso influjo del colegio de jesuitas donde MH se educó, han contribuido a catalizar la ideología católico-conservadora en que se formó MH como persona y como poeta. Durante su primera época, su etapa de formación, MH sólo escribe prosa y poesía. En prosa textos cortos como *El niño Flores*, o el proyecto de su primera y única novela, *La tragedia de Calisto*. Esta etapa se cierra con su primer poemario, *Perito en lunas* tras su primer viaje a Madrid en busca de la fama literaria. Si bien no halló el éxito, sí se empapó del aire artístico y cultural de la gran ciudad que le marcó de forma definitiva.

1930-1933, el peso del nacional catolicismo

Los años de orientación y búsqueda que siguen marcan el inicio de la producción dramática del joven MH. Bajo la influencia de su gran amigo y guía Ramón Sijé, Hernández trata de alcanzar la promoción social, que tanto anhelaba, y el éxito económico, que tanto precisaba, bajo el manto protector del nacional-catolicismo y así sus trabajos encuentran acogida desde el primer número de la revista *El Gallo Crisis*, publicación que con una orientación en ocasiones filofascista, dirige Ramón Sijé. Dentro de este ambiente tradicionalista en 1934 publica su auto sacramental ***Quién te ha visto y quién te ve y sombra de lo que eras***, y el mismo año terminada ***El torero más valiente*** drama perdido durante años y hoy felizmente recuperado gracias al magnífico trabajo de recomposición que realizó Sánchez Vidal en 1986. El auto sacramental, aunque gozó de un cierto renacer en el primer tercio del siglo XIX, es un género característico del Siglo de Oro de carácter alegórico y simbólico que trata el tema del misterio de la eucaristía u otro tema sacro con una marcada intencionalidad didáctica. En este caso es un texto dividido en tres partes que transcurren respectivamente en "El Estado de las Inocencias", el "Estado de las Malas Pasiones" y el "Estado del Arrepentimiento". En la primera, los Cinco Sentidos provocan una revolución que tendrá como fatal consecuencia la caída del Hombre-Niño. En la segunda se pasará del edén paradisiaco al mundo del trabajo. En la tercera y última, el Hombre aparece haciendo penitencia en el desierto y después de que la Carne acabe con la Voz-de-la Verdad, el Buen Labrador conseguirá vencer la impiedad del Hombre, la Carne y los Cinco Sentidos. En venganza se unirán al Deseo los Siete Pecados Capitales que acabarán con el Hombre, incinerarán su cadáver y finalmente su espíritu subirá a los cielos. Todo este largo entramado, de corte indiscutiblemente calderoniano, desemboca como conclusión en una condena de la revolución y de aquellos que tratan de transformar el orden previamente establecido. Los cinco sentidos representan al proletario y exigen mejoras laborales. Ante las evasivas del patrón, los jornaleros amenazan con "las hoces" y "el martillo" y acaban gritando "¡Abajo el capital!". Una vez más el amo hace oídos sordos a las justas solicitudes, y los rebeldes incitados por el Deseo gritan lo siguiente:

Oír	La sangre de las venas es para liberarla en ocasiones.
Oler	No hay límites.
Gustar	No hay tuyo.
Tocar	No hay cadenas.
Carne	No hay corderos guiados por leones.
Deseo	(Así: ¡más!, ¡más!)
Oír	¡Abajo los explotadores!
Mirar	¡Abajo!, yo repito.
Oler	¡La huelga general, trabajadores!
Gustar	¡La huelga general!
Tocar	¡Dios es un mito![5]

Una vez terminada la redacción de este texto, MH lo envía a Madrid donde es inmediatamente aceptado y publicado por José Bergamín en su prestigiosa revista *Cruz y Raya* (julio-septiembre de 1934). La circunstancia de aparecer en una revista de reconocida tendencia neocatólica marca aun más el sentido católico del auto hernandiano. Se cierra este primer ciclo con una tragedia española, *El torero más valiente*, donde se dan cita los temas típicos y tópicos de la rivalidad taurina, el amor, los celos y la muerte gloriosa en la arena de la plaza. Este binomio de toros y religión está dentro de las más tradicionales coordenadas del nacional catolicismo que caracteriza esta etapa hernandiana, cabe aquí recordar las líneas finales de su escrito titulado "Mi concepto del poema" en el que opina: "Con el poema debiera suceder lo que con el Santísimo Sacramento…¿Cuándo dirá el poeta con el poema incorporado a sus dedos, como dice el cura con la hostia: 'Aquí está DIOS' y lo creeremos?"[6] Su segundo viaje a Madrid y la relación que comienza a mantener con los intelectuales progresistas que en aquel entonces se daban cita en el Madrid republicano, en especial su amistad con Pablo Neruda fueron el hito que marcaron un cambio transcendental en su vida.

1934-1935 la concienciación social

En los años 30 la politización cobra fuerza. Dice Podestá de estos años al referirse a la estrecha relación que existe entre arte y política, que "si bien ésta siempre existe, es indudable que la década de los 30 fue privilegiada por el énfasis que grupos con muy diferente orientación, pusieron en hacer explícita dicha relación."[7] Fue a partir de la proclamación de la II República Española, en 1931, cuando los teatros populares comenzaron a florecer. Su misión era tanto la de dar a conocer obras nuevas, como la de revisar y recuperar a muchos de los clásicos que ya en su época habían efectuado obras de carácter social y reivindicativo. La fina sensibilidad de MH no podía permanecer ajena a los aires de libertad que soplaban y la concienciación social se hace patente en 1935, cuando expone por carta a su amigo Juan Guerrero Ruiz:

> ...estoy harto y arrepentido de haber hecho cosas al servicio de Dios y de la tontería católica. Me dedico única y exclusivamente a la canción y a la vida de la tierra y sangre adentro: estaba mintiendo a mi voz y a mi naturaleza terrena hasta más no poder, estaba traicionándome y suicidándome tristemente.[8]

En ese mismo año de 1935 da su Conferencia sobre Lope de Vega, compone *Los hijos de la piedra*, afianza su amistad con Pablo Neruda, conoce a Vicente Aleixandre, además la prematura muerte de su amigo Ramón Sijé en la Nochebuena de 1935, alejará definitivamente a Hernández de los círculos católico-derechistas.

Al año siguiente termina *El labrador de más aire*. Si en su primera obra fue Calderón el modelo a seguir, en esta segunda época es Lope de Vega quien guía la inspiración de MH. Al menos la visión populista que entonces se tenía de un Lope preocupado por promover la justicia popular ante las arbitrariedades y abusos de las autoridades intermedias. Con posterioridad a estas lecturas, ha habido otras interpretaciones, la de Maravall es la más conocida, que presentan la obra de Lope como reforzadora del papel real en un intento de acabar con la escasa descentralización permitida por los Austrias. Aunque así sea, no fue esa la lectura contemporánea a MH ni la que el propio poeta hizo de *Fuenteovejuna* o de *El mejor alcalde el rey*, este sentido Sánchez Vidal apunta que Lope de Vega fue leído por Hernández como "dramaturgo revolucionario"[9]. La consideración que MH tenía de Lope está recogida en un borrador de la conferencia que dio el poeta en la Universidad Popular de Cartagena en 27 de agosto de 1935 con motivo de conmemorarse el III centenario de la muerte de Lope. Dice así: "Lope está en la tierra, con los hombres que viven entre raíces y cepas, Voz del pueblo, sus problemas, sus modos de vidas, sus coplas y modos de decir únicos."[10] El modelo inspiratorio que ahora es Lope se patentiza en *Los hijos de la piedra* desde el título. Sánchez Vidal recuerda que en *El perro del hortelano* se lee "Que soy hijo de la tierra / y no he conocido padre", utilizando esta fórmula como declaración de bastardía. También Cervantes empleó esta idea con los mismos fines, en *Pedro de Urdemales* dice: "Yo soy hijo de la piedra / que padre no conocí". En el texto de MH, que como he dicho es del año 1935, el argumento viene dado por la sublevación que los mineros asturianos protagonizaron en octubre de 1934, y que fue duramente reprimida por el general Franco al mando de la Legión extranjera y mercenarios africanos. Entre las luchas directas, la tortura y los fusillamientos que siguieron, los mineros tuvieron más de cuatro mil muertos, y otros muchos fueron enviados a campos de concentración. También existe una clara referencia a los sucesos de Casas Viejas que tuvieron lugar los días 11 y 12 de enero de 1933. En aquella ocasión la Guardia Civil acabó con todos los revoltosos al grito de "tiros a la barriga", exactamente ese es el mismo grito con el que acaba el "drama de monte y sus jornaleros" como subtituló MH a la obra que me estoy refiriendo. El héroe de esta obra es todavía un ser individualista que responde a la agresión del señor más con pasión que con reflexión y aún existen en el texto unas claras referencias a la vida del más allá donde la justicia divina reparará las injusticias sufridas por los trabajadores en este valle de lágrimas que es la tierra.

En *El labrador de más aire*, el otro texto dramático de la época que ahora nos ocupa pues aunque se publico en el 37 fue escrita en 1935[11], el predominio de lo individual sobre lo colectivo también se hace presente. El profesor Rovira ha escrito a este respecto: "el planteamiento social del drama tiene en Hernández una articulación individual, constituyendo un héroe que representa a la colectividad, pero que no llega a convencer a ésta de la necesidad de rebelión". La ideología que Juan, el protagonista, expone es de marcado carácter revolucionario: "Nadie merece ser dueño / de hacienda que no cultiva"[12] . Pero no logra levantar el ánimo de sus camaradas:

Juan	Me entristece cuanto pasa: hace días merodea, amenazando la aldea, el hambre casa por casa, y la gente labradora su protesta no levanta como una solo garganta viva y amenazadora.
Lázaro	Déjanos beber en paz.
Lorenzo	No vuelvas al mismo asunto.
Roque	No toques más ese punto y como nosotros haz.

Al final tendrá lugar el sacrificio de Juan, pero su semilla caerá en tierra inculta y no se generalizará su protesta. La obra acaba con un planto en el que su enamorada afirma: "¡Ha muerto Juan, el airoso / de voz y de movimiento, / y a quedar él en reposo / se quedó el aire sin viento!"[13]

La etapa que viene a continuación está marcada por un viaje que si bien fue mínimo en distancia, debe considerarse histórico por su trascendencia. El 18 de julio de 1936 la sublevación fascista le sorprende, como a otros muchos españoles, cuando está disfrutando sus vacaciones estivales en su pueblo natal.

1936-1938, la euforia antifascista

No habían transcurrido aún dos meses cuando MH ya se encuentra en el frente de Madrid picando trincheras. Su enrolamiento como voluntario del Quinto Regimiento ha dado lugar a un malentendido que es conveniente aclarar si se quiere precisar la posición ideológica de MH. Para poder alistarse en el ejército republicano y evitar que sus filas se convirtieran en un refugio de fascistas, hacía falta el aval de un partido político o sindicato. MH realizó su ingreso avalado por el Partido Comunista y este aval ha querido verse en ocasiones como carnet de afiliación al PC. Pero no es así, este documento sólo significa que la entidad expedidora conoce a quien avala y garantiza su adscripción a la legalidad republicana contra la que algunos militares se habían sublevado.

En esta etapa, como en las anteriores, dos títulos componen su producción dramática. El primero de ellos abarca bajo el título genérico de *Teatro en la guerra* cuatro obras cortas de un acto cada una, y una "Nota previa" de indudable valor programático. Comienza así la citada "Nota": "El 18 de julio de 1936, frente al movimiento de los militares traidores, entro yo, poeta, y conmigo mi poesía, en el trance más doloroso y trabajoso, pero más glorioso, al mismo tiempo, de mi vida."[14] Sin dejar lugar a ninguna duda, MH expone su declaración de guerra "provocadores de la invasión"[15], por lo que expone: "Creo que el teatro es un arma de guerra contra el enemigo de enfrente y contra el enemigo de casa. Entiendo que todo teatro, toda poesía, todo arte, ha de ser, hoy más que nunca, un arma de guerra."[16] Estas obras están pensadas para poder ser representadas en cualquier circunstancia, no precisan ni de decorados, ni utillaje, ni vestuario específico, y por su brevedad y corto reparto no hay impedimentos para presentarlas en fábricas, calles, plazas o en las mismas trincheras. Las cuatro piezas representan un magnífico ejemplo del teatro de agitación y propaganda, modalidad que además de ser tan legítima como cualquier otro subgénero dramático, gozaba en Europa de una sólida tradición.

Como una premonición de su propio destino el título de la última obra de MH es *Pastor de la muerte*. Este texto fue acabado el 26 de noviembre de 1937 poco después de que MH asistiera al V Festival de Teatro Soviético y visitara la URSS[17] . La influencia que este viaje produjo en MH fue enorme. Tanto así que decidió dedicarse por entero al teatro y al cine abandonando la poesía. Las influencias de esta época ya no vienen del siglo de oro español, sino del ruso Ostroski, el alemán Piscator o el hispanoamericano Cesar Vallejo que después de una prolongada estancia en París, vino finalmente a Madrid.

En esta última etapa combativa y antifascista el héroe ya no es un personaje aislado y solitario, pierde el carácter aristocrático que había presentado anteriormente y se convierte en un personaje anónimo del pueblo o en una serie de personajes secundarios que juntos representan la heroicidad de un pueblo.

Con el triunfo por la fuerza de las armas de los militares sublevados, otro viaje cierra la etapa más gloriosa en la vida de H. Por desgracia Miguel se equivocó al elegir a Portugal como destino, pues nada más cruzar la frontera fue detenido por la policía política salazarista, la temible PIDE, y devuelto a las autoridades franquistas. Comienza así el principio del fin del poeta.

la época de derrota y cárcel 1939-1942

Durante esta etapa las condiciones físicas en las que le tocó vivir al autor, le imposibilitaron el escribir teatro. A duras penas fue capaz de escribir poemas utilizando, en ocasiones, pequeños pedazos de papel higiénico. Además, la motivación que tenía para escribirlo, la propagación de su ideario político-social, era imposible en aquellas circunstancias. Comenzó un peregrinar de cárcel en cárcel. En alguna como ocurrió en la Prisión del Conde de Toreno donde encuentra a Buero Vallejo, sus conversaciones tuvieron como tema el teatro, pero nunca llegó a ver el momento que había soñado: "cuando descansemos de la guerra, y la paz aparte los cañones de las plazas y los corrales de las aldeas españolas, me veréis por ellos celebrar representaciones de un teatro que será la vida misma de España, sacada limpiamente de sus trincheras, sus calles, sus campos y sus paredes." MH murió en una cárcel franquista el 28 de marzo de 1942, a los 31 años de edad, mucho antes de que la libertad por la que tanto luchó le llegaran a él y a España. Una última nota, el corpus dramático de MH fue presentado por el fiscal militar como prueba de cargo en el consejo de guerra donde fue condenado a muerte.

Endnotes

[1] Delay, Florence. "El teatro de Miguel Hernández" en *Entorno a Miguel Hernández*. Ed. Juan Cano Ballesta. Madrid: Castalia, 1978. pp. 109-135.
[2] Lentzen, Manfred. "Del teatro social al teatro político: sobre la evolución de los dramas de Miguel Hernández" en *Encuentros y desencuentros de culturas: Siglos XIX y XX. IV*. Juan Villegas. Ed. California: The Regents of the University of California, 1994.
[3] Serrano, Virtudes. "Las mujeres del teatro de Miguel Hernández: Construcción dramatúrgica del personaje" en *Estudios humanísticos filología*, 1996 18. León. pp. 71-91
[4] *Obra completa*. 101.
[5] *Obra completa*, 1325
[6] *Obra completa*, 2113.
[7] Podestá, Guido. *César Vallejo: Su estética teatral*. Minneapolis: Institute for the Study of Ideologies & Literature, 1985. p.33
[8] *Obra completa*, 2345.
[9] Sánchez Vidal, Agustín. "Literatura entre pureza y Revolución. La poesía" en *HCLE, VII*, pp. 668-680. p. 672
[10] *Obra completa*. 1197.
[11] *Obra completa*. 1201.
[12] *Obra completa*, 1730.
[13] *Obra completa*. 1781.
[14] *Obra completa*. 1787.
[15] *Ibid.*
[16] *Ibid.*
[17] desde el 2 de septiembre de 1937 hasta el 5 de octubre

Contributors

John Anton is Professor of Philosophy at the University of South Florida. He is the author and editor of numerous books and articles in ancient philosophy with particular focus on Plato, Aristotle, and Plotinus.

Linda Ardito is Associate Professor of Music at Dowling College. She is a composer of music and the author of articles in the history of music.

Robert Berchman is Associate Professor of Philosophy at Dowling College. He is the author and editor of books and articles in later ancient philosophy with particular focus on Philo of Alexandria, Origen of Alexandria, and Plotinus.

James Caraway is Professor of Education at Dowling College. He has authored books and articles on Whitehead and process theology.

Donald Duclow is Professor of Philosophy at Gwynedd-Mercy College. He is the author of books and articles in medieval philosophy with particular focus on Nicolas of Cusa.

Robert Helm is Worrill Professor of Philosophy at Wake Forest University. He has published widely in the history of philosophy.

Richard Henn received his Ph.D. in Philosophy from the University of Kansas. He has published articles in ancient philosophy with focus upon Aristotle.

Helmut Kohlenberger is Professor of Theology at the University of Salzburg. He has published widely in medieval philosophy and theology with particular focus on Anselm of Canterbury.

Jean-Marc Narbonne is Doyen of the Faculty of Philosophy at the University of Laval. He has published widely in Neoplatonism with particular focus on Plotinus and Proclus.

Antonio Noguera is Professor of Romance Languages at the University of Wisconsin-Madison. He has written extensively in Cuban and Latin American drama, theater, and literature.

Horst Seidl is Professor of Philosophy at the Pontifical Lateran University in Rome. He has published extensively in the history of philosophy with a focus on Aristotle and the Aristotelian tradition.